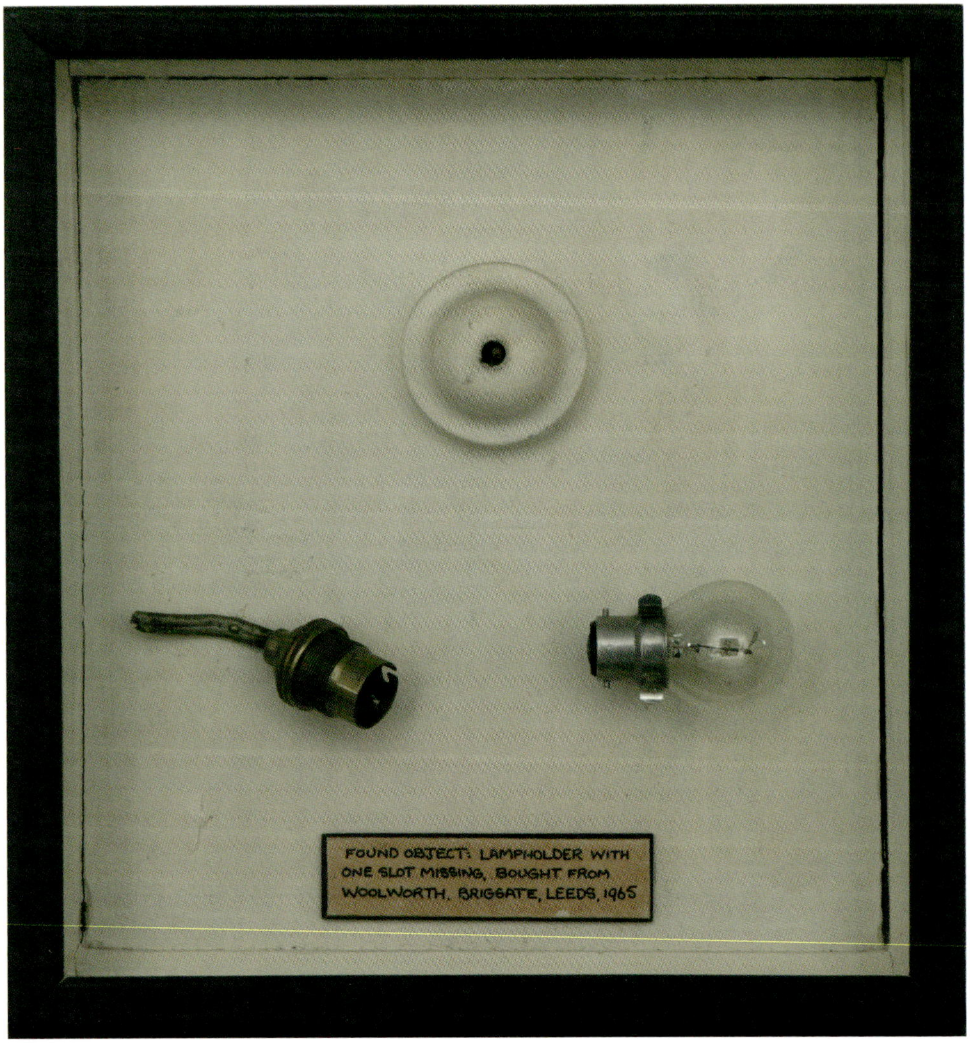

Found Object, 1965

A sport, or freak of nature, is something that has gone wrong, an accidental variation. In what might be Earnshaw's first box, he has singled out this socket intended for a bayonet lamp, which with only one slot cut is useless. As a factory worker he shared that enthusiasm mechanics have for improper products, like screws without slots, a kind of mechanical rejection of the industrial system: just as in older times, country folk were taken with the two-headed calf or the knot of rats' tails (a 'rat king').

—James Heartfield and Patrick Hughes

Edited by Les Coleman

Anthony Earnshaw

The Imp of Surrealism

RGAP 2011

In Memory of Eric Thacker

First published in 2011 by RGAP
(Research Group for Artists Publications)
Yorkshire Artspace
21 Brown Street, Sheffield S1 2BS
www.rgap.co.uk

ISBN 978–0–9558273–8–9

www.anthonyearnshaw.com

Designed by Colin Sackett
Printed and bound in China by C&C Offset Printing Co. Ltd

Distributed in the UK and Europe by
Cornerhouse Publications
70 Oxford Street, Manchester M1 5NH
www.cornerhouse.org

Supported by The Henry Moore Foundation

Anthony Earnshaw is represented by Angela Flowers Gallery, London
www.flowersgalleries.com

Contents

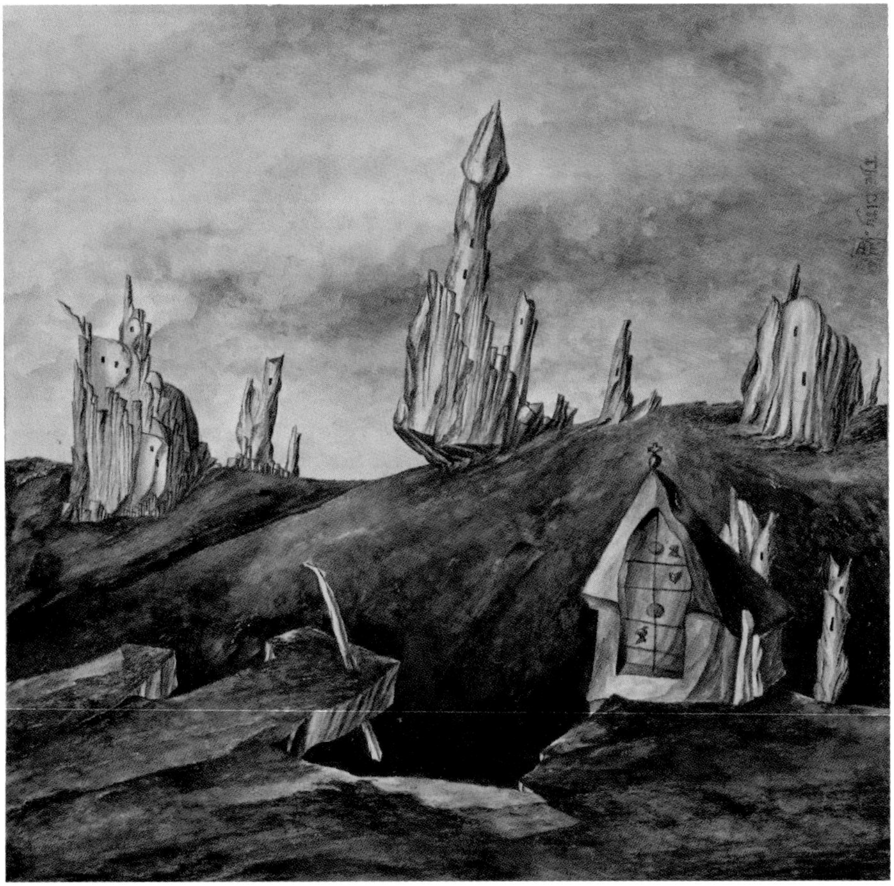

The City, 1950

Preface

It was not until I started editing this book that I became aware that Anthony Earnshaw considered me to be his archivist. It is true that during our friendship I bought his books, saved his catalogues and kept his correspondence. Furthermore, I kept a file of reviews and photographs that he would send me. My interest in his work overrode any sense that I was in the process of compiling an archive. One of the pleasures in putting this book together has been to discover how many other archivists Tony had among his friends.

I met Tony while I was studying at Leeds College of Art in the mid 1960s. At the time he was teaching at Bradford and Harrogate Colleges of Art while living in Leeds. I would regularly find myself in his, and Patrick Hughes', company while drinking in The Nag's Head, "up Chapel Allerton". In 1966 Patrick, a close friend and admirer of Tony's art, organized a retrospective of his paintings at the Institute Gallery connected to the Art College. I went to the opening and bought my first painting, an early watercolour titled 'The City'.

Although listed in the catalogue as NFS (Not for Sale), 'The City' was the painting I was most interested in. I decided to buy a different watercolour in the same series but at the moment I made my decision a woman walked over and placed a red dot against the painting. I explained what had happened to Patrick, telling him at the same time that the painting I *really* wanted to buy was NFS. "Why don't you go and talk to Tony, you never know he might sell it," he said. After another glass of wine I went over to Tony. He listened intently as I recounted my story. On finishing, Tony said without pausing for thought, "Would £11.00 be alright?" I still regard it as the best £11.00 I ever spent.

In spite of my moving to London our friendship continued, mainly through letters. Tony never liked talking on the telephone. On several occasions we exhibited alongside each other in group shows.

Sometime before Tony died, Gail, his wife, recorded him discussing his life and work with a view to producing a book with the working title 'Floodlit Shadows', supplied by Tony. I often thought a book on his rich and varied creative life should be published but there was no indication that this was about to happen. Gail approached me in 2007 to help organize Tony's disorderly library and papers ("brag sheets", and particularly his own, were something he considered with disdain). I travelled up to Harrogate not knowing what I might find but after some order had been achieved it became even more apparent that a book should be compiled. It was only a matter of time before Gail invited me to act as editor of a book about Tony's life and work to which I happily agreed.

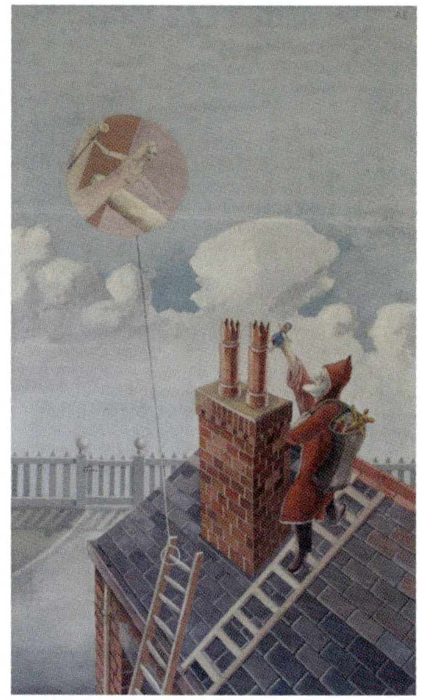

Distribution of Wishes, 1965

A year later, at the time of Patrick's seventieth birthday, he thought to buy 'Distribution of Wishes', a painting by Tony made in the early years of their friendship. He asked Di, his wife, and myself what we thought. I suggested to them that an appeal be set up (something that Patrick had done previously for Tony and myself) and invite friends to donate towards the purchase of the painting so it could be given as a gift to Patrick.

Gail readily agreed to the idea. Seeing the money raised from the sale as Tony's, she decided to use it to finance this book.

Les Coleman

Acknowledgements

To Gail for her tireless support and generosity in all respects to help in the realisation of this book.

To Dawn Ades, Gail Earnshaw, Paul Hammond, George Hardie, James Heartfield, Patrick Hughes, Michel Rémy, Michael Richardson, Roger Sabin and Chris Vine for their marvellous essays.

To Glen Baxter, John Bell, Liz Berry, Doug Binder, Tony Blundell, Jack Chesterman, Frances Earnshaw, Dudley Edwards, Peter Ellis, Marie-Odile Gain d'Enquin, George Hainsworth, Sonny Hayes, John Hyatt, Michael Randle, Phil Shaw, Wedgwood Steventon, Jean Thacker, Stephen Wierczewski and John Welson for writing their anecdotes about Tony.

To Vic Allen, Di Atkinson, Mary Rose Beaumont, John Bevis, Bill Bingham, Isabelle Blondiau, Alastair Brotchie, Louisa Buck, Michael Chestnutt, John Clayton, Ken Cox, Ruth Earnshaw, Angela Flowers, Matthew Flowers, Nancy Fouts, Kathleen Fox, Michael Gibbs, Dave Hanger, Frank Jennings, John Kirby, Alex Marengo, Jeffrey Sherwin, Kirsten Simister, Nigel Walsh, Ted Wilks, Dudley Winterbottom, Gareth Winters, Michael Woods, and the Random House Group Archive for providing invaluable material and support.

To Colin Sackett for his design work and editorial advice. To Martin Rogers at RGAP (Research Group for Artists Publications) for acting as publisher.

And all those friends, too numerous to mention, who generously contributed to the FOP (Friends of Patrick) appeal.

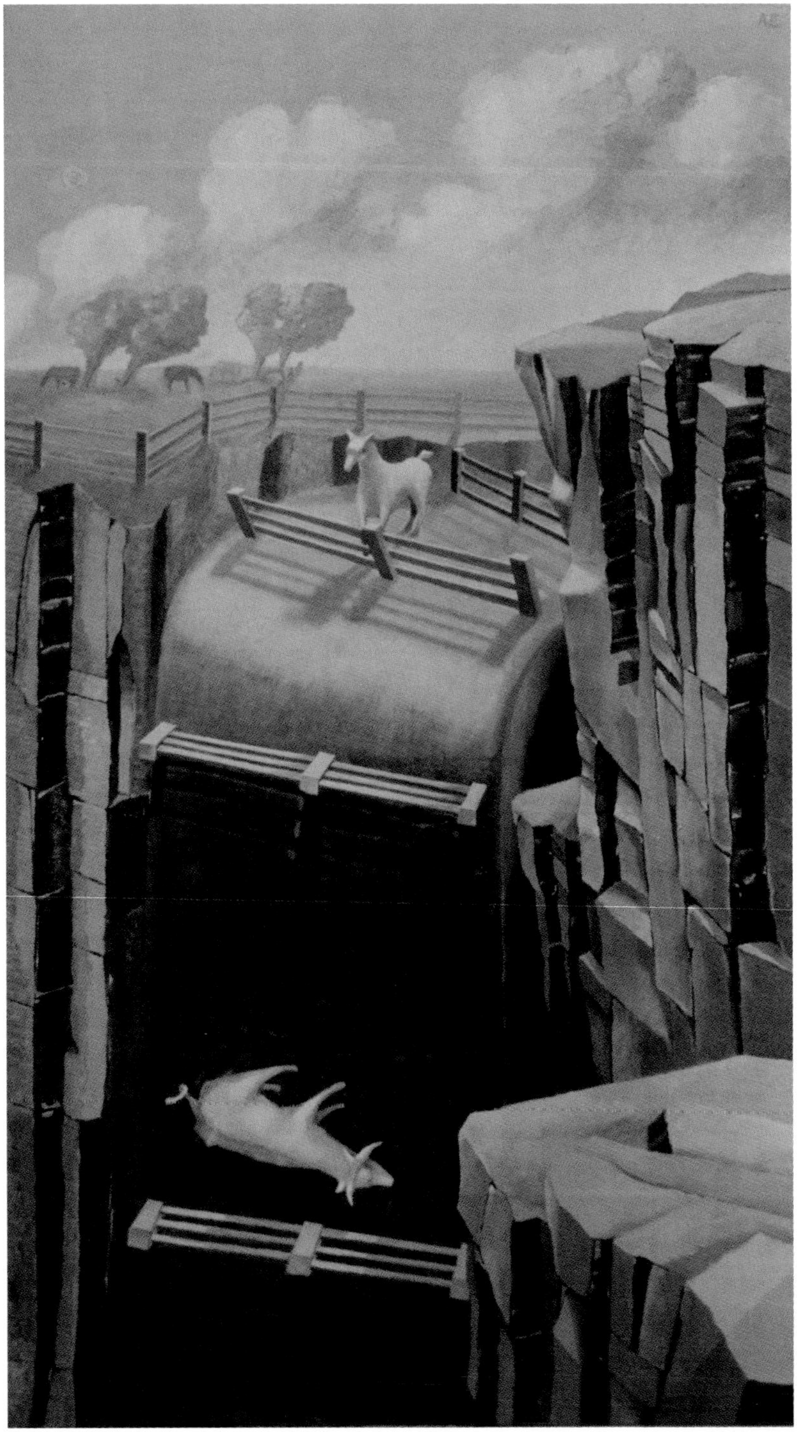

Field Fall, 1965

Michel Rémy

The Contagious Surrealist

"Elephants are contagious"—a surrealist note distributed in the streets of Paris.

In the ideal world, "all submarines shall be crewed by ex-miners" and "energetic sleepwalkers will go to bed with rucksacks strapped to their backs". Aphorisms such as these would no doubt appear in what one would like to imagine to be an expanded, augmented version of André Breton's *Anthology of Black Humour*. Indeed, there is no gainsaying that Breton would have recognized and welcomed Tony Earnshaw as one of the contributors to the anthology, had the course of history decided otherwise.

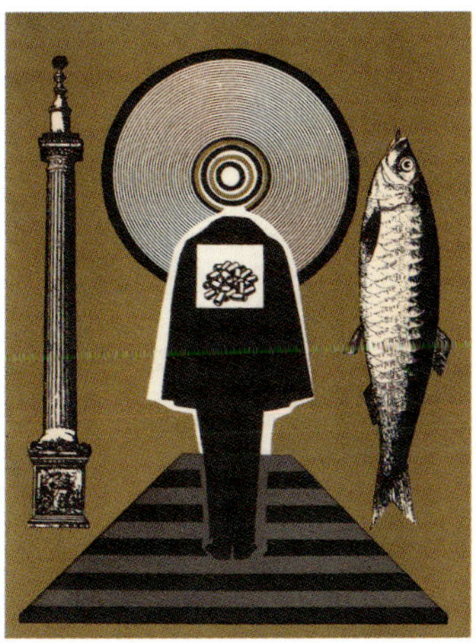

The Enchanted Domain, (Cover: Conroy Maddox), 1967

This course, however, was redressed by E.L.T. Mesens, John Lyle and Conroy Maddox's warm welcome of Tony at 'The Enchanted Domain' surrealist exhibition at Exeter City Gallery in 1967. In the catalogue, Tony made a brilliant, albeit brief, display of the self-ironical stance which he will never depart from when he declared "Paintings in an exhibition are subversive documents fallen into the wrong hands", adding "I think Bakunin's ukase 'If they give you ruled paper, turn it through 90° and write your piece across the lines' is surreal".

Tony's real ancestry was then clearly stated—anarchism—inseparably from his deep surrealist commitment. In the wake of Rimbaud, Blake, Lautréamont, Jarry, but also jazz and bluesmen like Jimmy Yancey and the Armstrong Hot Fives, and women like Bessie Smith, he would launch himself into the celebration of the marriage of heaven and hell, anarchism and Surrealism, regardless of the difference between the two—and this is as it should be since, like all surrealists, Tony never ceased to proclaim the death of dualism.

This is what humour is all about, isn't it? Refusing all kinds of categorization, including the supreme one, that of what is moral and what is immoral. Humour is a-moral. Unless one prefers to view it as belonging to a radically revolutionary moral, just as madness, love and poetry are fundamentally revolutionary activities (or should be!), inhabited as they are, possessed one should say, by the strict disinterestedness of the subconscious. There is, in humour, and even more in black humour, a deeply anarchistic quality in the sense that humour suspends itself from, and refuses to hear about, any of the consequences it might bring about, unwittingly or not. Humour proclaims its constitutive irresponsibility for what may ensue—the responsibility for its consequences being handed over, so to speak, to the one humour addresses. This is why one can speak of the *work* of humour taking place in the interlocutor's mind. Hence its salutary, restorative quality.

In *Grains et issues* (1935), the Dadaist poet Tristan Tzara sees humour as a factor of hope, a means to reduce "the monstrous antagonisms between the individual and modern society", a way to throw light on our relationships to things not only by negating the object which is made fun of but also by destabilizing the rational thinking which had hitherto comfortably pigeon-holed that object—as in "a sieve to sort big lathes from small ones" or "a blotting-paper boat" or "penicillin-tipped arrows".

Humour is a factor of survival, the revenge of the individual over his own limits and the limits imposed on him by society's language.

Hence the colours worn by Anthony Earnshaw's words, stories, drawings, paintings and objects, black and red, two colours, flying high, which interact and mix to the greater glory of the pleasure principle.

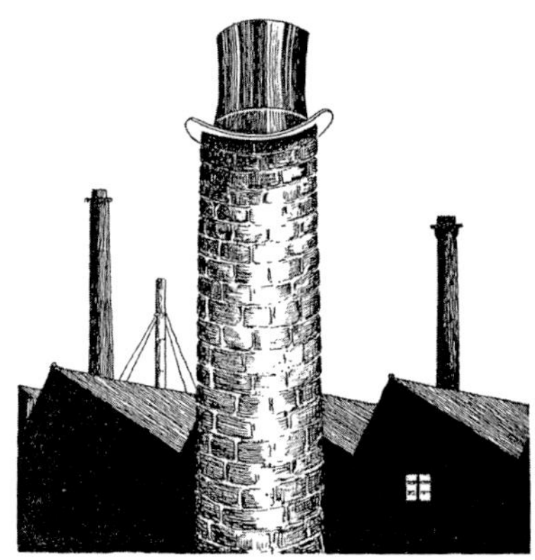
A Pillar of Society, c.1983–86

Tony, then, emblematizes the irresistible permanence of the surrealist spirit. But a form of Surrealism openly taken to its radical extremity, fertilized by the anarchist spirit which has inspired and fuelled Surrealism from its inception, and which surrealists have fully recognized as theirs, especially after the war when the hopes they had placed in political revolutionary solutions had been crushed by Stalin's blind dictatorship and by the news of Trotsky's assassination by Stalin's henchmen. Indeed, anarchism is constitutive of the surrealist enterprise. Let us remember the surrealist call to action in *La Révolution Surréaliste* as early as 1925: "Open the prisons. Disband the army. There are no common-law crimes". Maybe these orders are to be read between Tony's lines when he imagined that "in Arcadia, stiles over prison walls are a common sight".

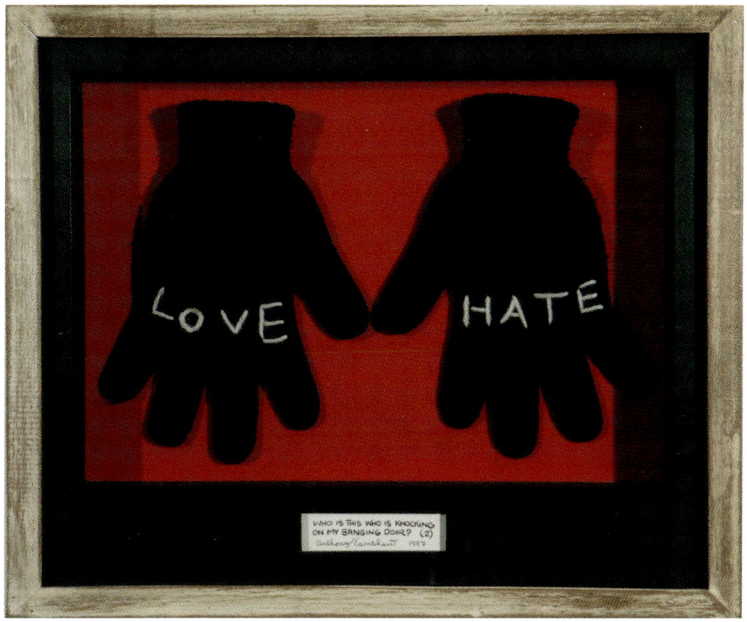

Who is This Who is Knocking on My Banging Door? (second version), 1997

In that respect, Tony Earnshaw's humour founds a radical deconstruction of reality. This signifies a destruction of the moral codes of a bigoted, neutralised (or should one say, neutered?) society, a scathing criticism of the mood of conservatism and blaséism which thrives on the untouchable values of order and social-stability-at-all-costs—the poor will be poor, and the rich will be rich, as one says boys will be boys. But it also signifies a desperate hope for the emancipation of the mind and the ever-renewed reconstruction of our mind's landmarks in the name of Desire—a deconstruction of all systems into a systematic questioning of systems—at the crossroads of Dada, socialism and libertarianism.

Let us remember André Breton's famous answer to a journalist of *Indice*, a Canary Island review, in 1935. When asked "Confronted by an immediate social action, can art put itself into the service of a definite political idea?", he unambiguously answered: "It must unreservedly put itself into the service of the idea during the period in which the idea is transformed into action… It is indispensable however, that art regain its independence if the artist wishes to escape serious contradictions objectively

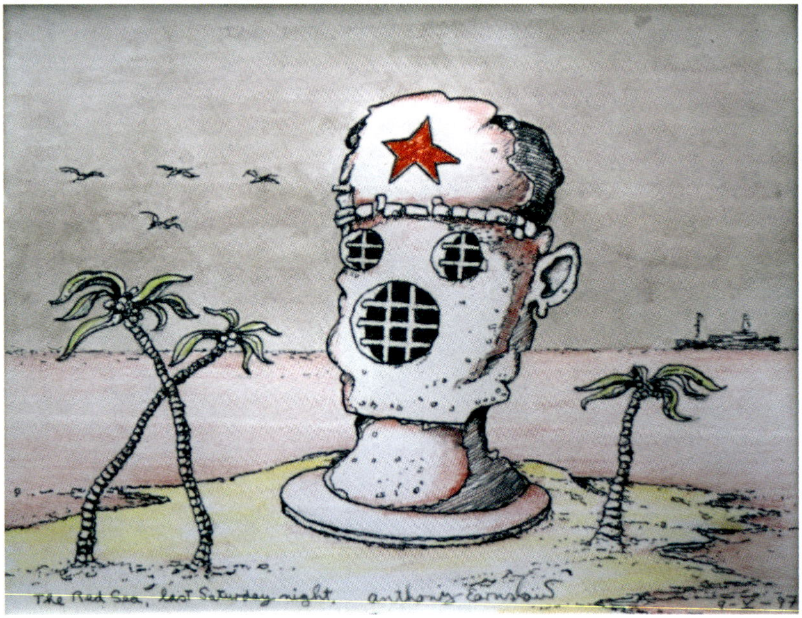

The Red Sea, Last Saturday Night, 1997

harmful even to the idea which he wishes to serve." Tony never ceased to exalt the struggle of the workers and the underdogs, he never faltered in his defence of those oppressed by inequalities and exploitation, working, weaving this commitment into his poetical work, and weaving his poetical work into this everyday struggle.

What Tony has clearly demonstrated is that that struggle goes on, the pressure of economic conditions and social constraints is far from coming to an end and it is essential, *vital* to resist and manifest one's resistance over and over again. "Warning", he once wrote, as if it were a public notice, "this slag-heap has been undermined by the working-class"; poetry and political protest making love.

Reading Tony's stories, relishing his aphorisms, gazing at

one of his objects or paintings is to catch a glimpse of another world—not a world elsewhere, but a world here. The title of one of the most stimulating British surrealist texts, written by Roland Penrose when he embarked on a journey of love and poetry through the Balkans with Lee Miller, is *The Road is Wider Than Long*. It says it all: Tony has managed to widen our roads, the question being not to walk *along* them, rather to walk in a lateral direction.

Earnshaw's collaborative writing with his friend Eric Thacker is the writing of anarchy raised to a disorganizing, deconstructing principle. The adventures of Musrum in *Musrum* and of Christmas in *Wintersol* are the imperturbable provocation of limits in extremely subtle ways—the alchemical magic of humour again. When Tony writes "the hooded thief scooped the booty into his sack, and disappeared into the dark cave which is always close at hand", the fall of the sentence is all the more abrupt and stunning as its beginning is ordinary and 'realistic'. At the core of *Musrum* and *Wintersol*, there is a discrepancy, a rupture, a change of level, a displacement at work which precipitates and telescopes two realities, so much so that we often have to read his statement a second time or to leave our immediate reality, forget the world around for a while and delve into a kind of day-dreaming underground world. "For that spell of time while the eclipse lasted, the miners demanded night shift rates" or "for the sea, an island is an unfathomable mystery" —the mind vertiginously comes back on itself, only to be caught in the logic of the illogical.

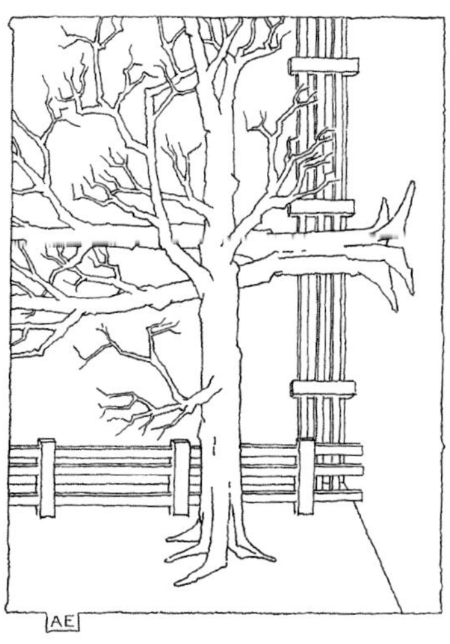

Drawing, *Musrum*, 1968

Any student of Freud's theories will know that this displacement is necessary for, and preliminary to, any operation of condensation which will throw us into surreality, i.e. into a universe in which "the communicable and the incommunicable, the high and the low, life and death..." are not seen as contradictory—and it is true that *Wintersol* and the Musroid world are the secret, vertiginous countries which evoke the poetic creations of Péret, Breton and Prévert in France and Hugh Sykes Davies and Ithell Colquhoun in England—secret countries secreted by "nightingales' sea-shanties".

This process of condensation is unforgettably achieved in Earnshaw's *An Eighth Secret Alphabet*, which is based on the deviation, expansion and mutation of the letters of the alphabet, or rather in their opening out to other shapes without relinquishing their recognizability. An "A" is a woman seen from the back and bending forward with her knickers half-way down her legs, with the caption "A for Ah haa", "W" is two opened books placed next to each other like two flying birds, "M" is two men facing each other and pissing with the caption "M for Mind my feet", "T" is a dove opening its wings perched at the tip of the index of a hand with the caption "T for Touch and go". In these examples taken from one of the many versions he made, Earnshaw reveals the secret life of the alphabet, the revolt of letters against the stereotyped appearance given and imposed on them by dictionaries, in other words by repetitive mental habits and the subsequent loss of imaginative powers. The alphabet conjugates a secessionist agenda, the unhinging of the signified through the slippage of the signifier, so that individual letters actually *mean*, independently of the words they are supposed to form. A revolution indeed when we realize that the minimal duty required of letters is to keep quiet until other letters join them to build words and phrases.

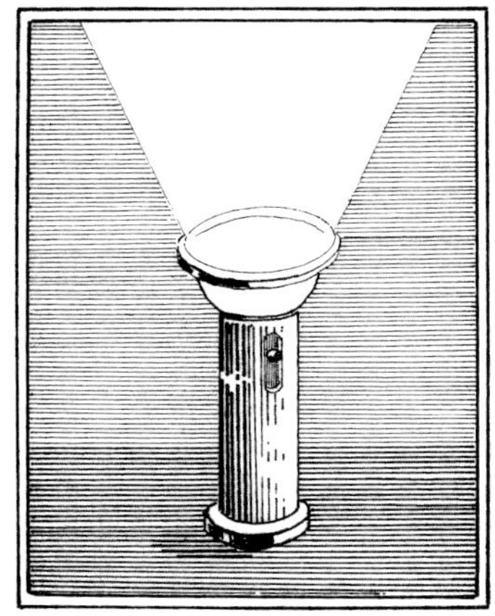

Y for Yeggman, from *An Eighth Secret Alphabet*, 1988

Here, indeed, through a kind of unilateral declaration of independence, letters are given free rein by Tony; they develop, from their own forms, a visual language which tells its own story, keeping umpteen other stories in stock. The literal and the

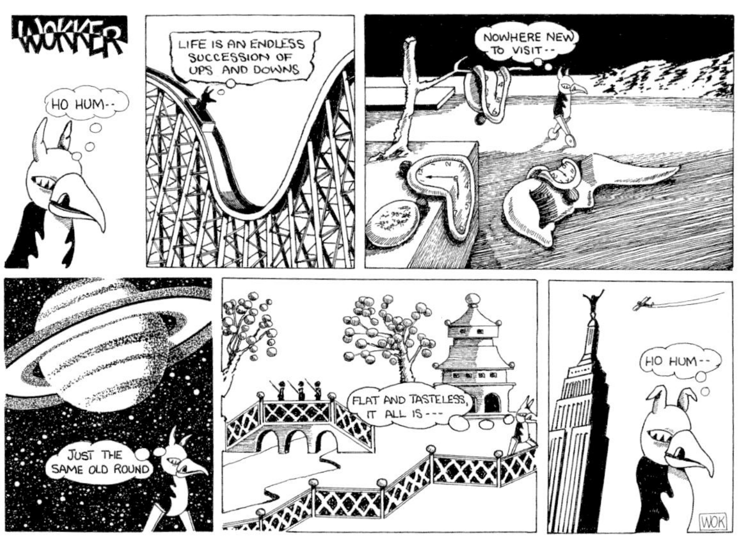

Wokker, previously unpublished, n.d.

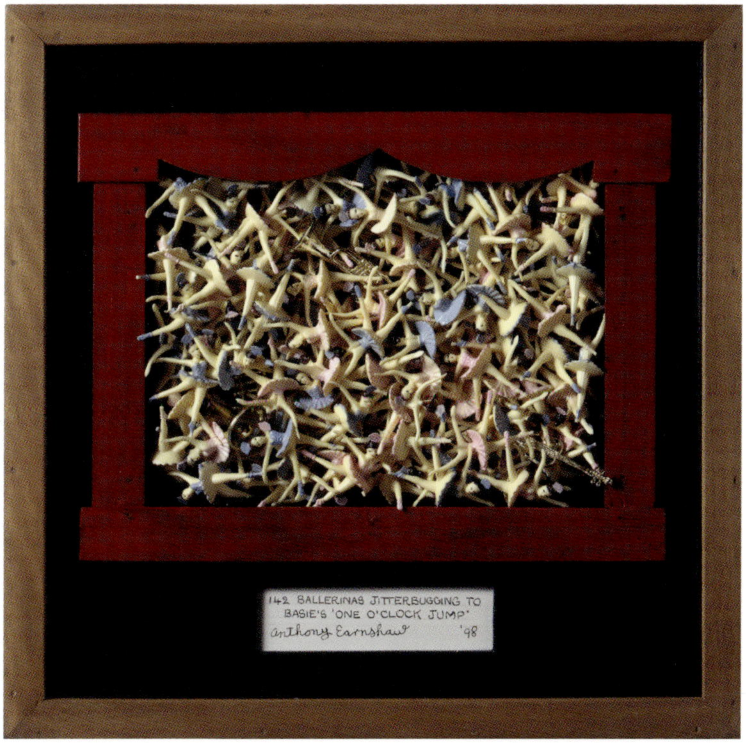

142 Ballerinas Jitterbugging to Basie's 'One O'Clock Jump', 1998

visual coalesce into a hybrid which, paradoxically, prevents us from writing, let alone *voicing*, the letter. We simply cannot write with those refractory letters. Tony kills letters by raising them to a new life. He has become 'literally visual'. This is neither more nor less than an appeal to renew our vision, epitomized in the vibrant call to empathy, to a new 'act of seeing': "We normally disregard our windows with crucial negligence, looking through them but seldom *at* them", he writes in *Musrum*.

E.L.T. Mesens, the once leader of the Surrealist group in England, loved to say that he was born "without God without master without king and without rights". Let Tony join him in this resounding, uncompromising statement, as one of Breton's Great Transparents, stealing the right at night to shake us into "la vraie vie".

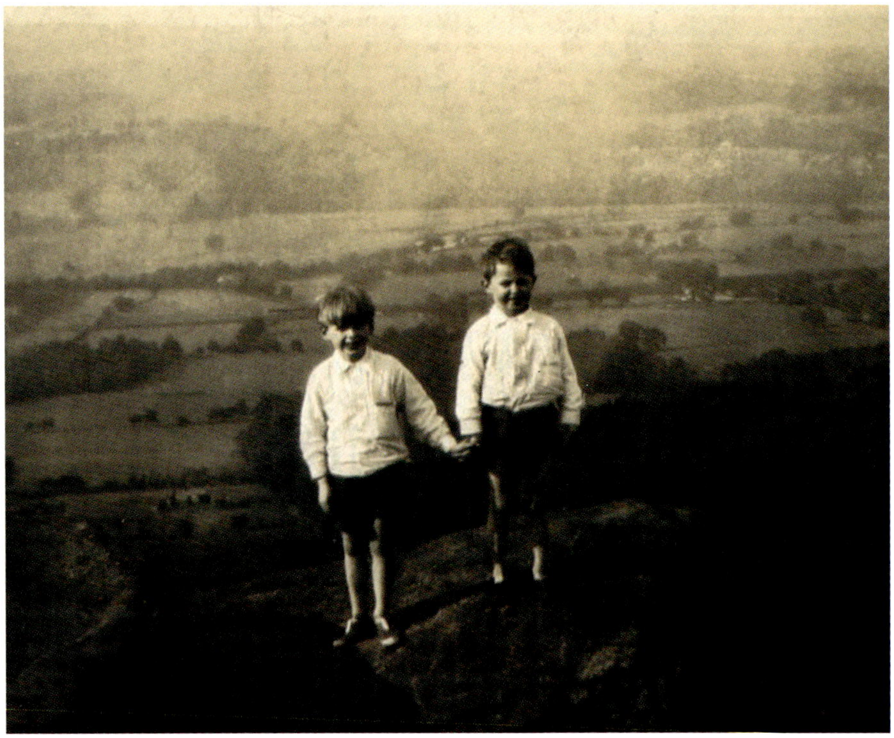

Tony and his friend Jack Swales, Ilkley Moor, 1930

Gail Earnshaw

The Boy in the Man

One day in 1930 six-year-old Anthony Earnshaw, along with his best friend Jack Swales, set off across Ilkley Moor on a journey to find America. The boys somehow knew that, to reach America, you first had to get to Liverpool and the sea. They also knew vaguely that to get to Liverpool they needed to cross the moor and then drop down into the Aire valley and keep heading west. Once there it was their intention to hide on board ship as stowaways and land in America after, in their innocent minds, encountering adventures with killer whales, sharks and pirates. But the Cow and Calf rocks were as far as they would get before being apprehended by a policeman. Earlier in the day, Dorothy, Tony's mother, had left the family jewellery business where she was working to check on the two boys who she had left playing in the yard. They were nowhere to be seen and after checking with Mrs Swales as to their whereabouts without any success, she reported the matter to the police as it was getting late.

"Hello lads! Now where are you two going?"

"Liverpool and then America", replied young Tony, "It's over there isn't it?" he asked the policeman, pointing to the west. After explaining that their mothers might be worried about them, the policeman persuaded the two youngsters to accompany him back to their homes. Earnshaw would not step onto American soil until 1997, where there was an exhibition of his work at the Belloc-Lowndes Fine Art Gallery in Chicago.

Anthony Earnshaw was born in Ilkley, on 9 October 1924, where he spent the first six years of his life. As he describes it: "I first saw the light of day, or for that matter the shades of night, in 1924, the year Lenin died and Breton published his first manifesto. I was born, doubtless bawling and kicking, above the shop at 42 Brook Street, Ilkley. A posthumous child I was, my father having had the unforgivable ineptitude to go ahead and die a month before the event." [1]

In the late summer of 1924, his father, Ernest Earnshaw, who ran the family jewellery and watchmaker's business in Ilkley died after developing pneumonia, complicated by meningitis. In the days before penicillin became widely available meningitis was often fatal and within two weeks of contracting the disease Ernest Earnshaw died.

From family accounts Ernest lost control of his senses having developed a brain fever. According to an aunt he took hold of his razor and attempted to cut his throat only to be restrained by the family doctor who happened to be present. At the time his wife Dorothy (née Myers) was seven months pregnant and their first son Peter was three years old. But Ernest would not live to see his new son born.

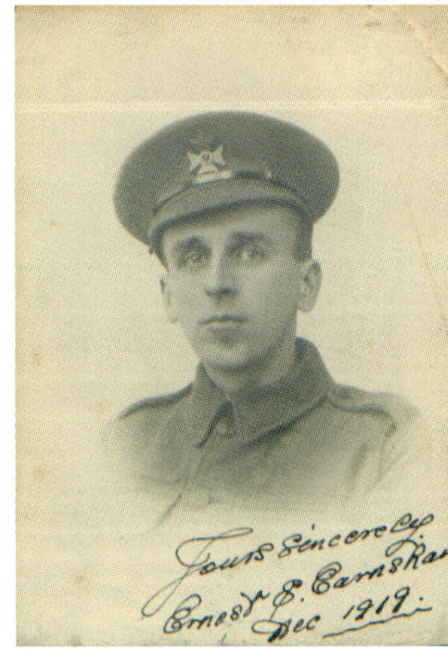

Ernest Earnshaw

Dorothy went into labour, enduring a difficult and distressing time. Later, Tony's aunts told him that she didn't want to live or give birth to him imagining the bleak future stretching ahead. The prospect of bringing up two small children on her own was overwhelming.

Her sisters, Winifred and Gertrude, were at her bedside trying to console and support her. Having finally given birth, she broke down unable to cope, overcome with worry and grief. Winifred, affectionately known to Tony as Aunt Winnie, took the baby away from the distraught Dorothy to lovingly wash, comfort and welcome him into the world. A special bond formed between them that lasted until her premature death in 1940. For the first hours of his life, Tony had temporarily lost both his parents.

Tony spoke of a childhood memory he felt ashamed of. Aged about five years old, and just before the family moved to Redcar, he convinced himself that his mother was not his real mother. He thought he was the offspring of parents who had gone off and left him in the hands of a surrogate mother. He convinced himself he was a changeling, someone of some importance who had been exchanged at birth. He entertained this delusion for some years, not telling anyone, but believing it to be true. He

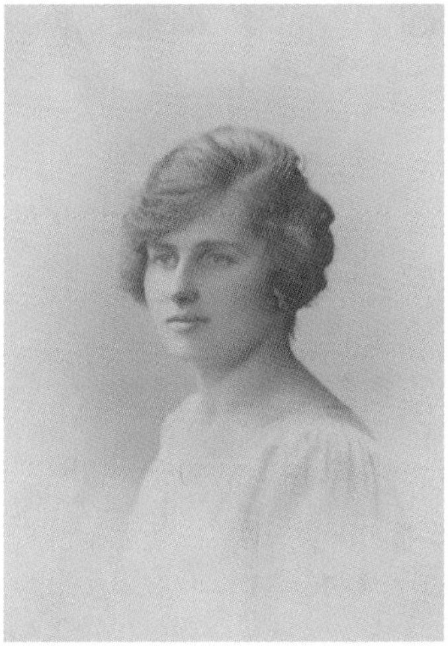

Dorothy Earnshaw

recalled, "As time passed, I realised I had been silly thinking such thoughts. It was obvious that she was my mother. I'm told it is quite commonplace for children to think this, especially when there isn't a father around. The fact that I did not have a father did bother me in the early years, everyone had a dad and I did not. This put me in the 'outsider' category, I felt cheated. I felt the odd one out and ashamed. Like all children, I wanted to be the same as everyone else. However, as I grew older, I liked being different. I began to understand that I was spiritually 'out of step' and felt a kinship with minority interests."

The Earnshaw family seemed to be beset by disaster and death. In the late nineteenth century, Grandfather Earnshaw, as he was called in the family, established a jewellery and watchmaker's business in Ilkley. Legend has it that in 1910 he visited Bradford to sell a pouch of diamonds, where he had arranged to meet a dealer. After successfully closing the transaction and collecting several hundred pounds, he put the money in his wallet. Being of a sociable nature he made his way to a public house to celebrate his good fortune before returning to Ilkley. After buying drinks for everyone he left the pub to be attacked by 'footpads' who stabbed and robbed him, leaving him dying in the gutter. The police were alerted and took him to Bradford Royal Infirmary, where he died. He was twenty-seven years old. The murderers were never apprehended.

Obviously the running of the business became complicated by Ernest's premature death while Dorothy struggled to bring up the two boys. Far from being a prosperous enterprise Dorothy inherited debts and, after six years of uncertainty, financial ruin. As Tony summarised it: "1930 brought a further nosedive in the family fortunes for the shop went bankrupt and we, my mother, brother and I moved to 6 Cedar Grove, a council house in Redcar on Teeside. There, summer visitors in the season, and lodgers in the snowy winters, were put up."[2]

Earnshaw vividly describes his childhood memories, in these formative years spent mostly on his own devising games and exploring his imagination: "I recall playing alone on the beach in mid-winter, building sand cities, labyrinthine constructions with many streets, each with a name known only to me, indifferent to the flurries of snow whirling in the wind from the sea. Another memory is of myself on the beach when a gull which must have died on the wing, plummeted to the sand at my feet, its feathers brushing my head as it did so. Taken aback I was. At the age of seven, it was my first encounter with death."[3]

The family spent four years in Redcar, before moving again, this time to Leeds, where Dorothy had found a job at Lewis's department store. Earnshaw was to live at various addresses in Harehills and Chapel Allerton until 1989 when Tony and I, by then married, moved to Saltburn-by-the-Sea. But he always regarded Leeds as his true home.

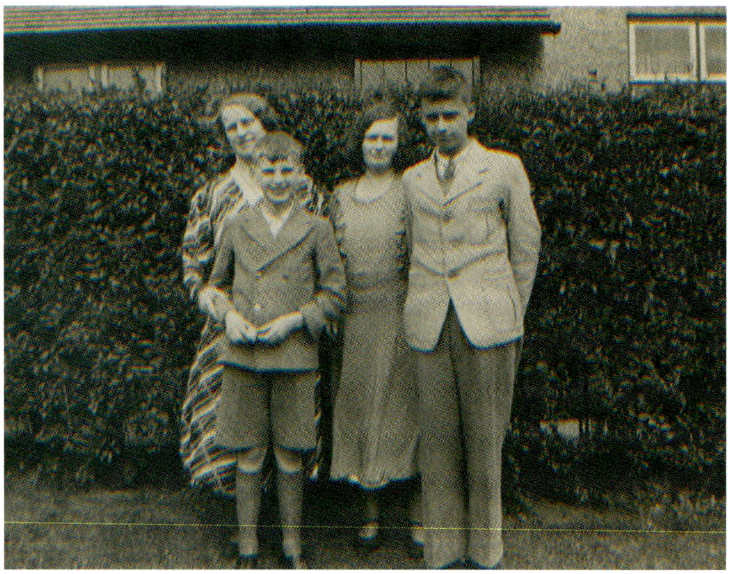

Aunt Winnie, Anthony, Dorothy and Peter, Redcar

Tony and his elder brother Peter always had enough food to eat, shoes on their feet and warm clothes to wear. In 1934 during the Depression an event took place that affected Tony profoundly. It was a cold December day and snow and slush covered the ground, a north wind blowing off the nearby sea. Tony, aged ten, and his mother were on a shopping trip to Middlesbrough when he witnessed a scene he never forgot. A woman with a shawl covering her head was walking towards them, a boy and a girl by her side. They were the about the same age as Tony and he immediately identified with them. The children were trudging barefoot in the slush without any shoes or socks. The look of anguish on their faces showed their suffering and desolation. Tony stared at the boy who wore a scruffy jersey and ragged trousers. It was a scene he would never forget.

Like many children, Tony became a member of the local street gang. 'The Back Gathorne Terrace Gang' consisted of six boys who spent their time playing marbles, climbing lampposts and playing football. It was in the streets that he learned to 'muck in' with others. Around the age of ten an awareness took place when he realised that ethically he was at odds with his friends. On trips to the local woods to climb trees, dam the beck and 'rag and rob' birds nests of their eggs, he spoke in defence of the birds and their right to live. The gang listened and were persuaded not to 'rob the nests'. This triumph represented a sense of personal morality and the need to stick up for his own beliefs.

Tony attended Harehills School in Leeds which he enjoyed, but because of poor health and a diphtheria epidemic in the city in 1934 he had to be moved temporarily to live with his grandparents in Saltburn-by-the-Sea, a small seaside town on the north-east coast of Yorkshire. They lived in a large rambling property called Arlington House and took in summer lodgers.

The previous occupants of the house had left behind an extraordinary cabinet that fascinated him and would be an influence in his boxed assemblages in later life. This was a Victorian glass-fronted natural history showcase about the size of a wardrobe. It contained a 'jungle' of dried plants in which were arranged stuffed pelicans and humming birds, ostrich eggs and exotic butterflies. Tony and his grandfather were the only members of the family who enjoyed it so it was moved to the cellar workshop. They would stand in front of the showcase imagining far-away places. Occasionally Tony was allowed to step inside the cabinet where he could handle the birds eggs. The cellar became a magic place and it was here that he would watch his Grandfather making toy boats out of wood and showing him how to use wood-working tools. Grandfather Myers was a formative influence on Tony's early life. Most of the time Tony was surrounded by female relatives who, although kind, were unable to provide him with the male role model he wanted. It was Grandfather Myers who showed him the value of patient workmanship, thought and precision. Later in life he used

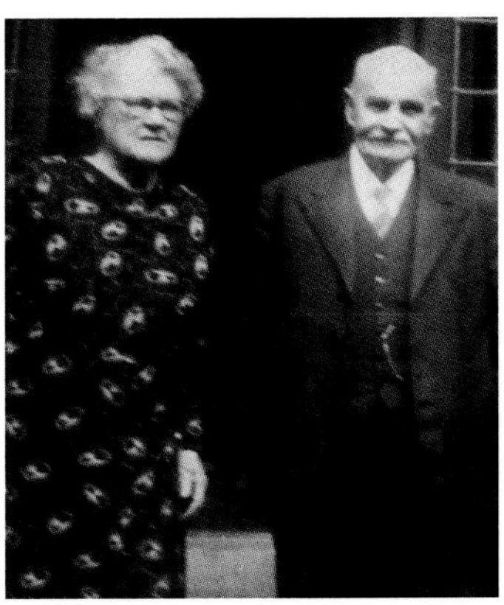

Alice and Fred Myers

this philosophy in his own work, always believing that it was important to give an idea the best possible home.

On one occasion his grandfather gave him two stuffed birds and some eggs which Tony took home to Leeds. Inspired by what he had seen in Saltburn, he tried to make a display case of his own using an empty shoebox. This would be his first attempt as a box maker.

Tony's childhood was lived against the backdrop of the social and political turmoil of 1930s Britain, witnessing several events of historical significance. On the 27 September 1936, he witnessed Oswald Mosley and his Union of British Fascists (Blackshirts) being chased and fighting with trade unionists and members of Jewish organizations in Leeds city centre. These incidents followed a public meeting held by the Fascists on Holbeck Moor. A month later, Tony watched the Jarrow Marchers waving banners and protesting, as they marched through Leeds. These early experiences were important in helping to shape his political awareness.

He developed a special interest in 'uncanny' tales and American science fiction. He particularly liked stories that described strange phenomena and events. These were often stories of the everyday world, suddenly interrupted by circumstances that had no rational explanation being set apart from cause and effect. Every week with his shilling pocket money he took the tram to town and visited Stringers bookshop in Leeds market, which provided him with a wealth of pulp fiction magazines, comics and paperbacks. He would spend hours looking at copies of *Astounding Sci Fi*, *Amazing Stories*, and his favourite *Unknown Worlds*.

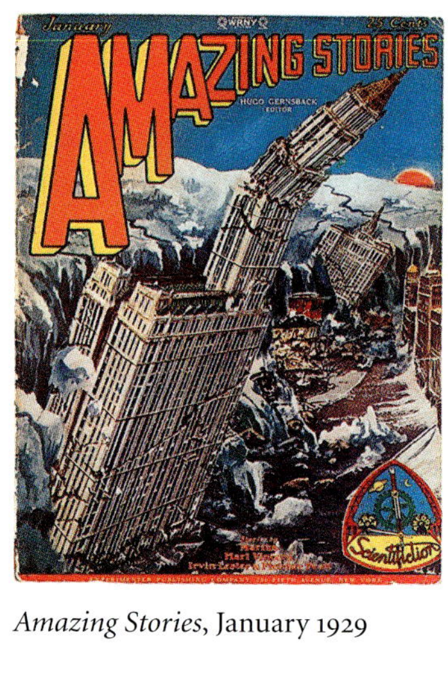

Amazing Stories, January 1929

In one particular story the world is presented as a film set with the human race cast as bit actors taking part in a third-rate movie made for the entertainment of superior beings, namely the gods. This world was to coincide with the emergence of cinematography and what we regard as history was just an intervention by the film scriptwriters. In the story when we die we would become unemployed and available for the next film. Throughout his life, Tony remained an avid reader, enjoying ghost stories and science fiction. Three authors he constantly returned to were Edgar Allan Poe, M.R. James and Arthur Machen.

During their early teens Tony and Peter became closer. Dorothy bought Tony a bicycle, a JT Rogers which cost six pounds and five shillings, a lot of money for her to pay out with the family finances so precarious. She paid for it in installments over the next year. Cycling gave the boys the freedom to discover and explore the Yorkshire Dales. They would spend the weekend cycling and staying at youth hostels. Tony had great respect for the Youth Hostel Association and became a life member.

Peter liked American swing music, in particular Benny Goodman, Woody Herman and Duke Ellington, and Tony heard him listening to his 78s played on an electric gramophone which he had made himself. This interest rubbed off on Tony, who

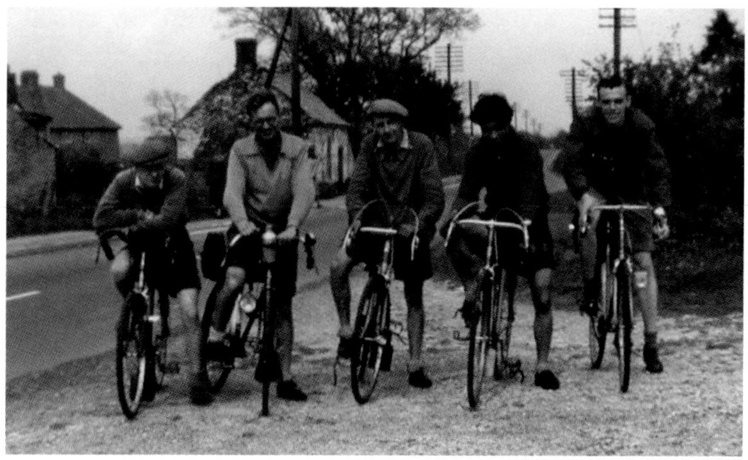

Anthony (centre) and Peter (centre left) with friends, Yorkshire Dales

then developed his own musical tastes. Ellington's records such as 'Harlem Airshaft' and 'Black and Tan Fantasy', captured Tony's imagination. At fourteen he developed an interest in the history and origins of New Orleans jazz and blues. He fell in love with the rough emotional appeal of Armstrong's Hot Fives and Hot Sevens, and the warm humanism of Bessie Smith.

At the time there were a number of dance-halls in the centre of Leeds, ballroom dancing being part of the entertainment for young people. The Mecca, Majestic and Capitol were popular places to go and meet girls on a Saturday night. Disliking dance music and being shy, Tony looked for an alternative social life. Although he felt alone he was not completely isolated, establishing close friendships with 'comrades' such as Eric Thacker, who shared many of Tony's interests.

Eric and Tony both left school at the age of fifteen, and one year later, in 1940, they would meet at Leeds Rhythm Club, where members brought their jazz 78s to play. Their friendship was built around their common interests and was often conducted through the post. Their mutual interest in poetry would lead to their written and illustrated collaborations *Musrum*, *Wintersol* and 'Wokker'.

Tony went to work at Ingleby Motors, an engineering works in Leeds making electric motors and dynamos, as an apprentice lathe turner. It was necessary for Tony and his brother to start work at a young age to help with the family finances. This responsibility brought an abrupt end to their childhood and formal education.

It was a different story for their cousin George Earnshaw who had the support of the wealthier side of the Earnshaw family. Dorothy and her two boys were looked down upon, because it was believed that Dorothy's late husband, Ernest, had married beneath himself. Meanwhile, George went to Bradford Grammar School where he received an education from which he would benefit. During their childhood, Tony and Peter knew little about George. Although of similar ages they had very different experiences growing up. Edward Earnshaw, George's father, was a bank manager and the family lived in a leafy suburb of Bradford. Through the qualifications he gained at school he was able to pursue an academic career, teaching Spanish in an Adult Education College. Tony thought the reluctance to offer financial help to Dorothy was shameful as they were a wealthy family and could have paid for Peter and Tony to continue their education. He knew that it was a real struggle for his mother and felt they had come down in the world through the misfortune of their father's early death.

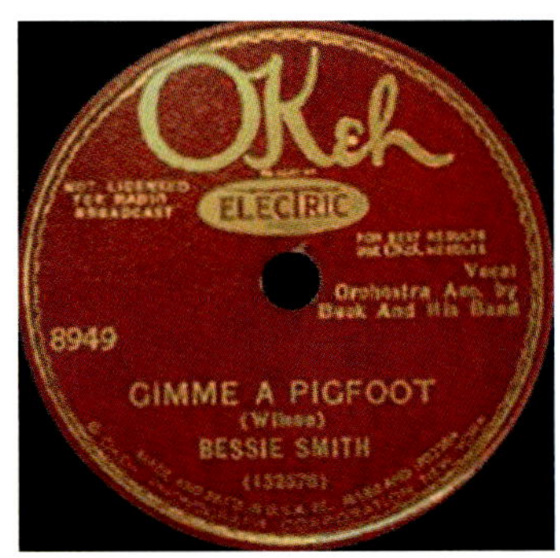

Record label: Bessie Smith, 'Gimme a Pigfoot', 1933

The abrupt end to Tony's formal education troubled him deeply throughout his life. The brutalizing experience of manual drudgery in poor factory conditions left him angry and frustrated. He knew he had been deprived the opportunity to further his capabilities. One of the reasons for his politicization was the experience of working in an environment where he felt exploited by 'the bosses'. It was his natural curiosity that led him away from work to Leeds Public Library where he would discover Surrealism and poetry. Books became Tony's education, an education that eventually enabled him to turn his back on factory work.

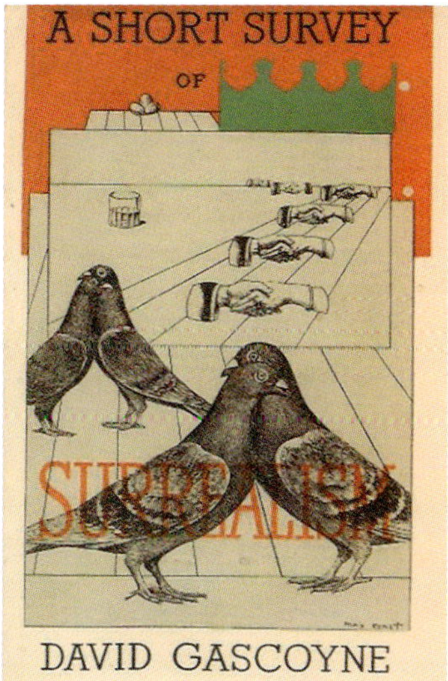

David Gascoyne, *A Short Survey of Surrealism*, (Cover: Max Ernst), 1935

Despite the harsh conditions at Inglebys there was no union to fight for the workers' rights. Tony felt rebellious. He had little respect for his employers who he considered greedy, often quoting the science fiction writer Robert Heinlein: "We go to work to earn the money to buy the food to get the strength to go to work to earn the money to buy the food to get the strength to go to work, and so on, until we fall over dead!"

After six years working at Ingleby's he was sacked in 1946, for pinning a poem that he had written on the factory notice board:

These ingled and angled engines
Shall be motored to a place
Where power has fused
And a new drive flows free.
When the Madams and the Sirs
Busy with eclairs
Order the goods
To be delivered to the woods.
The power of St. Barnabus
Speeds through the wires
Up above the Spires
To harm us.
Hammer and turn
Cut and wind
Money is short
When the boss is long.

Skilled engineering work was plentiful and he immediately found employment at Thomas Green & Sons, North Street, Leeds. The conditions at Greens were much better. There was a union which he was pleased to join. He had to work shifts, described as 'fortnights about'. Two weeks on days and two weeks on nights. He saw this as a new and interesting experience but had to adjust himself to this change in conditions. Working nights seemed strange. He describes it as, "you step out of the daylight world into a different world. Ten of us worked nights as opposed to thirty working on the day shift. You became more intimately involved with your workmates."

Tony was given the job of operating an indoor crane. There were long gaps between lifts and it was usual for the driver to read a paper. Instead Tony took this opportunity to paint small watercolours. Working nights meant that he could continue to paint during the daytime. Previously at Ingleby's he had used 'found objects' to make small metal sculptures; now he had started painting and it was this that would gradually become his route out of factory work.

In 1942, on his eighteenth birthday, Tony received his call-up papers to join the army. He attended the customary medical. Throughout his life he suffered chest problems and on examination, together with his own doctor's report, he was graded C3, which meant he was unfit for active service. Being exempt from military service his part in the war effort was to make electric motors. He was relieved, as he dreaded the idea of being drafted into the army and the way that would impact on his life. In later life I asked if he would have been prepared to go to prison as a conscientious objector. Tony responded by saying that he probably would have joined up and fought Nazism, as it was an authoritarian tyranny, so destructive that it had to be resisted and the only means of doing this was by war. Like many others he had no real idea of what was happening in Europe during the war years. He was shocked when after the fall of Hitler he saw pictures showing the sinister truth of Belsen on British Movietone News at the cinema. A few months later further horror committed in the name of democracy, came to the cinema screen showing what the USA had achieved by dropping their atomic bombs on Nagasaki and Hiroshima. This knowledge only propelled Tony further in the direction of anarchism, feeling that these devastating events cast doubts on the idea of government serving the best interests of the populace at all times.

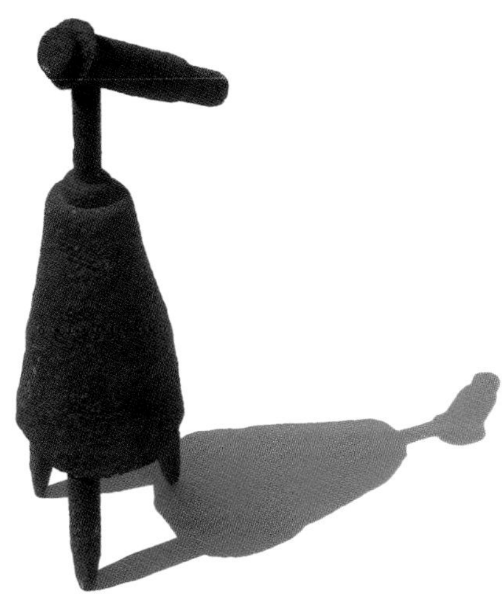

Me Mam, c.1944

Around 1945, Tony contacted Freedom Press, publisher of the long standing anarchist newspaper, encouraging them to print an invitation, asking anyone interested in forming an Anarchist Discussion Group in the Leeds and Bradford area to contact him. Ironically, only Donald Rooum who worked for *Freedom*

Phantoms & Shadows Playing With Ropes & a Rusty Helmet, 1949

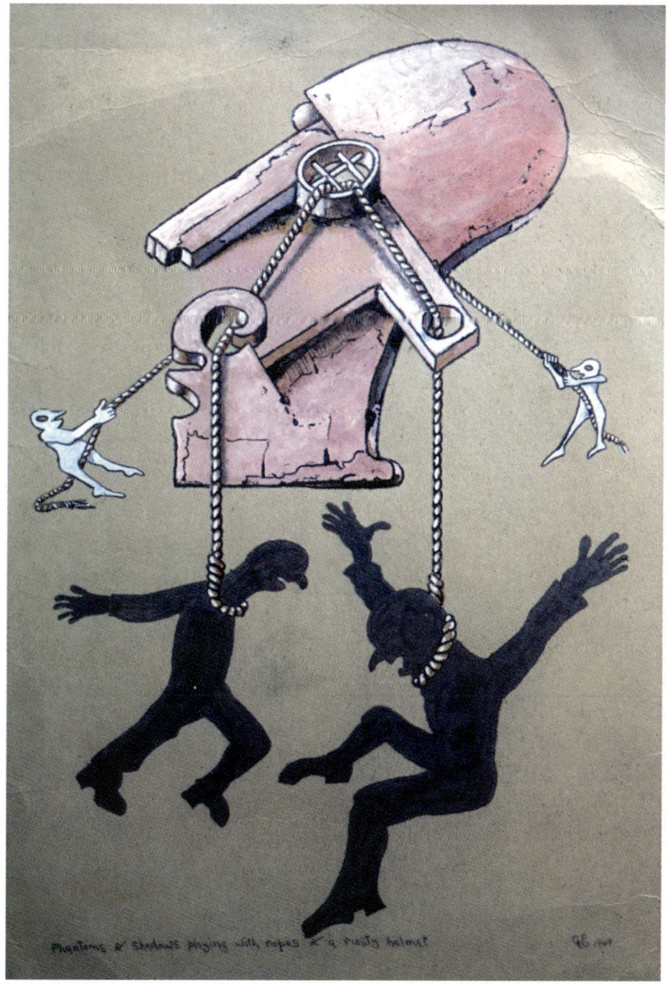

and lived in Bradford at that time, responded. Politically the Labour Party was not radical enough and trade unionism, in Tony's words, was "just a compromise set up to get a few more crumbs from the table of capitalism. It would not overthrow capitalism and set in motion a new socialism which would have been a revolution that would have changed society for the better."

Tony's pre-war friendship with Eric Thacker had been interrupted when Eric received his call-up papers, but they maintained a correspondence throughout the war. In 1947 they got back together again, to visit bookshops and discuss Surrealism, poetry and jazz. For their amusement, they would elect to meet up in unusual places, for example, in a prearranged cinema. Having separately entered the cinema, a voice might be heard in the darkness: "Eric are you there?" and from another part of the cinema, the reply might come, "Yes, I am here!" Having met up they would leave the cinema, without watching the film, then on to a bookshop or tea-room.

"It was in the late 1940s that, enamoured of Surrealism, I came to see my home city—Leeds—in a new light. Restless and not knowing what to do, I spent my Saturday evenings walking… seeking, I suppose, some avenue of astonishment. (Occasionally I was in the company of another but most frequently alone.)

These walks were in fact elaborate games. From some arbitrary starting point, I would walk to the other side of town using, as far as possible, only backstreets and side-roads—secret passages of yet another species.

Again, other evenings were spent tram-riding, I boarded and alighted from trams at random for two or three hours. It was my custom to carry a book to read on these swaying, nocturnal journeys.

It was only later that I learnt that the (actual) Surrealists had engaged in very similar activities in Paris in the 1920s."[4]

In 1947 Tony made three visits to the London Gallery, in Brook Street, which specialised in surrealist art. The gallery was run by E.L.T. Mesens, who had been a central figure in the Belgian surrealist group in Brussels throughout the '20s and '30s. Here, Tony would see paintings by Magritte, Ernst and Tanguy, amongst others. Too reticent to introduce himself to Mesens, Tony did get into conversation with a young George Melly, who was employed by Mesens and gave Tony a tour round the gallery. This was the first of many meetings, and a loyal friendship developed between them, with Melly becoming a champion of Earnshaw's cause and a collector of his work in later years. Although Tony was aware of a surrealist group active in London, being a retiring young man, he lacked confidence to make contact. As he later put it to Melly: "I saw myself as a scruffy working lad, no money, uneducated, no talent. I'd only just started to teach myself to draw and paint (from rock bottom). Nothing to offer but my restlessness. The idea of a real surrealist like Mesens overawed me."[5]

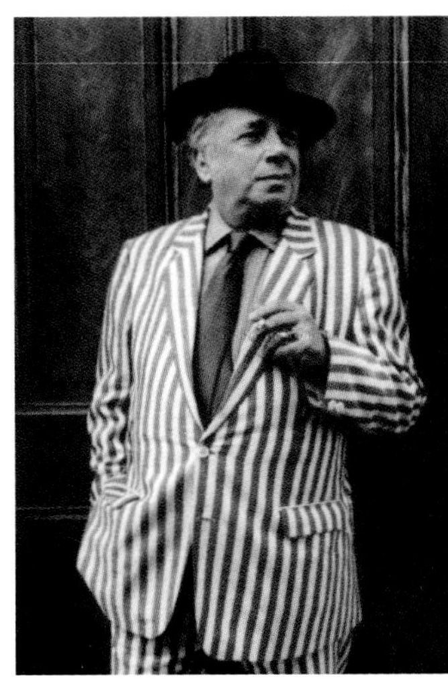
George Melly

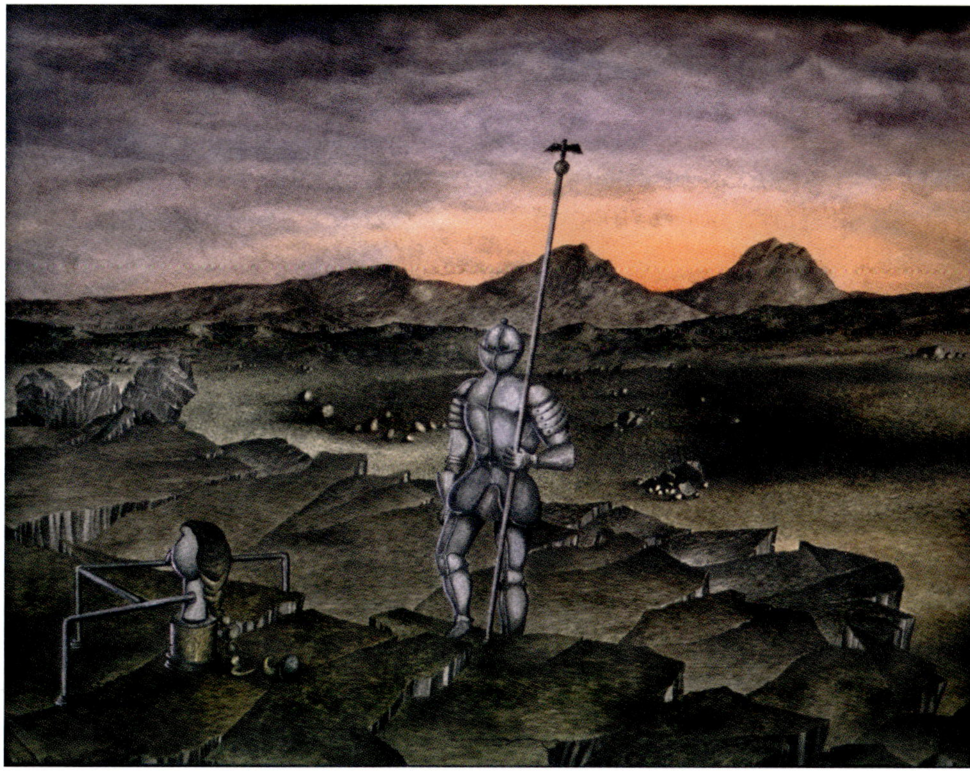

Untitled, 1946

In 1956 Tony gained employment at Leeds College of Art working as a portrait model for painting evening classes. Here he met Monica Simpson who attended his class. They became close friends and in 1957 married. In December their first daughter Ruth was born, followed by Frances in 1959.

Throughout the 1950s, despite his family responsibilities and the lack of interest in his work, he continued to develop his painting which drew heavily on the factory environment in which he worked, echoing its forms and colours. The shapes found in machinery, with their levers and cogs, were rendered in a rich range of browns reminiscent of rusty metal. His paintings were always adventures in personal discovery, with technique always secondary to poetic vision. This, coupled with his natural reticence, might have resulted in a drift into obscurity, but for several important encounters he made in the decade that followed.

One such encounter was with the young artist Patrick Hughes. In 1961 they met in The Wrens pub in Leeds, becoming

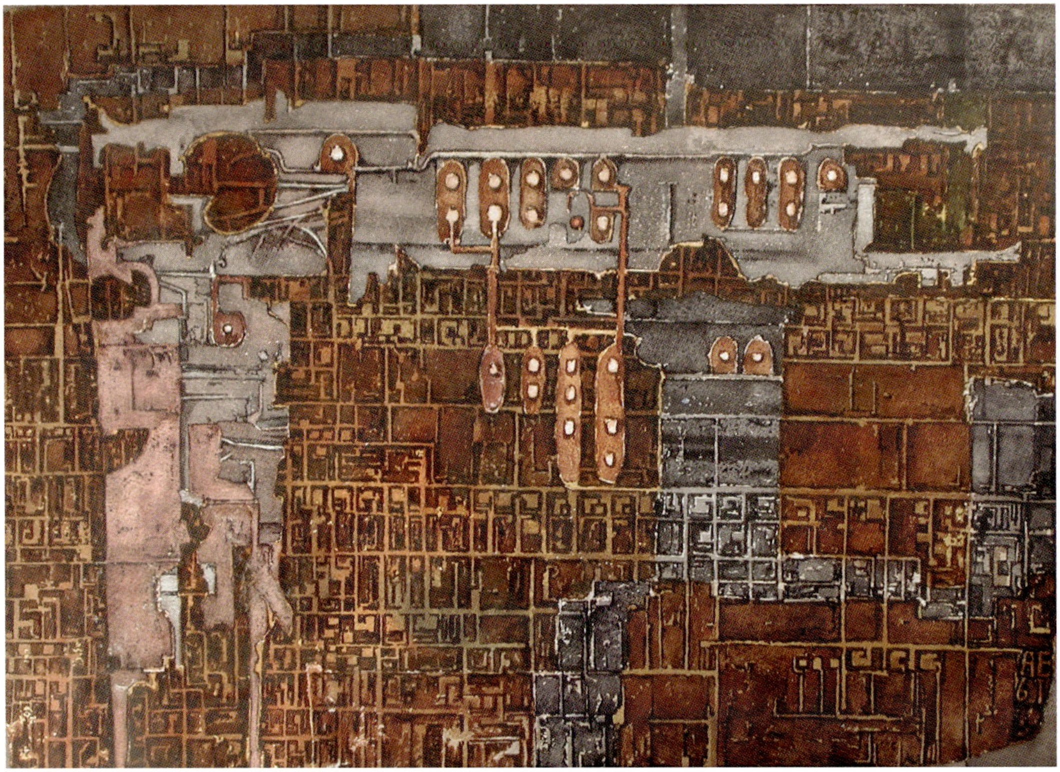

Many Levers to Push and Knobs to Pull, 1961

firm friends through their shared interest in poetry and also Surrealism, but through their wish to see the world from a different perspective. Patrick, then twenty-one, had just held his first successful exhibition in London and was a schoolteacher. Shortly after he started teaching at Leeds College of Art and invited Tony to hold a retrospective of his work in the Leeds Institute Gallery, which organized exhibitions with the support of the college. An exhibition of eighty paintings and drawings covering the period 1945–1965 was held in January 1966. This was a pivotal exhibition for Tony, provoking considerable interest in his work; it changed the course of his life. Later that year, Tony was offered one day a week teaching at Harrogate Art College, which in turn led the following year to two days teaching at Bradford College of Art. This move into teaching finally helped Tony to free himself completely from factory work.

From an early age Tony felt he was different from his peers, an outsider, or as he described it, "out of step". Due to the social and economic climate of the interwar period, his perception was coloured by an awareness of the injustice of the class and economic system of Britain. This drew him to discover anarchism, Surrealism and New Orleans jazz. For Tony, they were one and the same thing in as much as they represented liberty, imagination and poetry. Through embracing their rebellious spirit, he found his true home. "I was among friends at last." [6]

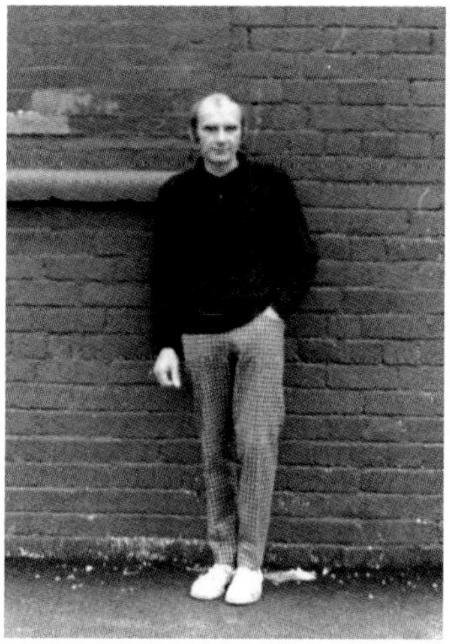

Bradford College of Art, c.1967

Notes

This account of Anthony Earnshaw's early life is based on conversations I shared with him during the thirty-two years we spent together. All unsourced quotes are taken from these conversations.

1. Anthony Earnshaw, *A View From Back o' Town*, Leeds City Art Gallery 1987.
2. *Ibid.*
3. *Ibid.*
4. George Melly, *Paris and the Surrealists*, Thames & Hudson, London 1991.
5. *Ibid.*
6. Anthony Earnshaw, *op. cit.*

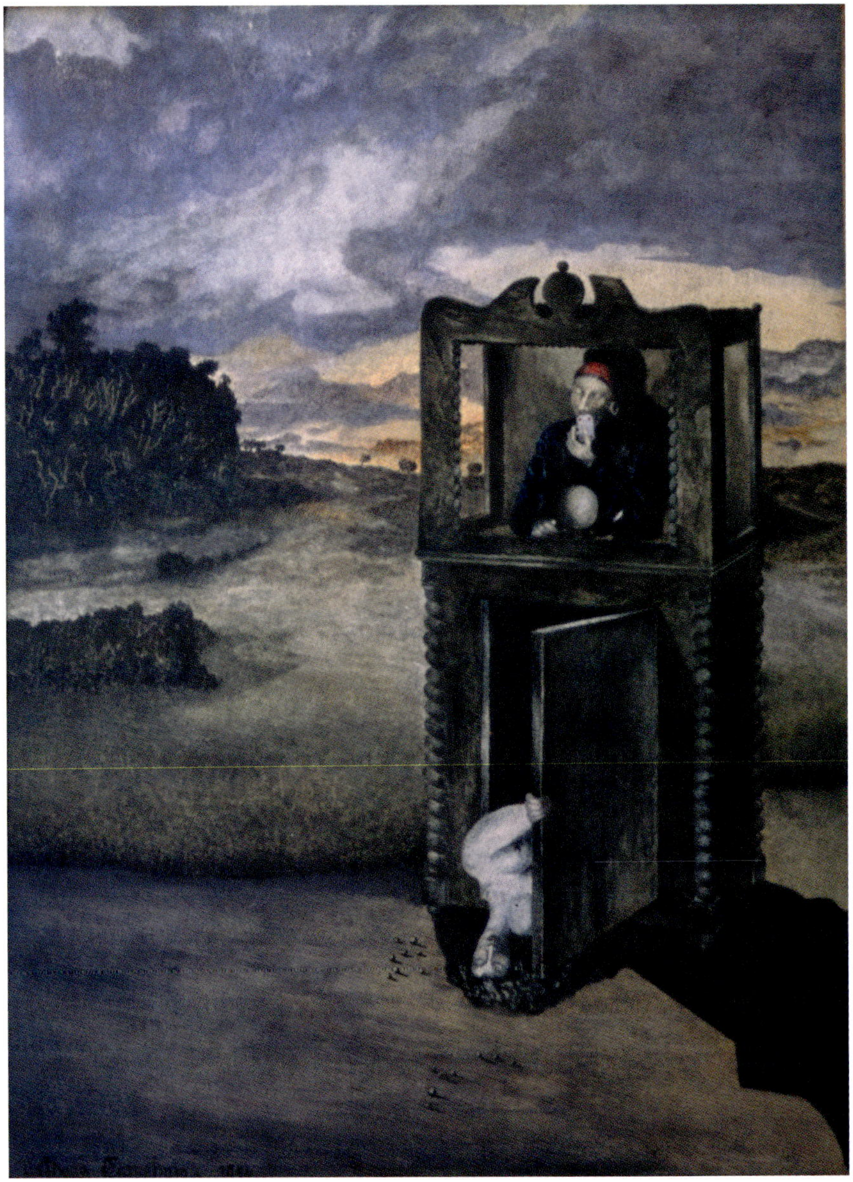

The End of a Perfect Day, 1946

Dawn Ades

Surrealism Discovers Earnshaw

Without any warning and, apparently, without any previous desire to do so, Anthony Earnshaw began to paint, and found he could transmit dreams, ideas, conundrums, perceptions in immediately graspable visual form. This seems to have happened quite suddenly, as an immediate consequence of his encounter with Surrealism. In 1945, he said, he discovered Surrealism, "and I will say that up to this date I was not interested in painting, later that year as a result of my discovery I made my first watercolour".[1] This was 'Landscape' 1945, (now lost), the first entry in the catalogue to his first solo exhibition (he had contributed to a mixed show in a shoe shop in Leeds in 1950). But enough of his drawings, watercolours and gouaches survive, from the 1940s, to support the notion that he sprang forth fully armed for visual combat, and by the mid 1950s he was making paintings of breath-taking originality. He continued to paint, usually in watercolour, until "towards the end of the 60s my activities as a painter virtually petered out. Apart from the occasional 'dabble' I haven't painted since then."[2] Compositions of other kinds took over—social-realist drawings, the albums of alphabets, stories, aphorisms, assemblages, and 'Wokker', a comic strip. Looking forward in 1987 he wrote: "These days assemblage is the thing. It seems to me 'the assemblage' is more real, therefore more powerful than 'the painting'."[3] Today Earnshaw is better known for his assemblages and box-constructions rather than his paintings, and his sense that they could be more powerful than painting echoes the triumph of the surrealist object in the 1930s and beyond.

The tension between action and expression was felt acutely by the surrealists. As Earnshaw wrote: "To make a lathe crack an egg, or have a hut cast a shadow over a mansion, is all the poet or artist can hope to do. But I fear it is not enough."[4]

Nonetheless, it is something, and the subversive disruptions of the proper order of things in his early drawings and paintings still startles.

Discovering Surrealism and through it, painting, was not a matter of seeing and emulating a visual style. As Earnshaw immediately understood, Surrealism was not and never had been definable by a style. "If this century only had Cubism or Futurism or the Euston Road School to offer, I doubt I would have been interested in painting. Surrealism is a spirit of rebellion which can express itself in humour, cocking the snook, upsetting the applecart to criticise Western culture with all its arrogance."[5] His unruly imagination was, marvellously, given visibility and for over twenty years Earnshaw produced paintings that owe little to external influences but at the same time are not in the realm of Outsider Art. Nor would it be doing justice to his work as a painter to suggest that the medium was just an expedient. The experiments, the extraordinarily subtle uses of colour, the effortless command of pictorial space argue his immense enjoyment of its possibilities. This became especially evident from the mid 50s, when Paul Klee became an important reference, and "revealed to me the serious content of painting as an activity in its own right".[6]

There is one oil painting completely unlike any other he ever made, a 'Self-Portrait' [p.178] from 1951. Had he wished to follow a conventional painting career this demonstrates how easily he could have done so and the young face looks at himself (and us) with a curious expression as if he is surprised at his own ability to flick the oil paint into life, to make it into flesh, light, hair and cloth.

Over the years Earnshaw has given a few clues to the origins of his images and to the artists that interested him. He has mentioned, for instance, Leonor Fini as well as Klee. On the whole, he said, it was daydreams rather than dreams that gave birth to his visual and written images. However, a number of his earliest drawings and paintings originated in a dream he had shortly after discovering Surrealism. "I had a dream featuring a powerful image which dominated my mind for

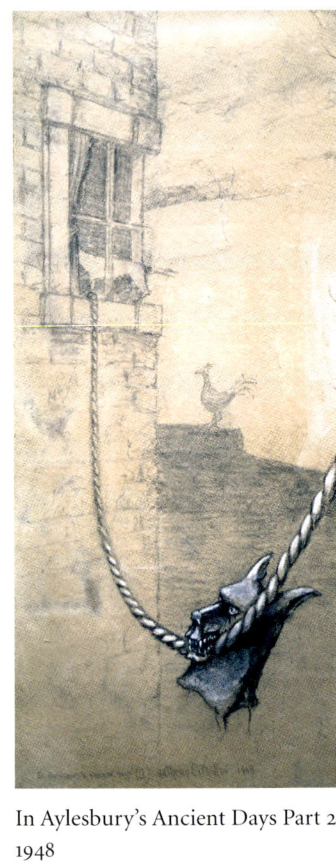

In Aylesbury's Ancient Days Part 2, 1948

many years. This image was, while simple in itself, sinister and gripping, it depicted the severed head of a wolf biting a rope with its teeth: the rope stretched from a window in a dark, otherwise featureless brick wall. It was twilight, a wind was blowing making the rope and the wolf's head sway. Since then I have drawn the image and variations of it many times, as well as painted two watercolour versions, plus an oil on canvas version."[7] The late oil on canvas version, 'The Future of Pets: Whatever Became of Rin Tin Tin', 1966, was very close to the first drawing of the dream. In the variations that followed the latter between 1948 and 1950 he seems unaffected by the interpretation offered by a friend versed in psychoanalysis to whom he told the dream: that "the image probably stemmed from the trauma of birth, the severing of the umbilical cord".[8] In this, as in his attitudes generally to the debates within Surrealism about psychoanalysis, Earnshaw preferred to take the dream as poetic fact in its own right, rather than material to be analysed.

In the first Wolf's Head drawing, 'In Aylesbury's Ancient Days', 1948, the dream space is thoroughly disorienting; there is no ground as the gulf between the buildings seems to plunge endlessly, while the brick building on the left extends up out of the picture. The plunging space is reminiscent of scenes in *Amazing Stories* , the world's first science fiction magazine, initially appearing in 1928, which often featured futuristic structures and buildings suspended in a void, although Earnshaw has anchored his to familiar, solid brick buildings with windows. The rope on which the wolf's head clamps its teeth swoops up towards the viewer, giving the sensation of reaching back into our space, as though the picture frame is a window from which we look onto the scene. Variations on the wolf's head and rope proliferated, in a numbered sequence, but all with the title 'In Aylesbury's Ancient Days'. Sometimes a deep horizon line, and tents or tepees are added, with a curious object, part-mirror part-staff, framing the wolf's head, while its body appears elsewhere, detached, its headlessness often disguised by the edge of a tent or door. Several of the series are framed together forming pairs; the links between the twinned images are elusive. Sometimes one scene seems to involve a close-up view of the other, or the same seen from a different perspective; in parts 3 and 4, an interior

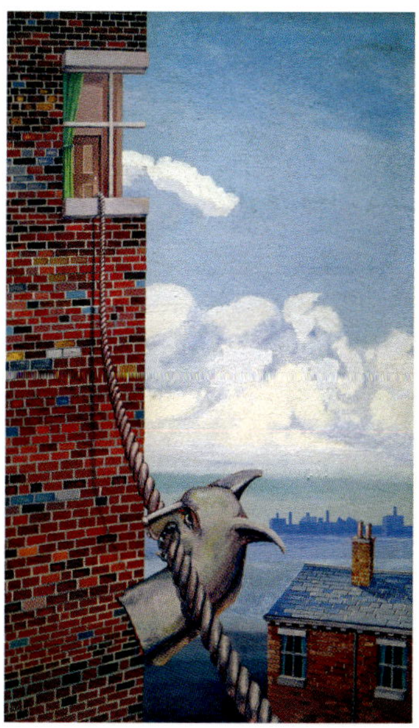

The Future of Pets: Whatever Became of Rin Tin Tin, 1966

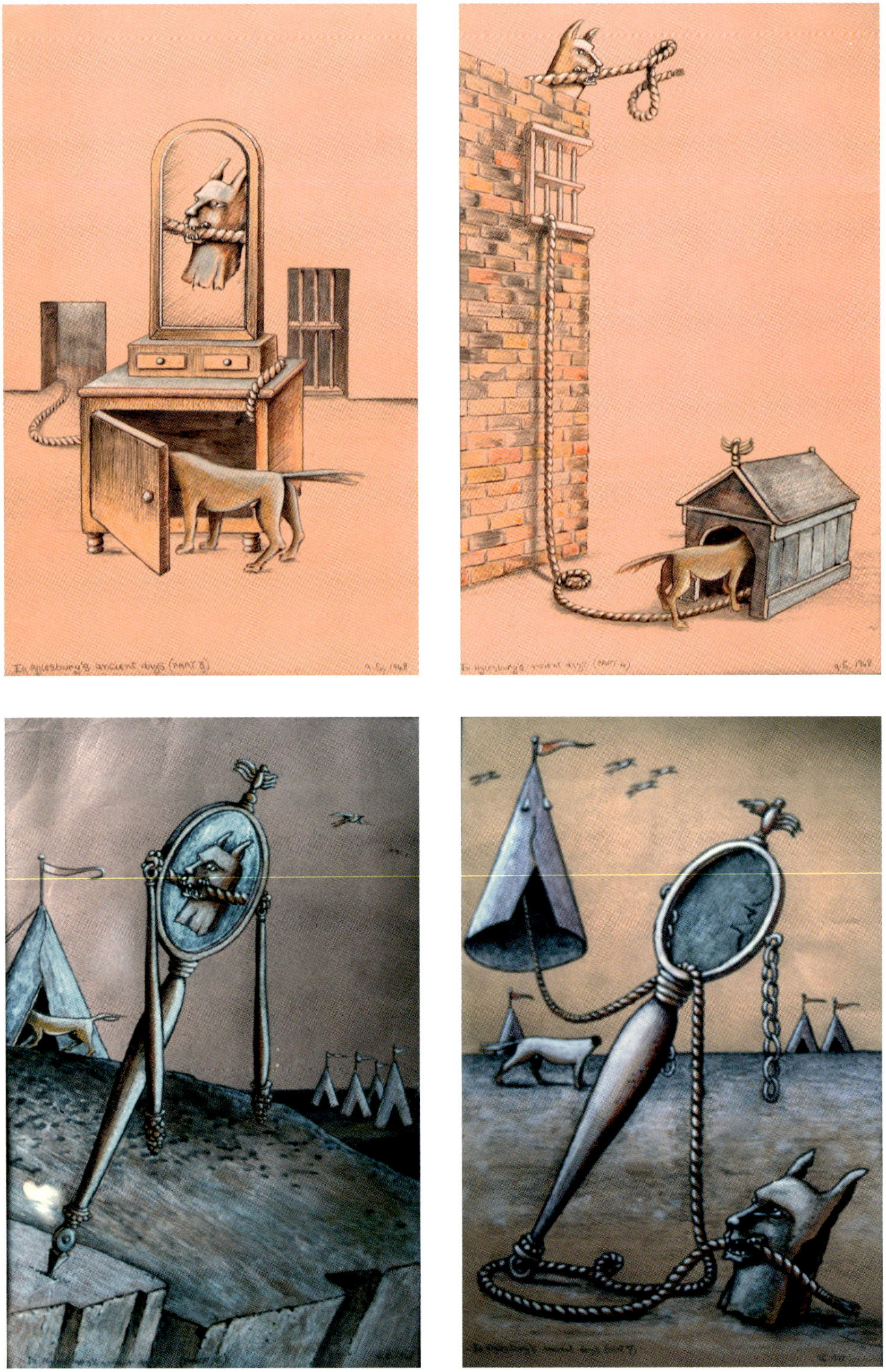

In Aylesbury's Ancient Days, Parts 3–4, 6–7, 1948

and an exterior both contain objects with openings onto dark spaces. Having already claimed that Earnshaw was not pursuing the 'birth trauma' analysis of the dream, I should probably modify it—these 'containers' would corroborate the idea, as symbols of the maternal body. One is a kind of dressing-table, the other a kennel in the form of a miniature temple, into the dark interior of each of which the (headless) wolf appears to poke his head, which also appears, severed, above.

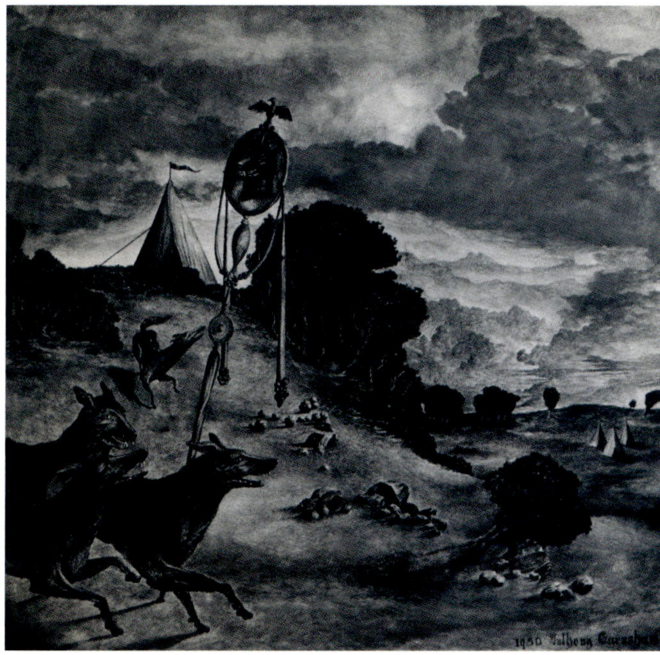

Black and Snowy Night, 1950

In the 1966 catalogue to his exhibition at Leeds Institute Gallery, Earnshaw noted that his "series depicting wolves engaged in human activities" had been inspired by the work of Fini, who painted "scenes of women engaged in recondite non-human activities".[9] It is likely that this series includes 'In Aylesbury's Ancient Days', though the work at Leeds was the 'Black and Snowy Night' of 1950, depicting a pack of wolves in a landscape, with a camp and Roman staff. Fini's sphinx women, such as those in her 1942 painting 'The Shepherdess of the Sphinxes', its bare landscape with distant horizon line scattered with lion-bodied women, curled round each other and with furry claws clutching plants and bones, could be the kind of scene Earnshaw had in mind.

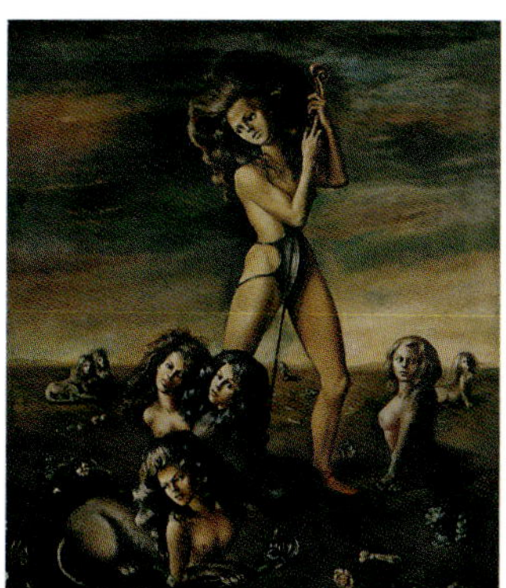

Leonor Fini, The Shepherdess of the Sphinxes, 1941

At about the same time as the series 'In Aylesbury's Ancient Days' Earnshaw produced a group of pencil, ink and gouache drawings which transform the elements of the dream into a scenario of machinery and humanoid puppets, part nightmare and part comic caricature, a forerunner of the black humour found in 'Wokker'. In 'One Bent Ventilator, One Severed Hand, Two Phantoms Playing With a Length of Rope', from 1949, the severed hand protrudes below a rusted sleeve-pipe with a button, ending in a kind of mechanical phallus with inset cog, while two ghostly figures play a lethal game with the rope. As an allegory of the capitalist system of production, and its dehumanising process, it is just as effective as any humourless social-realism and a precursor to Earnshaw's own later mock social-realist drawings.

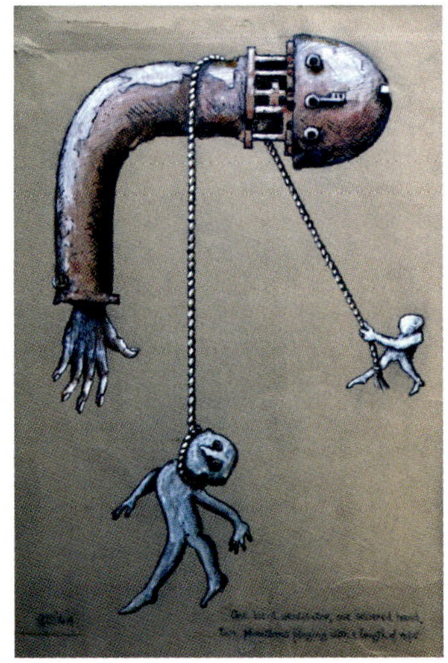

One Bent Ventilator, One Severed Hand, Two Phantoms Playing With a Length of Rope, 1949

His first painting had been a landscape, and he continued to paint imaginary landscapes with unexpected figures or objects in them. In one of the earliest, 'The End of a Perfect Day', 1946, [p.34] a puppet theatre oddly occupies what looks like a carved mahogany tallboy with barley sugar columns. A fortune teller is in the place of Punch, while a lifeless woman falls from the open door of the cupboard below, a scattering of balls around her suggesting the fairground game, Knock the Lady out of Bed. There is often an unsettling conjunction of past and future in the scenes of this period, characteristic of science fiction and its forerunner the Gothic novel, as in the untitled watercolour depicting a figure in armour, carrying a staff topped with a Roman, or perhaps German, eagle [p.31]. In front of him in the otherwise timeless landscape is a fragment of the modern industrial world, metal railings protruding from the side of a female bust. Rocky cliffs, plain, and ancient hills like extinct volcanoes resemble a lunar vista, eerily empty; perhaps a future earth wasted like the deserts in a J.G. Ballard story. The textures of the surfaces Earnshaw creates in the watercolour are extraordinarily precise—the slightly metallic stone of the clefts in the cliff echo the smooth metal of the armour against the mottled turf. In 'The City', 1950 [p.6], buildings emerge like outcrops from the land, troglodyte dwellings; it resembles the strange stone hills, inhabited and pitted with windows, of Cappadocia in Turkey.

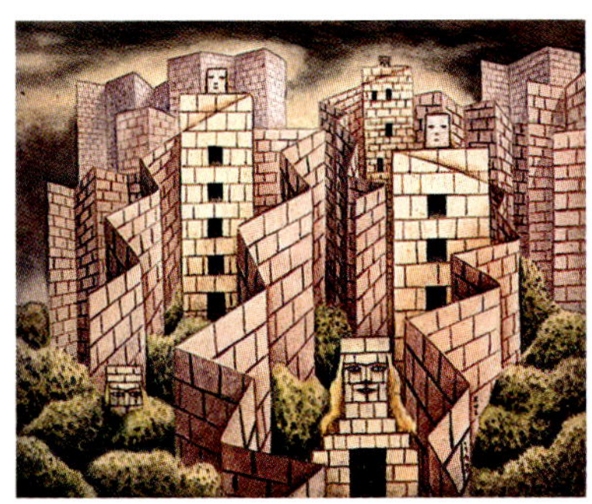

Xul Solar, Muros Biombos, 1948

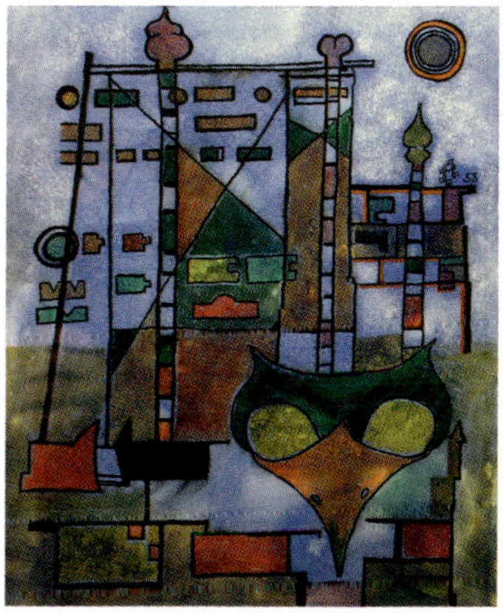

The Castle Where the Birds Live, 1953

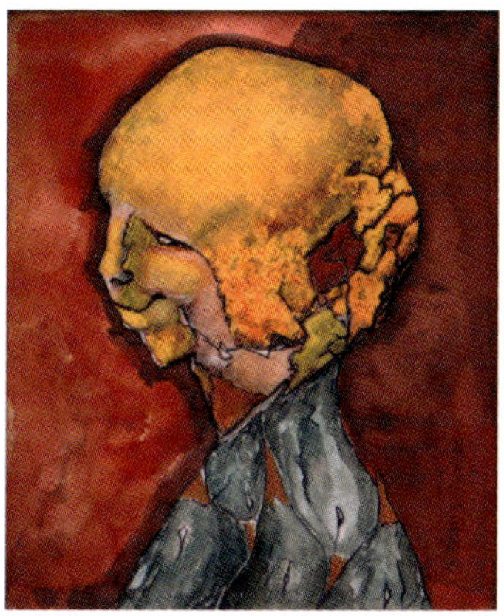

The Citizen, 1952

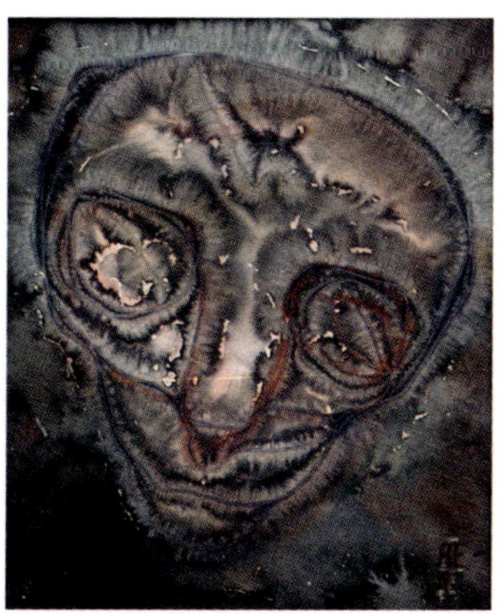

Luminous Skull, 1953

It is unlikely Earnshaw would have known the paintings of Xul Solar, but it is interesting to compare the imaginary landscapes and cities with those of the Argentinean artist, Borges' favourite painter. Although at very different times, both artists came under Klee's spell. Solar encountered the work of Klee while living in Europe during and after the first World War, and began to emulate the Swiss artist's delicate watercolour patches and spindly lines to create fantastic architectures, some of which are constructed using alphabets. Perhaps the closest to both Klee and Xul Solar of Earnshaw's watercolours is 'The Castle Where the Birds Live', 1953. But while there are some similarities, on the whole Solar's images conjure up pure fantasies while Earnshaw's imagination works in the terrain between the unconscious and experience. There is another difference too—Klee stimulated Earnshaw to make explorations of colour and surface, taking him in unexpectedly experimental and original directions.

There are some paintings from the early 1950s, however, in which Earnshaw is already making his own versions of chance encounters. 'The Citizen', of 1952, was, he wrote on the back of the painting, "a faithful copy of marks and scratches made by chance as seen on the wall of the machine shop at Thomas Green & Sons Engineers, North Street, Leeds". Earnshaw has seen into these random markings the configuration of a head, smiling and with the eye half hidden under yellow hair. He was probably aware, like Max Ernst and other surrealist painters before him, of Leonardo's advice to the young painter, to look intently at "the stains of walls, or ashes of a fire, or clouds, or mud or like places, in which, if you consider them well, you may find really marvellous ideas".[10] Another work that exploits chance though in a different way is 'Luminous Skull', 1953, in which watery bleedings of paint have been enhanced by the addition of string, which creates a fan-like halo round the skull. There is a difference between this and 'The Citizen', in that the latter was a transcription of an image seen by chance in the scratches on the wall, whereas in 'Luminous Skull' Earnshaw himself created the random markings then to be coalesced into an image. In other watercolours he was known to occasionally incorporate washing-up liquid whose bubbles burst to create random forms that could then be read, interpreted and over painted or left as they were.

From the early 1950s Earnshaw produced an extraordinary variety of paintings, mostly in watercolour, exploiting the innate character of the medium to invite accident but at the same time constructing intricate and carefully controlled configurations. He developed slat-like patterns, not unlike the kind of tiered ground in paintings by Klee such as 'Comedy', 1921. In several works, like 'The Wheel That Will Trundle Round the World', 1955, he built up segments into intricate formal patterns whose scale is mysterious. 'The Wheel That Will Trundle Round the World' resembles a map, the plan of an ideal city and the spokes of a wheel. In another watercolour from 1955 the shape of a head is embedded in mini-blocks, each carefully outlined, that resemble the circuit of machinery as well as an aerial map. In two watercolours of 1958, 'Two Ghosts' and 'Three Ghosts', the

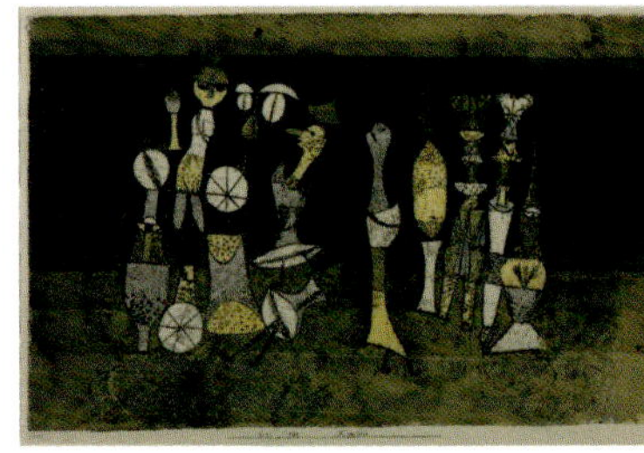

Paul Klee, Comedy, 1921

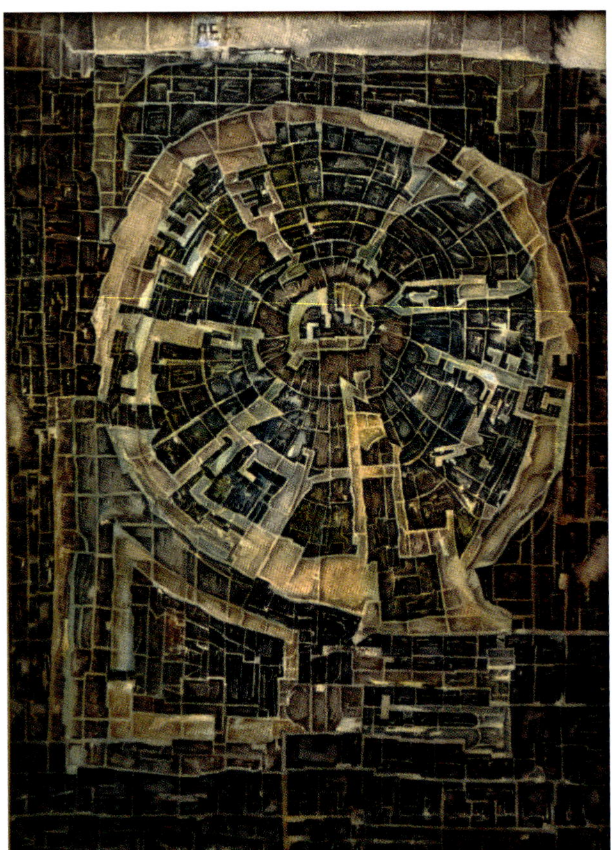

The Wheel That Will Trundle Round the World, 1955

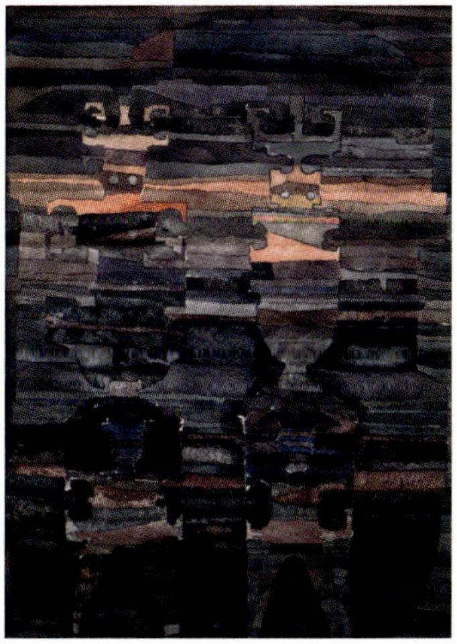

Two Ghosts, 1958

irregular but carefully controlled horizontal slats of lightly washed pigment are interrupted with darker and lighter bands, minimally outlined, to make ghostly, hieratic forms with eyes in their headdresses that resemble the Colombian gold figurines of Ancient America. In 'Pushing Knobs and Pulling Levers', 1960, small rectangular slabs fragment and disintegrate like rusted panels in the background, merging into an erect silver-grey machine manipulated by a robotic figure, wearing ear defenders—a familiar scene, as Earnshaw was still earning a living in an engineering works.

All this time, for twenty years, he painted when he could, usually at home. He worked long factory hours, as his daughter Frances recalled, often doing night-shifts. "For this reason he was often at home during the day, sleeping in the living room corner armchair. Sometimes he was at home recovering from an injury. The same corner armchair was studio space as well, where he was to be found, a piece of glass balanced on his knee with an anglepoise light shining up through it."[11] She remembers him painting watercolours on the sitting-room floor, working in the attic and the cellar, and making stretchers. He also always made his own frames. Occasionally he painted at work: "For six months in 1958 I drove a heavy overhead crane in an engineering works, in between lifts while sitting in the cabin I made a series of necessarily small watercolours".[12]

After an initial burst of bright colours in the first watercolours inspired by Klee, such as 'The Castle Where the Birds Live', 1953 [p.41], or 'Letter to a Bird', 1954 [p.44], the hues become quieter and the tonality very subtle. Greys, pinks, purples, browns and blues predominate, sometimes in close harmonies. In a short story that was not, presumably, intended to be autobiographical but nonetheless contains passages on colour that are so strongly worded that it is hard not to think it is the painter speaking, Earnshaw wrote "I have always held the symbolism of colour to be a trite device: red for danger, green for envy, and so on. All nonsense! For me, a certain leaden grey tinged with violet is the colour of danger, even as that wan ochre found in wrapping paper embodies the sentiment of envy." Colour is such an active element in these watercolours—it is not something that fills in a shape and is defined by it: "Colours have a power in their own right". They confer identity: "We each own colours in an intimate way, just as objects do. It is hard to recognize old, battered sofas that are not a particular shade of chocolate brown; faded, inconclusive and remote. Colours clothe the form of reality and make the secret seem austere… Colours in motion shift and assume new chromatic values."[13] Objects own their colours, they are part of the identity of the things that surround us every day.

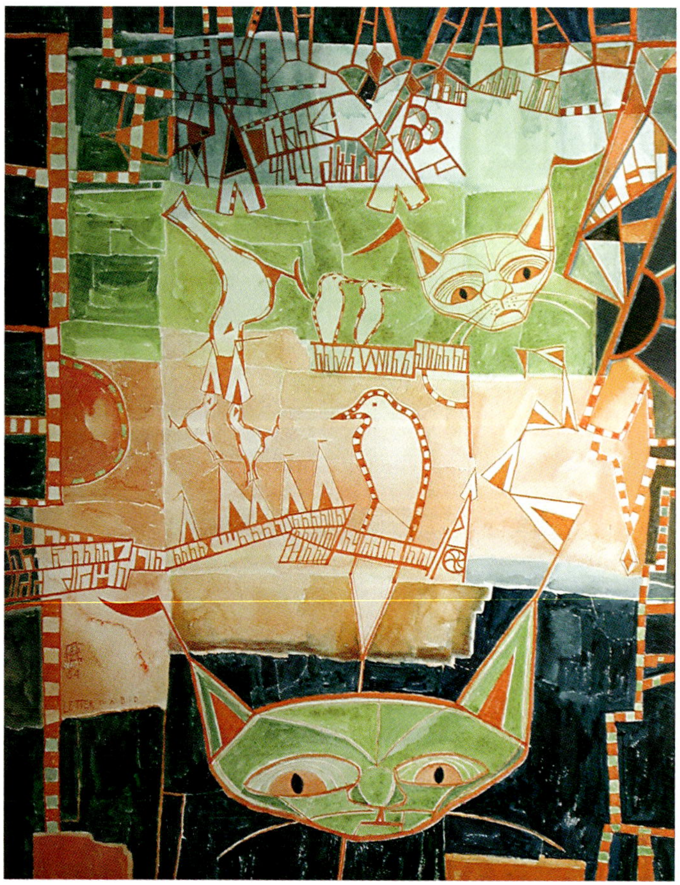

Letter to a Bird, 1954

A photograph of Earnshaw's last studio shows several of the early paintings, including 'Two Ghosts, The Wand' and two much larger paintings, one of a television, the other from the 'Dressing Table Series'. 'The Wand', 1960, which is shown vertical in the studio photograph, is one of the most complex of the compositions built up with intricate slats, the rusty hues of a scorpion-tailed creature or construction standing out from the violets and blues. The two jagged holes onto blackness could be eyes, or if the painting is seen horizontally, port holes in a barque or ark. If the latter, it also bears some connection to 'Cartrider after L.P. Hartley', 1954, and 'The Chinese Dragon', 1962, a machine animal, with railtrack-body and fangs like plug prongs. The forms in 'The Wand' glow like a magic baguette but also disintegrate, as if the whole structure is falling apart. "What kind of house will we have when the world is worn out and fallen to bits?"[14]

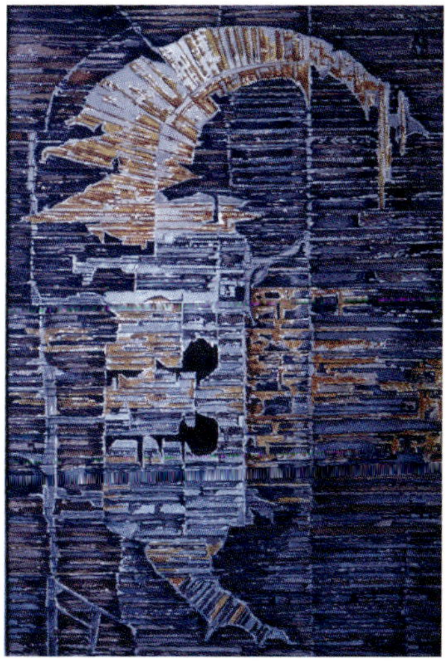

The Wand, 1960

In the early 1960s Earnshaw's painting took a new direction. He started working on a larger scale, in oils, often with thick impasto and the addition of sand. He had been interested in

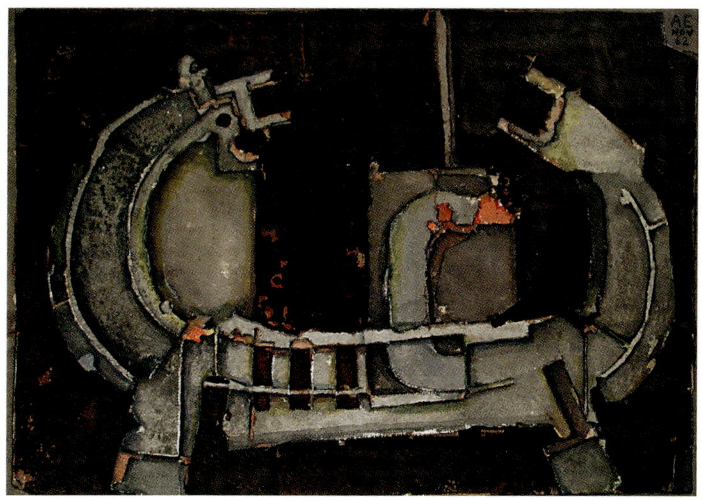

The Chinese Dragon, 1962

Tàpies, as is evident in 'Trellis', 1964, where we see what appears to be the back of the stretcher, but with a thoroughly original twist: the idea of the bare support picked up in the empty trellis in the lower half of the canvas. But many of these larger paintings are of large single objects, washbasins, dressing tables, bed ends, stairs, sometimes doubled or cropped, which fill the whole space. These unlikely things become the object of imaginative speculations and metaphorical, often humorous, transformation, sometimes residing in the title, as in 'Semi-detached Washbasins', 1963.

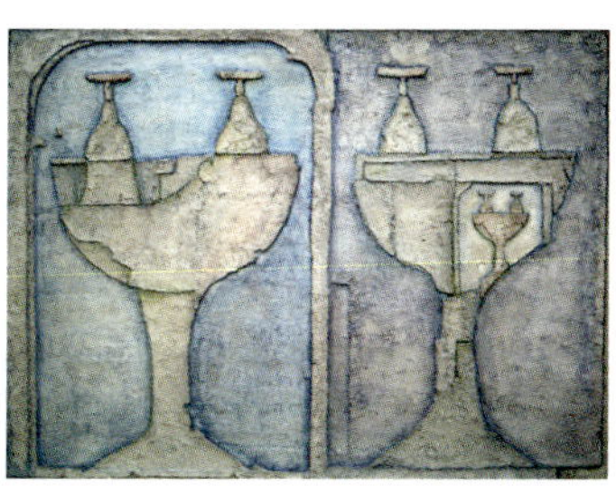

Semi-detached Washbasins, 1963

Eleven 'Dressing Tables' were exhibited at the Leeds Institute Gallery in 1966; the dressing-table itself seems to have been quite elaborate, almost theatrical, with its lamps at either side

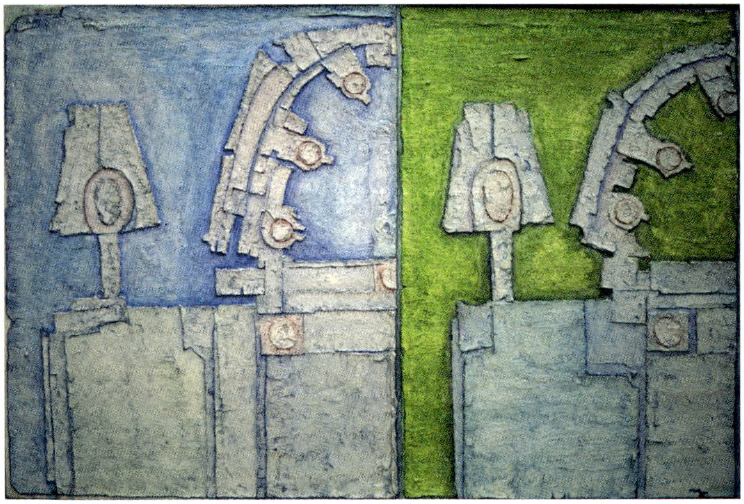

Dressing Table Number 4, 1963

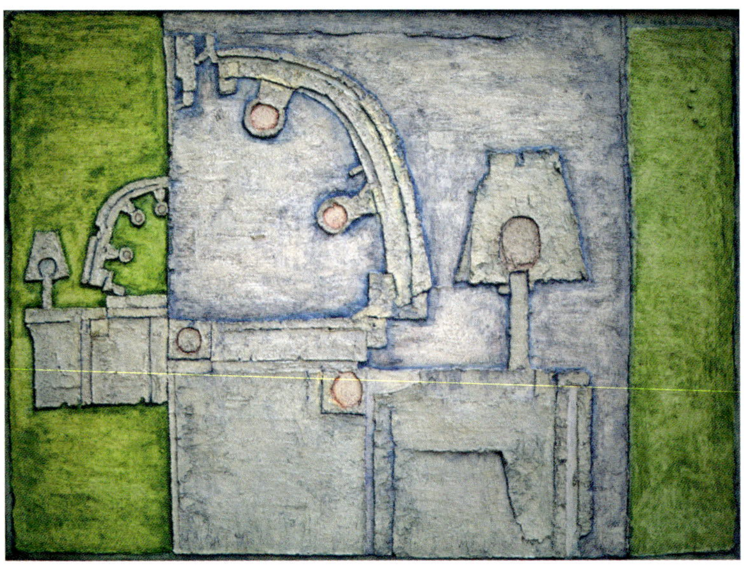

Dressing Table Number 6, 1963

of the mirror which is ringed by smaller lights in an art deco style, although he treats it/them in an austere, almost minimalist manner. Earnshaw added short sub-titles to seven of them in the catalogue, which have the effect of not supplying a comfortable description to fit them within recognisable categories, rather an irrational set of unrelated characteristics:

> 2. A single one sundered, or many perhaps an endless line
> 3. Disturbing, as when a burglar ransacks your house and disarranges familiar objects

5. All facing the wind
6. Scale
8. Back and front
9. One lamp to light two rooms
11. Inverted, the image becomes its own environment.[15]

The impasse between 'why?' and 'why not?' is funny, as well as disturbing, like the famous Chinese Encyclopedia "in which it is written that: animals are divided into a) belonging to the Emperor, b) embalmed, c) tame, d) sucking pigs, e) sirens, f) fabulous...".[16] Earnshaw must have delighted in the endless possibilities in painting these domestic objects, which are almost like readymades to which he has restored an imaginary dimension and an irregular anthropomorphism that is both comic and tragic. Paintings give the objects another life no more and no less real than their humble everyday one.

These familiar things are witness to the lives of those that use them. They accumulate the residue of endlessly repeated acts. As Earnshaw wrote in one of the aphorisms from *Carping & Kicking or My Shadow Floodlit*: "Stove and sink, life and death".

Notes

1. Anthony Earnshaw, *Paintings 1945–1965*, Leeds Institute Gallery, Leeds, 1966
2. Anthony Earnshaw, *A View from Back o' Town*, Leeds City Art Gallery, 1987
3. *Ibid.*
4. *Ibid.*
5. Patrick Hughes, 'Earnshaw', *Art Line*, April/May 1987
6. Leeds Institute Gallery, *op. cit.*
7. *Écoutons Voir,* Supplement to S.U.R.R... no.4, 2001
8. *Ibid.*
9. Patrick Hughes, *op. cit.*
10. *The Notebooks of Leonardo da Vinci*, selected and edited by Irma A. Richter, Oxford University Press, 1998
11. Frances Earnshaw, 'Some Words About My Father', 2007
12. Patrick Hughes, *op. cit.*
13. Anthony Earnshaw, 'Brooches for Typists', *Surrealist Transformaction* no.9
14. *Ibid.*
15. Anthony Earnshaw, Leeds Institute Gallery, *op. cit.*
16. Michel Foucault, quoting Borges, Preface to *The Order of Things*, Tavistock Publications, 1970

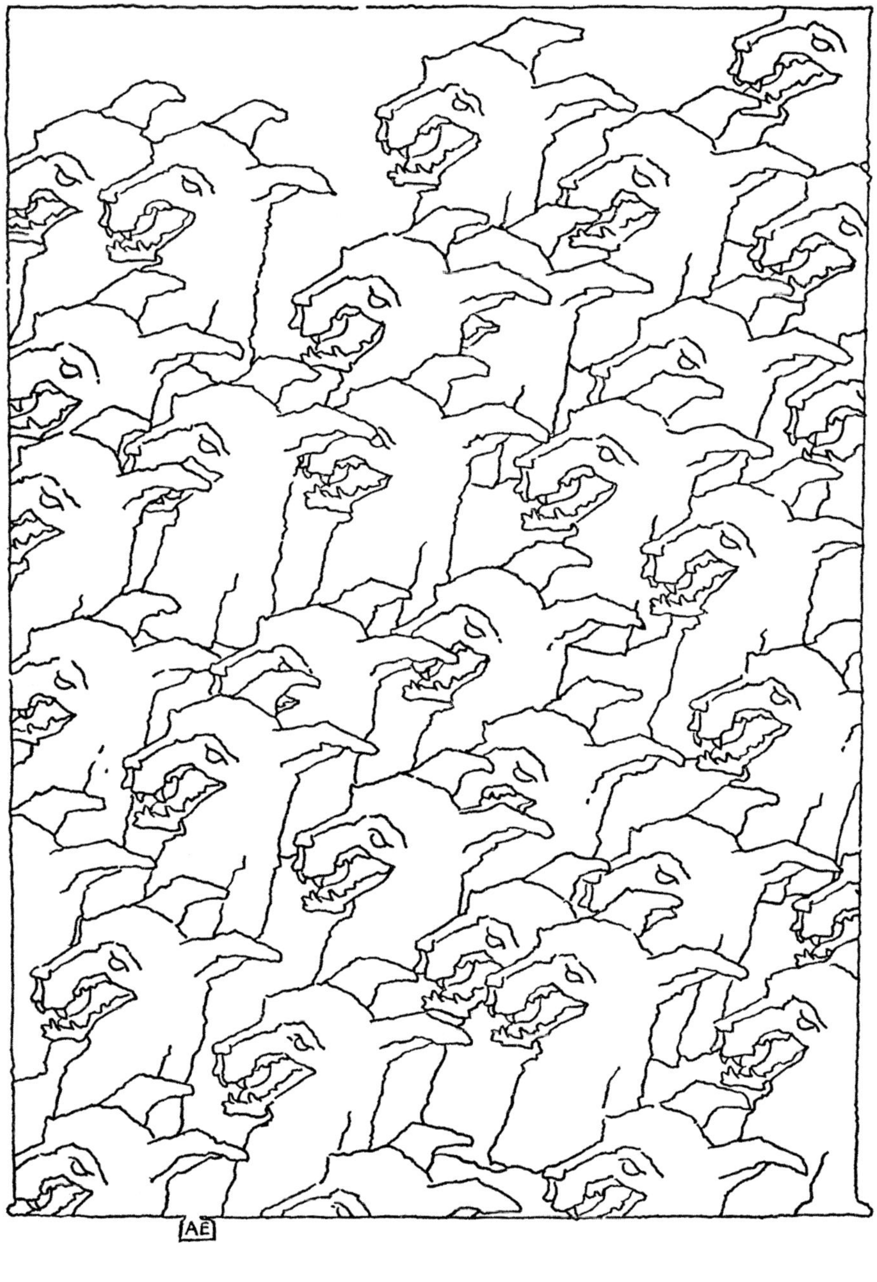
AE

Michael Richardson

Wolves at the Door of the Mind

As for all surrealists, creative expression was not for Anthony Earnshaw a matter of finding one mode of representation and then striving to perfect it. Creativity rather came from elsewhere, often unbidden, and it demanded of the one to whom it appeared a responsiveness to the broadest possibilities of expression. Thus, Earnshaw was not a painter, an image maker, a cartoonist, a maker of assemblages, a poet or a story-teller: he was all of these things simultaneously and his various activities cannot be separated one from another.

As a teller of tales, he has left us with a small number of short stories, recounting intriguing and often obscure, secret or private anecdotes of things that have happened (or not happened) and that lead nowhere. It was in his collaboration with Eric Thacker, however, that his narrative invention was given full rein, in the two novels, *Musrum* and *Wintersol*, they wrote together and in their comic strip, 'Wokker', whose cartoons, placed together, constitute a third wayward narrative text.

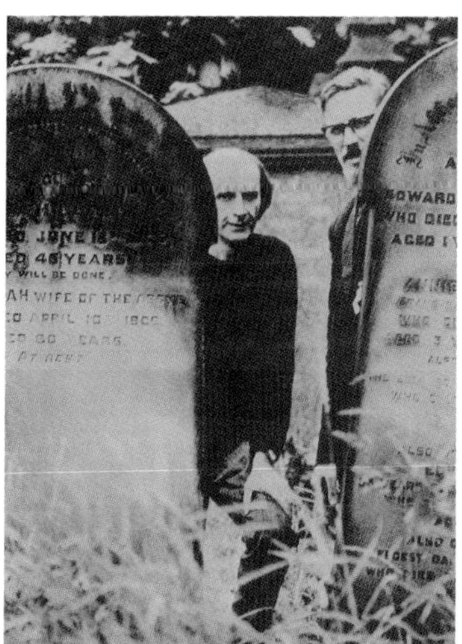

Anthony Earnshaw and Eric Thacker, Leeds, 1968

The two novels are, along with the 'Wokker', evidence of lasting friendship and collaboration from which, at times, it would be impossible to draw out who contributed what. This did not prevent reviewers at the time the books were published from hazarding that Thacker was principally responsible for the text, Earnshaw for the illustrations, ignoring the fact that half of the illustrations are by Thacker. This is an example of how difficult it can be for some people to accept collaborative creative working, something which undermines the still dominant notion of the genius of the Author. In fact, the book was written by means of a postal correspondence between them,

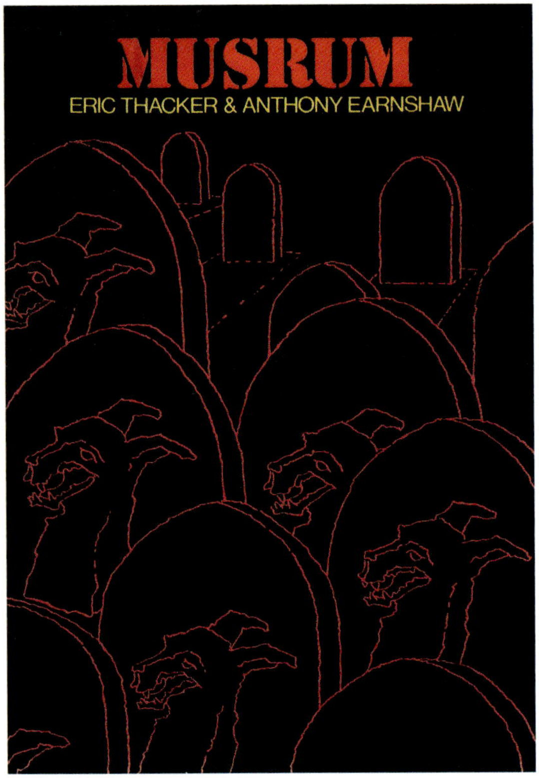

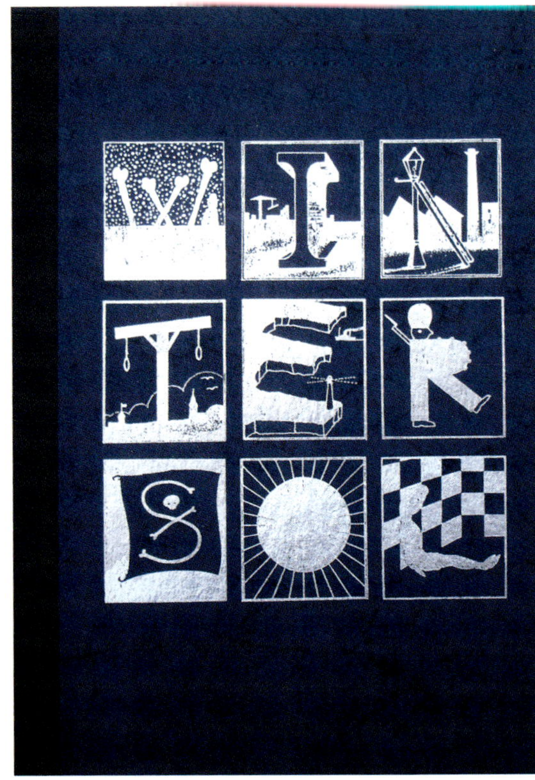

and one can imagine that the to-and-fro movement, through which each one played off the other, created, in the process, a kind of third presence, which was actually the author of the book. The two books are indeed one of the most successful extended examples of the many attempts at collective creation by surrealists, bearing comparison with Breton and Soupault's *Les Champs magnètiques* and most especially with Breton and Éluard's *L'immaculèe Conception*. Curious, then, that one of the collaborators was not a surrealist, indeed at the time was a Methodist minister, a vocation just about as far as one can imagine from inspiring a surrealist sensibility, even if we do not take into account the instinctive surrealist anathema for all things religious. Earnshaw, of course, was too much of an anarchist to allow dogma to stand in the way of a genuine and fertile friendship and their fundamentally differing philosophies of life seem to have engendered little discord, indeed appear to have stimulated a partnership based upon mutual respect across differences.

Musrum, Grove Press, New York 1970; *Wintersol*, Jonathan Cape, London 1971

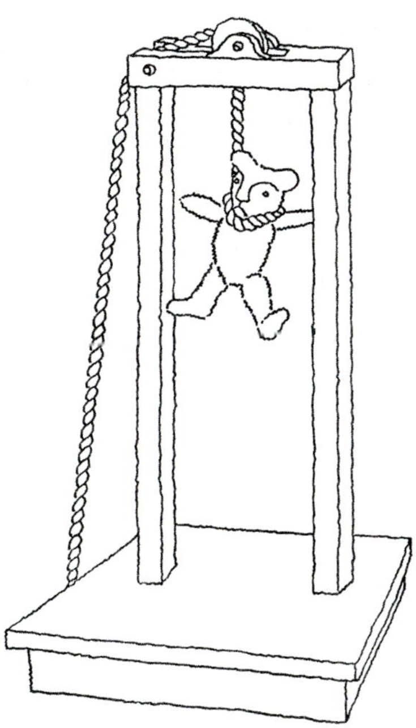

Musrum burst upon the world in 1968 in an environment, in Britain at least, that was in one sense extremely hostile to and ignorant about Surrealism. It was a time when hardly any of the key surrealist works had been translated and Surrealism as such was generally dismissed as 'old hat' and irrelevant. And yet at the same time it was an environment that was oddly responsive to its manifestations. In the following year, 'Monty Python's Flying Circus' would appear on British televison, the culmination of various inventive and irreverent forms of comedy that had followed in the wake of 'The Goon Show' on the one hand and the satire boom on the other. *Musrum* ties in with this tradition; indeed there is something very 'goonish' about its characterisations. But it also draws upon surrealist tradition, notably the 'Pataphysical adventures of Alfred Jarry's Dr Faustroll. It is interesting to contemplate that, even though knowledge of Surrealism has increased and diffused in the intervening period, it seems inconceivable that any leading commercial publisher today would for even a moment consider publishing a book like *Musrum*. Yet in 1968 not only did Jonathan Cape publish the book, they apparently did so with some fanfare, thinking that they had a potential cult classic on their hands. It was widely reviewed, in the main positively if not terribly insightfully, and the Institute of Contemporary Arts organised an event to launch it. A common comparison made was with the world of Tolkien, an association that seems quite outlandish viewed from today's perspective, but is instructive, especially if we bear in mind that around this time the cult of Tolkien's work was at its height.

The narrative of *Musrum* is actually quite conventional: a perennial struggle of good versus evil in which the 'good' in the end prevails. This could be seen as a Christian morality tale (and gives slight support to the comparisons made with the world of Tolkien), which is perhaps evidence of the input of Thacker, except that it is undermined both by the fact that the moral boundaries between the supposedly 'good' Musrum and the 'evil' Weedking are not at all clearly defined and the course of the story is so absurdly paradoxical that we are never allowed to take this struggle seriously in any literal sense. Indeed, our sympathies may lie with the Weedking, a gallant underdog fighting against the system, or anti-system, instituted by Musrum, which may turn the world upside down but is also in its way rather authoritarian—and in fact at the end of the story the Weedking is the witness and hapless victim of imperialist and colonialist conquest. But let us not get ahead of ourselves.

Musrum is the creator of worlds, a kind of demiurge, a crazed builder who constructed America (God finds out about this only later) but flees in advance of the appearance of

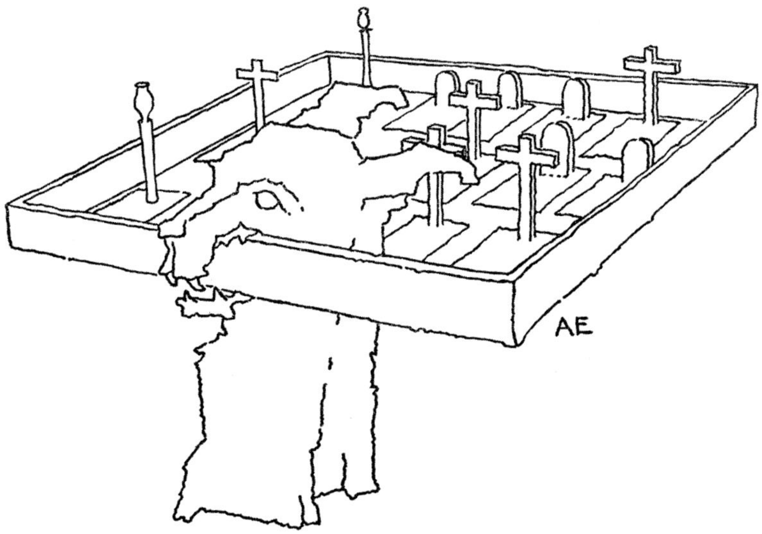

Columbus. He then constitutes Intersol, a found place, the place that exists between solids. This formless world contains a giant mushroom, which functions as its deity. When the Weedking steals the mushroom, war is declared. Musrum goes to Spain to seek followers, whilst effecting bilocation, that is splitting himself in half in order to be in two places at once. This double he names Palfreyman to deceive the Weedking's agents and in this form he aims to head the Weedking off by going to Russia, where he thinks the latter is headed. Musrum himself will join him later. There follow a series of monumental skirmishes in the course of which the adversaries generally seek to outmanoeuvre rather than confront one another. Finally Musrum defeats his rival and recovers the Giant Mushroom, the symbol of his power as well as the deity of his domain.

Like most surrealist narratives, *Musrum* is not a book to be read but one to be entered and engaged with. Musrum, a relative of Dr Faustroll, travels through forms rather than through actuality. This is not an imagined world, but one which unravels in the process of being formed and in which there can therefore be no certainties; it is a location of perpetual disorientation. This is where the comparison with Tolkien is most misguided, for where Tolkien creates a parallel, but perfectly consistent, universe, Earnshaw and Thacker take apart the world as it is and play with its absurdities. In this embrace of the arbitrary none of the convictions that sustain everyday life are of any significance. Work and ambition would get you nowhere. Money and property offer no security or assurance. What matters is to place oneself on the side of destiny and be able to recognise the signs and signatures which underlie existence.

Like many surrealists, Earnshaw was an inveterate writer of aphorisms and in some ways it might be said that the novel is less a story than a set of extended aphorisms, aphorisms strung together to create a story that might more accurately be said to be an anti-story. In this one might believe that he and Thacker were following the advice of Karl Kraus that "an aphorism does not need to be true, but it should out-wing the truth. It

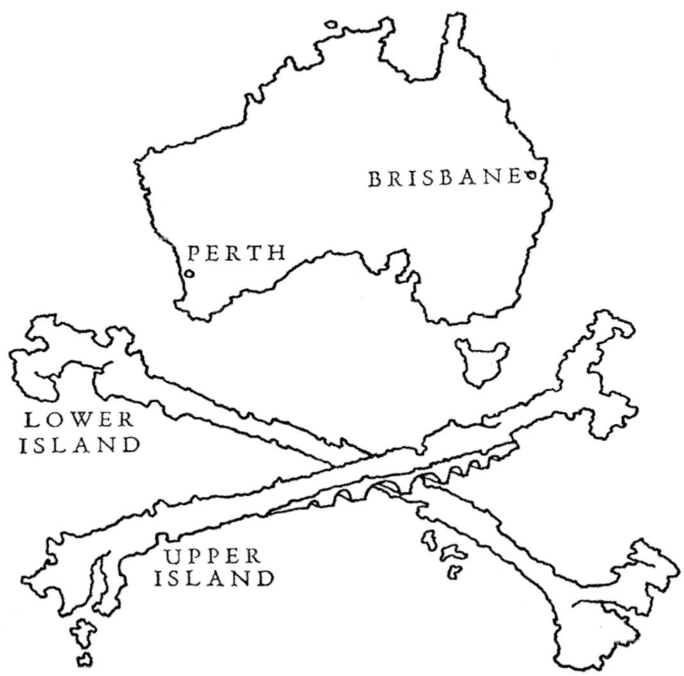

must get beyond it with a spin." And this spin is what *Musrum* undoubtedly performs as it outwits any attempt to pin it down: form is always non-form.

The second novel, *Wintersol*, is a continuation of the themes raised in Musrum. In it even the thin narrative structures that hold together the storyline of *Musrum* are dispensed with, as the two lead characters, Christmas and Bella, do not do battle against one another but rather struggle (and fail) to find one another as they contend with the polarities of their own being.

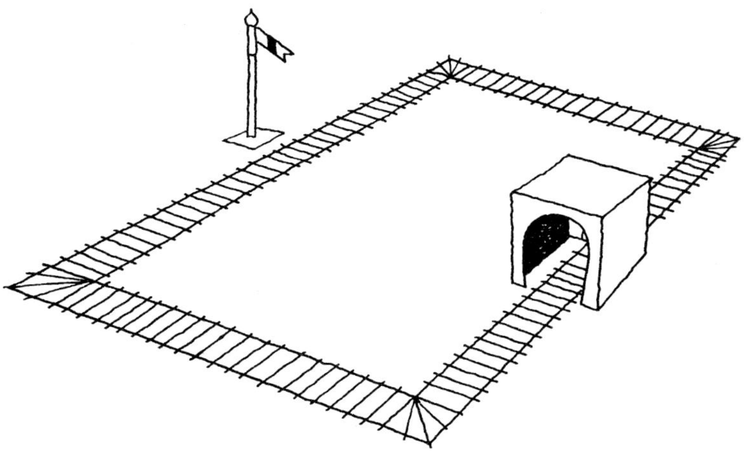

It is a kind of (and rather touching) love story *à rebours*, in which the lovers, instead of finding one another, arbitrarily set up barriers between them to prevent themselves from getting together despite recognising their common destinies.

As we are told at the beginning, "*Wintersol* is the tale of an enemy whom millions regard as a friend". This is none other than Father Christmas, a sinister character with a shady past and a none too laudable present. As a child he was a stowaway on a pirate ship and is the sole survivor when it is shipwrecked. Cast up on the shores of Intersol in the midst of a lawless town, the boy is given the name Christmas when he proves himself to be the most dextrous criminal in the land whose crimes have enabled him to build up a treasure chest and who had "decorated their lives with dreams of excess".

Still a child, he becomes enamoured of a Toy Factory, which he must seek to recover when it is apparently purloined by Bella, "the most beautiful woman in the Musroid world", with whose

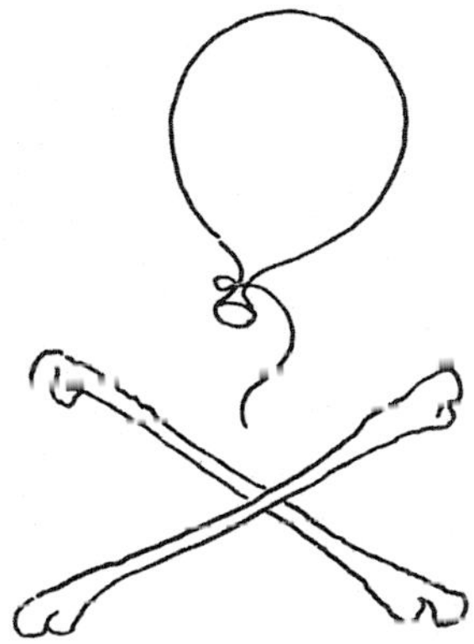

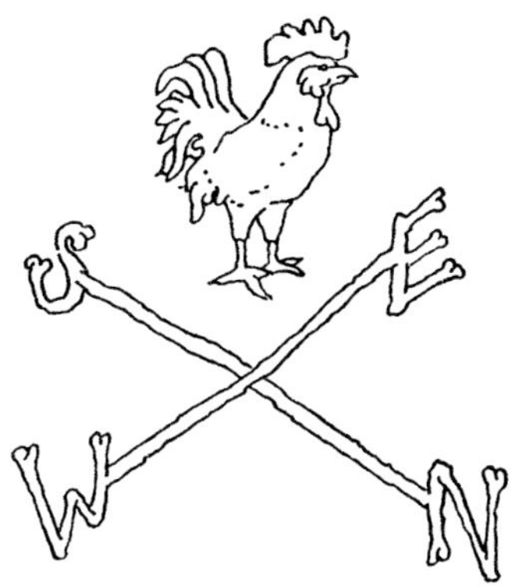

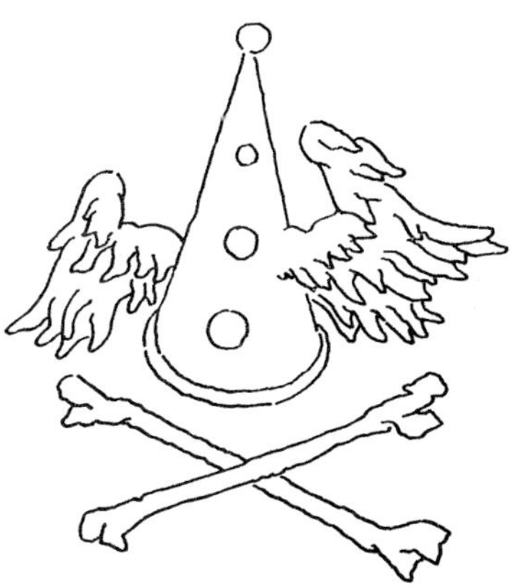

portrait Christmas becomes obsessed. The paths of Christmas and Bella cross and intercross, but never seem to meet and by the end of the story Bella is perched atop a chimney in the icy northern wastes of which she has always dreamed, while Christmas remains at its base, unable to climb up because the sack in which he carries all of his possessions is so bulky it weighs him down. Despite the fact that the only toy he really wants is Bella, Christmas, who we are told is also "in love with his factory", cannot bear to dispose of these treasures which keep him from his beloved. He has to spend his time learning to despise them so that one day each year he can palm them off onto the children of the world. In the meantime, however, Bella's workers will have produced many more toys that when he returns his sack will be fuller than ever. As a description of industrial alienation it illuminates a situation that is as ironic as it is just.

This synopsis gives a certain consistency to a narrative that is anything but coherent. *Wintersol* may not be as successful a book as *Musrum* in so far as it seems to have been put together with less care and attention (the illustrations in particular mostly lack the sparkling inventiveness of the first book). One has the impression that *Musrum* emerged from a joint enthusiasm and with no thought of publication, whereas the second suffers from the fact that it was the result of a commission by the publishers. As such it lacks *Musrum*'s exuberance and visual and verbal inventiveness. Nevertheless, the throwaway style of the book has a power of its own and in many ways it is a more disturbing tale precisely because of its narrative incoherence.

Although it is a follow up to *Musrum*, and takes place in the Intersol that we have learned from the first book is his domain, Musrum himself does not appear and none of the events recounted in his story are referred to, even though we are told that it takes place around the same year, 1896. The only direct link with the first book is Bella, who appears at its end as Musrum's lover, although this fact, too, is never mentioned in *Wintersol*.

We are, however, warned that "the Musroid world is a headstrong replica of the world we know, constructed on the principle that all conceivable and inconceivable things persist within reality, and that myth is the true history of this and any other world". As such it offers up a distorting mirror to the everyday world we know, whose apparent consistency is in fact the real illusion. Inconsistent with itself, the Musroid world brings our attention to the gaps and interruptions that are present within what we perceive as reality. It means that in reading the texts we should not expect narrative closure, even as regards the smallest detail, since as a story it contains contradiction within itself.

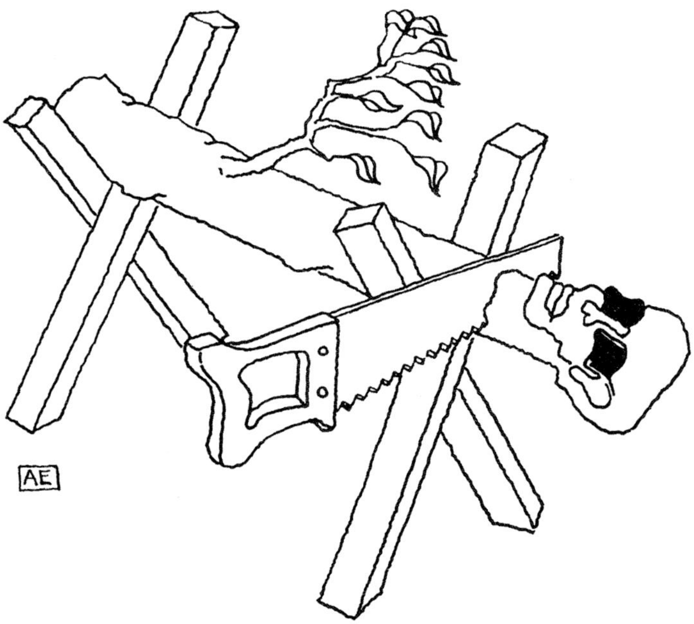

In the most intriguing review from the time of *Musrum*'s original appearance, Jonathan Miller compared the lucidity of the Musroid world with the schizophrenic state of mind. Since Miller was trained in the treatment of mental illness, he presumably knew what he was talking about. Yet, if the Musroid world is truly a reproduction, as Miller says, "of the accents of madness", this raises issues which are not so easily dispensed with as he thinks since neither Earnshaw nor Thacker appear to have ever had any direct involvement with insanity. At least, neither of them ever suffered from a mental illness nor, as Miller seems to imply, did they study the modes of expression of insane people in order to write their book. The equivalence therefore seems purely involuntary. How, in this case, did they gain access to such states of mind?

This sort of convergence is by no means unique. Miller cites the cases of *Alice in Wonderland* and 'The Goons' and of course in *The Immaculate Conception* Breton and Éluard consciously simulated different mentally-disturbed states in a way that suggests that insanity is not a sickness but rather a displacement of normal mental processes. The fact that its expression can be simulated involuntarily as well as deliberately indicates that such a disturbance of perception may be provoked in all of us under certain conditions and as such gives evidence for the surrealist confidence in the oneness of mental processes. From this perspective, it may be seen less as an aberration than as an opening-up of the latent or hidden parts of the psyche which become a problem only when it is extended so that the subject ceases to recognise it as disturbed. Moments of irrational lucidity are perhaps inherent to the creative process, which most writers will reject as aberrant or flatten them out into a rational form. Earnshaw and Thacker, however, had sufficient confidence in the mental process itself to accept this lucidity as

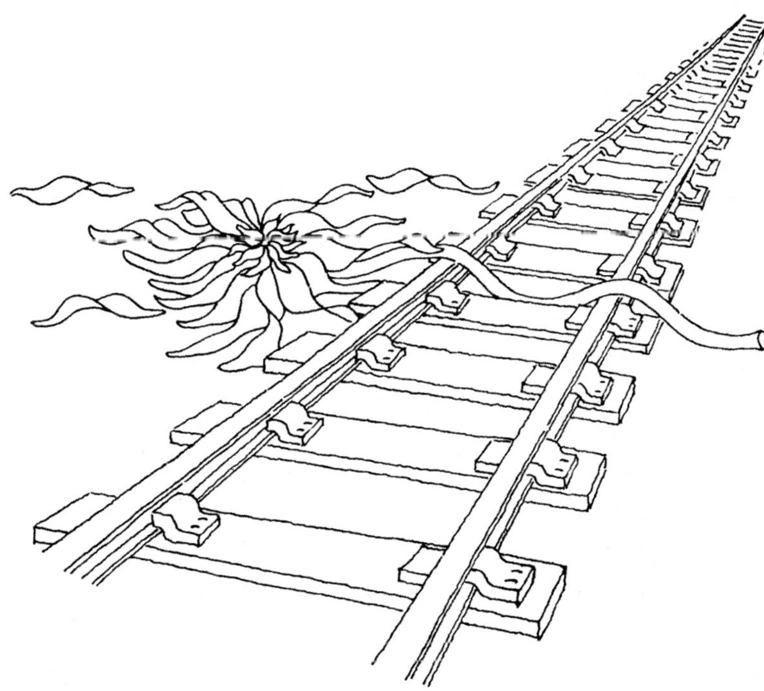

it is, untrammelled and pure in its nakedness. Doubtless this was aided by their collaborative process, which must have functioned as a challenge to each of them to enter parts of their own minds that perhaps would have been closed off to them if they had been working on their own.

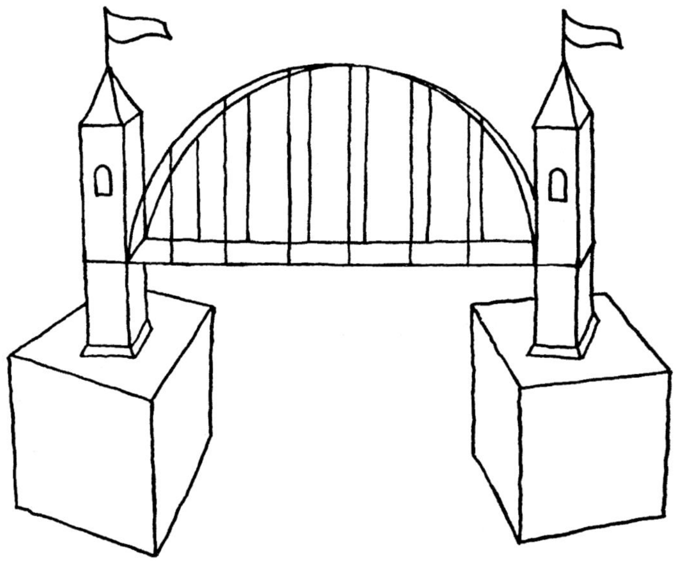

It was also aided by the enthusiasms they shared for poetry and for traditional jazz and blues. In working together, they incorporated in their own way important lessons about improvisation and (re)integration of the given learned especially from the latter. Poetically, this was extended to the play between word and image that is a striking aspect of the books. Conventional visual or pictorial signs are overturned as the authors' awareness of how the inter-relationship between images and words brings each into question. We are presented on the one hand with the pictorial qualities of written language and on the other with the linguistic potential of visual images. Scenes and situations are mysteriously transformed from one moment to the next in a way that brings to mind what may be done with the frames of a comic strip. In this respect it is indeed not difficult to discern the influence of *Krazy Kat* (which is even more apparent in the 'Wokker' strips), as perspective is constantly being changed and the reader is thrown off guard by being taken in a direction different from that expected. This audacity is perhaps best conveyed by the example of the cartographer in *Musrum* who makes a chart of a group of islands using invisible ink, which immediately causes the islands themselves to vanish. Indeed, the 'love' between Bella and Christmas has something of the uncanny quality of that of Krazy Kat and Ignatz. As in Herriman's strip, nothing between them is what it seems, as Christmas's infatuation is not for the woman herself but for a portrait of her, but this portrait is actually a window which actualises her presence and thus representation shades into living reality, and vice versa, for here, "sight is an excretion of darkness".

The imagery throughout is enigmatically precise: "Every sound", we are told, "is a scratching or tearing of silence which liberates the darkness behind". This suggests an engagement with the nature of language itself in tune with Walter Benjamin's observation that "the language of nature is comparable to a secret password that each sentry passes to the next in his own language, but the meaning of the password is the sentry's language itself".* Each of us knows the password but we will realise it only if we have respect for the nature of language itself. It is a recognition that is constantly present throughout Earnshaw's and Thacker's two novels.

In a world whose staple industry is "the manufacture of bloodstained bandages" we are confronted with what, for all its incongruity, is oddly familiar. The splendidly idiosyncratic mythology they have conjured up is above all a testimony to friendship, a friendship that persists through the work even though the two men are no longer with us.

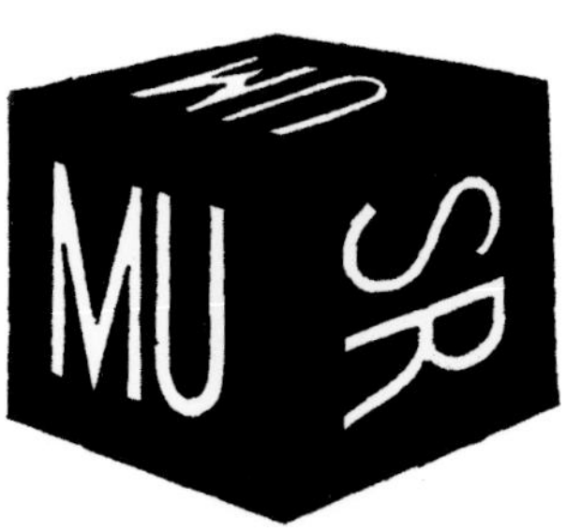

*Walter Benjamin, 'On Language as Such and on the Language of Man', *Reflections*, Schocken Books, New York, 1978

The drawings in this essay originally appeared in *Musrum*.

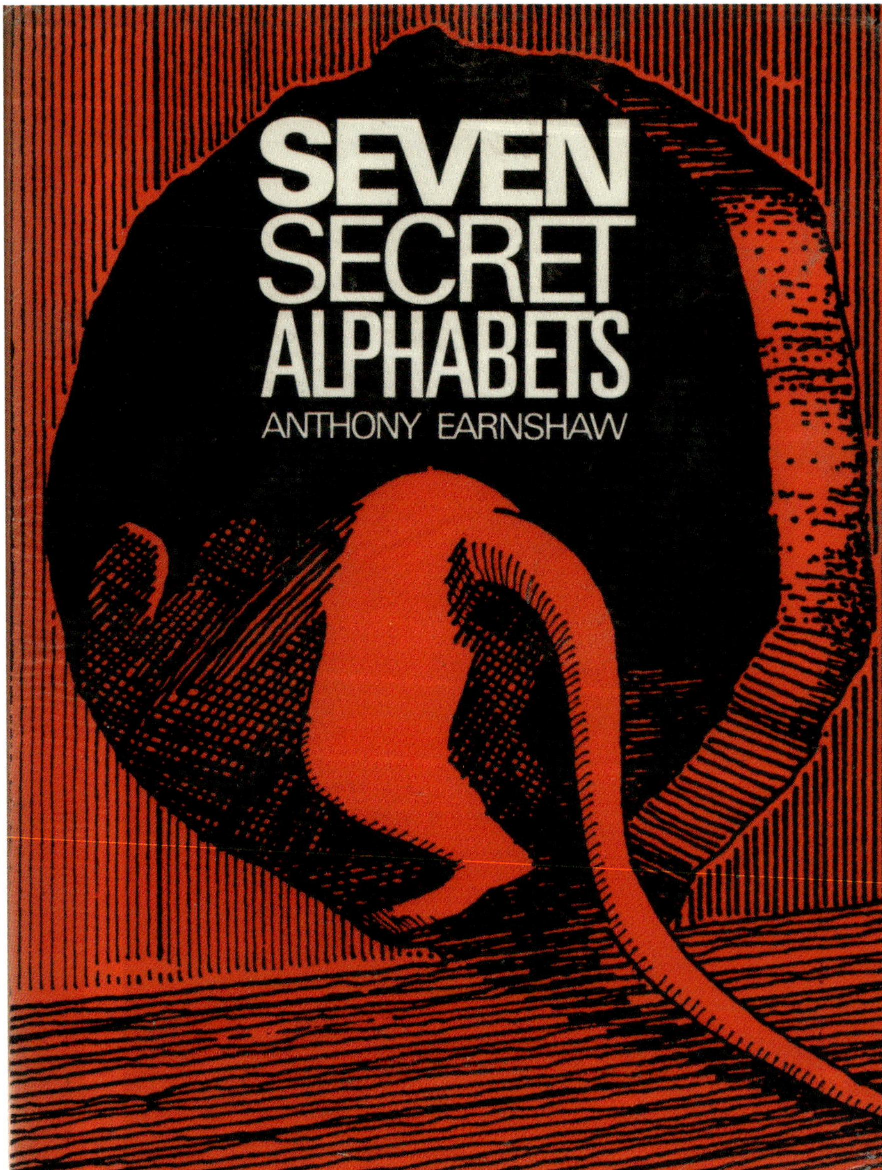

On the cover a rat, coarsely cross-hatched like the enlarged detail of a Victorian engraving, enters its dark hole. Its body is in shadow, its left hind leg and tail brightly lit. In isolation it seems to be no more than a rat entering its hole. In context it turns out to represent the letter Q in the fifth of Anthony Earnshaw's *Seven Secret Alphabets*, a very remarkable book.[1]

—George Melly

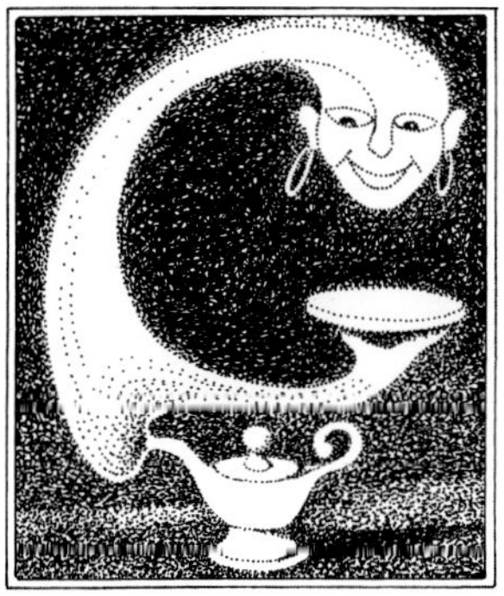

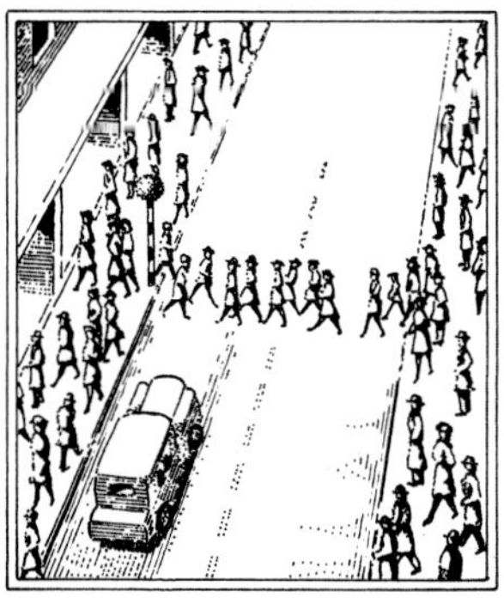

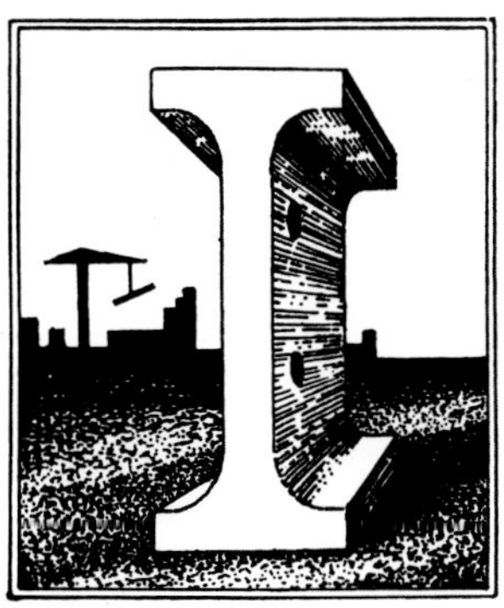

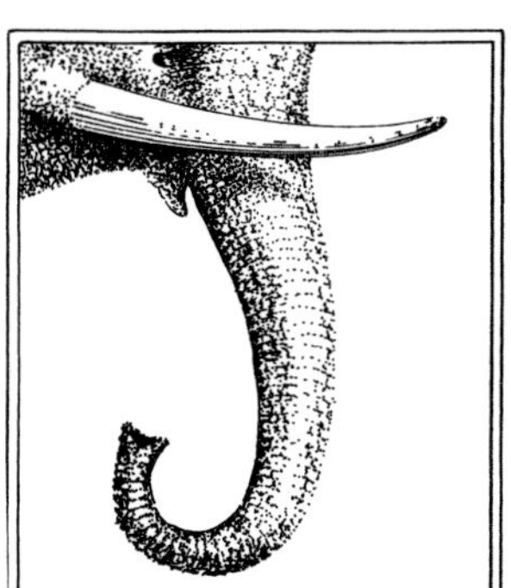

benefit, in terms of forming a set, with a single implement only, often followed by further unification using the medium of wood, or metal engraving undertaken by craftsmen. This opinion is supported by Marcel Jean in a letter sent to Earnshaw commenting on the unusual amount of invention involved in the alphabets: "Do you think they might be adapted, preferably by a graphic artist specialising in lettering, to become typographically drawn—I mean, to look like printing letters, but keeping, of course, their metaphoric ideas? A difficult proposition, I am sure."[3]

Earnshaw's alphabets are the antithesis of functionality. My approaching the seven alphabets in an analytical manner is of course to stack the absurd upon the absurd. The law governed policeman meets the actions of an anarchist.

"Earnshaw enjoyed 'upsetting the apple-cart'. I get a sense that he is giving his alphabets a holiday from their daily work. The drawings are suggestive of letters and although they can be 'used' they are also individual vignettes; a cornucopia of visual ingenuity".[4]

Examples of Earnshaw's Approaches to the Letters

Finding and noticing letters
A is for a pair of hobbled legs, a step-ladder with its stretched safety cord, a drawing compass with a fixing bar. P from a U-shaped magnet stuck to a nail. Z seen in the bars of a garden gate.

Seeing scripts in nature
B is smoke curling above a cigarette. S is a hose held over a fire-man's shoulder. An airplane's vapour trail. An octopus fighting a diver forms a B, the wood shaving from a box plane another S. The tail of a devil. A letter B made from a straight needle and a curved thread.

Invented coincidences
Lit windows in a building at night form M. Three falling factory chimneys and three shooting stars make chance Ks. Crossed searchlights an X. Bees fly to a hive in formation for Z.

Altering objects
A bite out of a piece of bread and a toothless comb become C and E. The numeral one stands in for an I. Thirteen for a B and sixty-nine for an O. An open book makes a V. W is an opened folding rule. Cigarettes are carefully arranged in a packet to make an E.

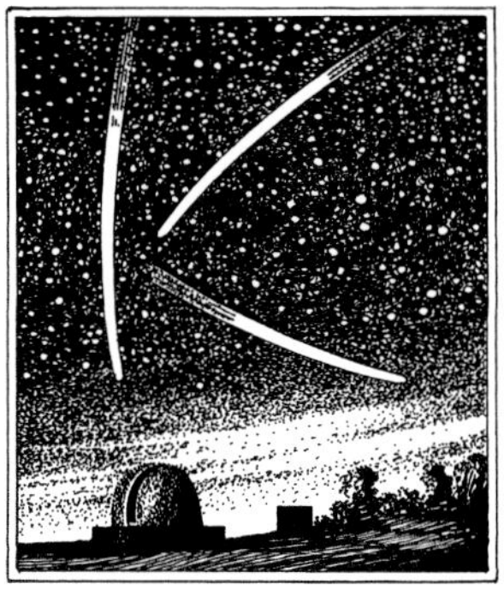

Dotted lines
V and W as a kangaroo bounces along. Sportsmen's moves, balls being juggled, a race, a pass at football. A fly's path. Stars in the sky. Tracing a boomerang's circular path. Smoke signals. A snail track crosses a bicycle track. A circle of footprints. Bubbles form the diagonal between submarine and convoy to make a Z.

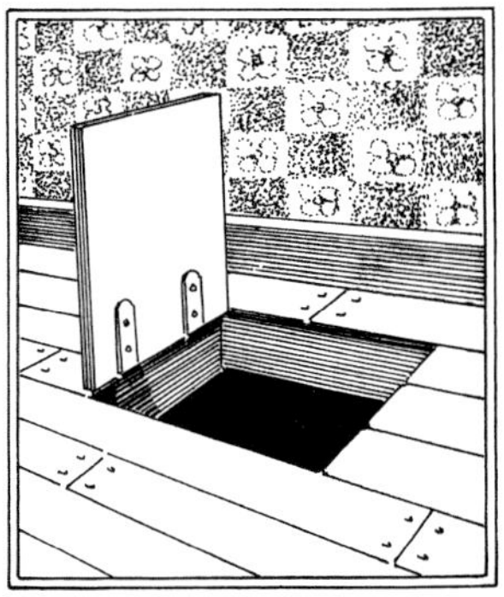

Cropping
A bed to make an H. A round table to make a C and a D. A clock face L. Using a brick wall to crop both a keyhole, and a man in a flat cap playing with a yoyo, to produce two different Rs. An obscuring prison wall to turn a ladder into an H. A spanner head for a C. A crucifix cropped by a head forms an X. Half a pie for a D. A pudenda for a W. Beaded breasts for a B. A slot for turning a coin into a D. An enlargement of a saw blade becomes a W.

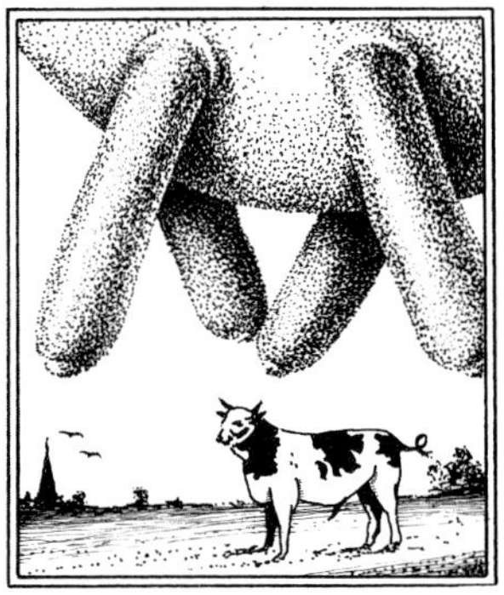

Unusual viewpoints
A crowd in a street makes an H. A climbing accident forms a D. Three funnels of a liner posed vertically just before sinking form a E. An open trap door becomes an L.

Juxtaposing
Straight and leaning towers form K and N. Broken bones a W. A porthole and a piece of rope a Q. A bridge, its reflection, and a rope another Q. Two stetcher-bearers become an H. A man buying a posy from a girl with a tray of flowers another H.

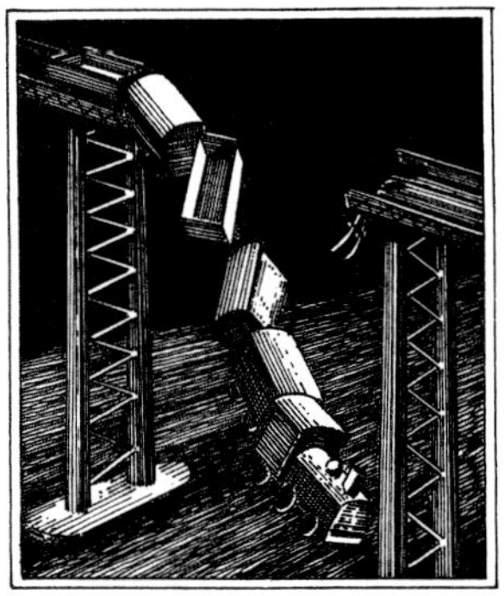

Telling stories
Many of the images appear to be part of a story implying that something has just happened, or will happen. The broken link in a chain making a U. The girl tied to the railway track. The empty

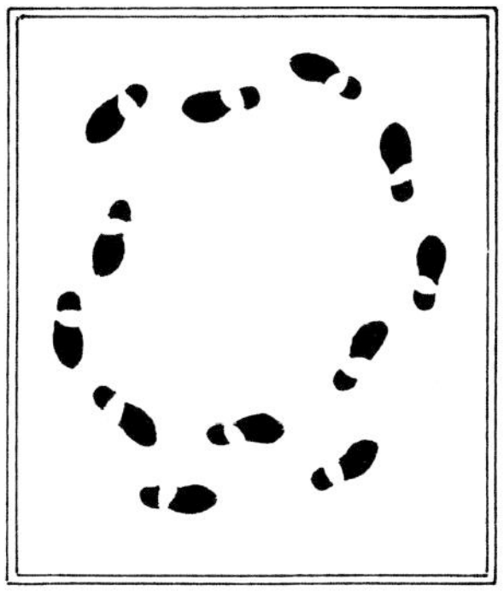

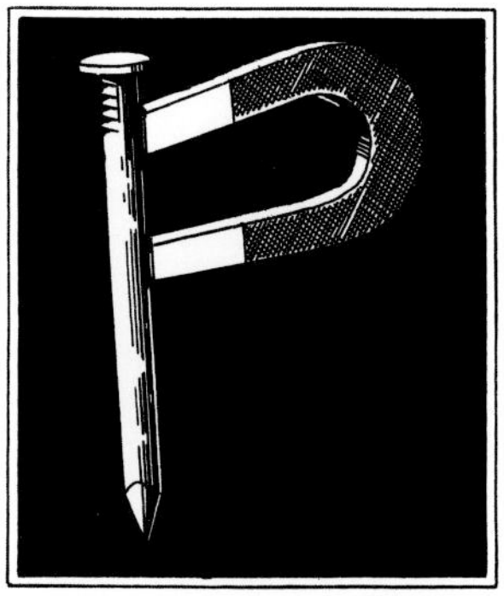

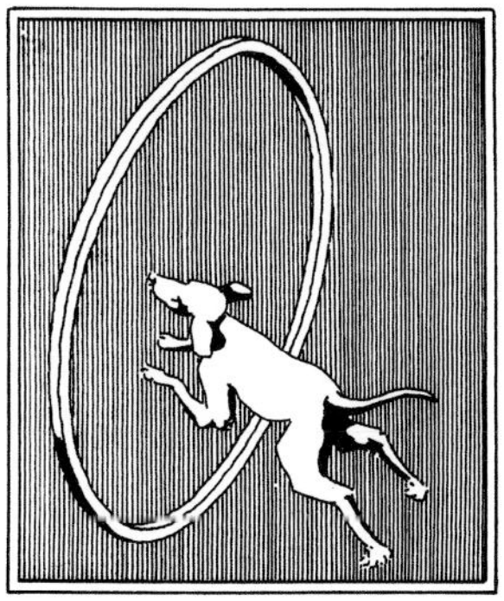

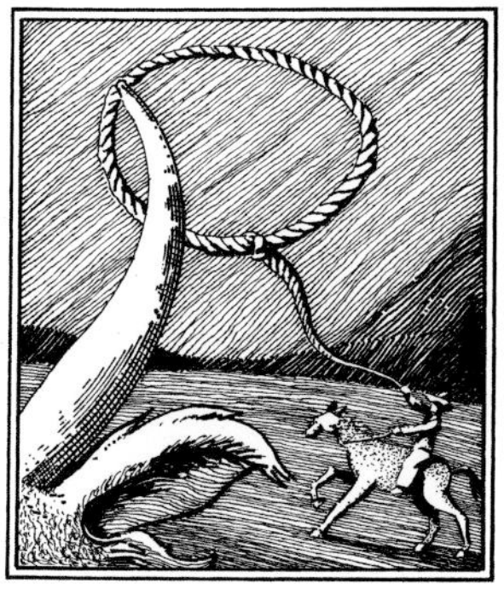

sardine tin. The returning boomerang. The falling man. The overwhelming wave. The open trapdoor. The convoy of ships attacked. The sinking liner. The crack in the ice. The urinating dogs. The crossed tracks of a bicycle and a snail.

Breaking rules

In a world of no rules Earnshaw finds two to break; he allows a kangaroo and an aeroplane to break his established double line frame; he alters a first letter to create the next letter in the alphabet on three occasions, once with E and F and twice with V and W (in effect 'spotting the difference' and telling short stories).

The Content of *Seven Secret Alphabets*

Earnshaw's visual vocabulary appears endless. He refers to a vast range of subject matter and in very different ways. He is able to "reinvest the cliché".[5]

The cast in order of appearance are hobbled, racing, juggling, drumming, fishing, trying to escape, caught red-handed with a gun, doubly stabbed, throwing boomerangs, smoke-signalling, playing football, falling off a cliff, fleeing an erupting volcano, standing on breaking ice, drinking, watching Punch and Judy, marching with rifles, licking their lips, snoring, naked, in front of a firing squad, transfixed with pins, lassoing steers, running away from a tornado, tightrope-walking and being removed to the morgue. This is all in the service of the alphabet, not a story.

The *mise-en-scène* contains coastlines, gulfs, railway trains, tented camps, double gibbets, half-buried bones, coal mines, castles, falling chimneys, brick walls, lighthouses, garden gates, high streets, skyscrapers, guillotines, cliffs, waves, stairs, oceans, volcanoes, ice, trains crashing off viaducts, mountains, forests, pyramids, graveyards, planets, tornados and big dipper rides.

When it comes to flora and fauna, he includes trees, sharks, snakes, bees, whales, rabbits, octopuses, cows, dogs, leaves, seeds, elephants, mice, rats, wasps, snails, whales, scorpions, bats, swordfish, horses, steers and kangaroos.

At first sight it looks as though he has avoided the Apples and Zebras approach. Looking closer there are occasional similarities to a child's abecedary but these are probably just coincidental: B for boots, F for flag, G for genie, J for juggler, R for rope, T for totem. The various styles and themes and occasional sequences seem to be fairly carefully spread across the alphabets.

Everyone takes for granted the one rule that no alphabet book ever breaks—the letters come in a fixed order. Earnshaw employs the four or two images to a page grid to make further connections. In the second alphabet the adjacent letters C and D are two separate halves of a circular table. In the third alphabet, V and X are made by a tick and a cross marking a right and a wrong mathematical sum. In alphabet five, tiny figures flee the I of an erupting volcano, and also from K, the cracks of an earthquake.

The last letter of the last alphabet in the book shows a log being sawn by two saws. The sawn log, a symbol for sleeping and snoring, from the world of comics.

In the original dummy Earnshaw submitted to his publisher Jonathan Cape, there is a hand written note signed by Earnshaw. It reads: "These Alphabets are the off-spring of certain work Eric Thacker and I did for our book *Wintersol.* Seven Alphabets, one for every day of the week—each Alphabet is followed by a 'sampler' in which the letters are used to form some common place notice or prohibition."

These proposed samplers were designed to fill up the final page which always consisted of the final two letters of the twenty-six. A further note in pencil indicates Earnshaw's thoughts on the title *Seven Private Alphabets.* In capitals and surrounded by a drawn box the following words are written: "Strange Odd Secret Outlandish". At the end of each alphabet the samplers are indicated in pencil capitals: "Spitting is Forbidden. Now wash your hands. These Animals are dangerous. No hands wanted. Sound your horn deaf persons crossing." The best, and penultimate, was not about trespassers and copyright but seems to refer to the possible arrangement between an author and a proposed publisher, "No bets taken after hare starts running". The final sampler reads "Emergency Exit."

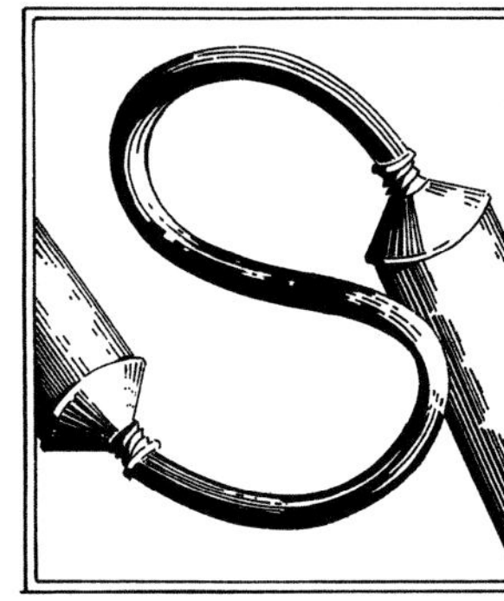

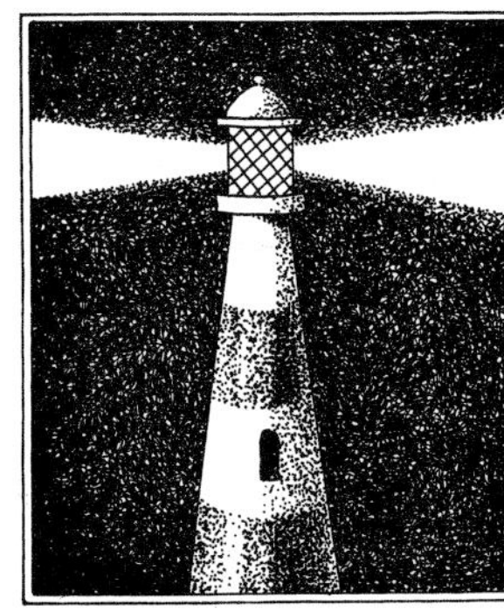

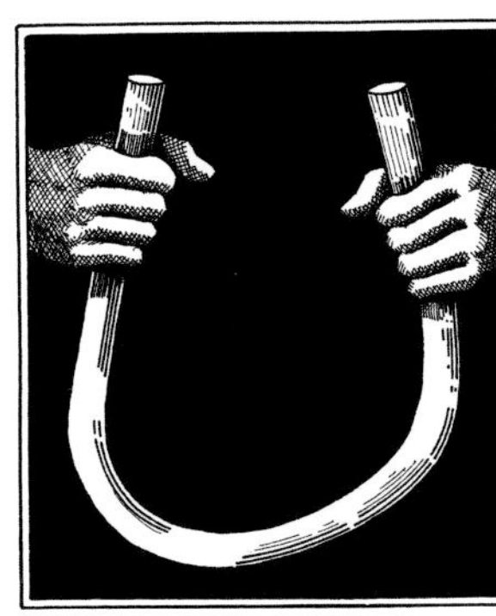

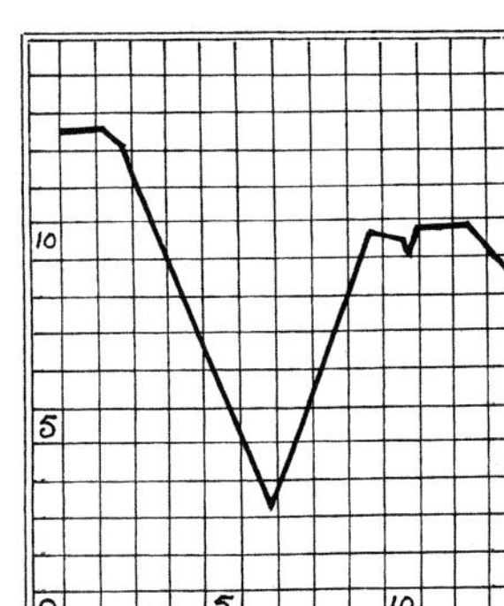

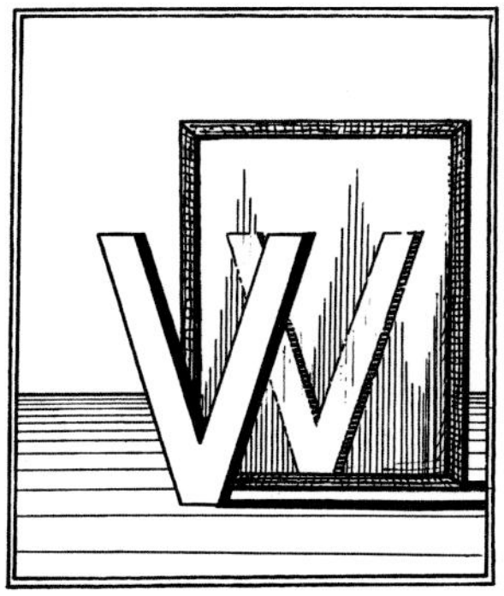

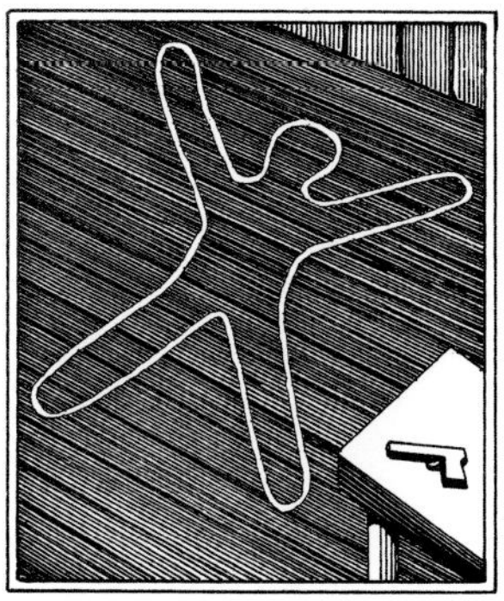

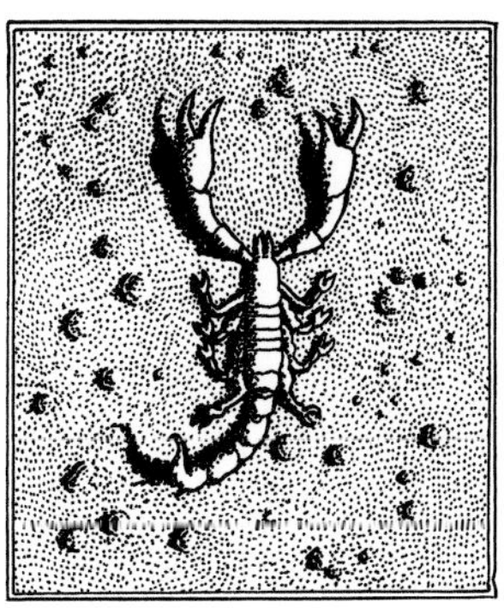

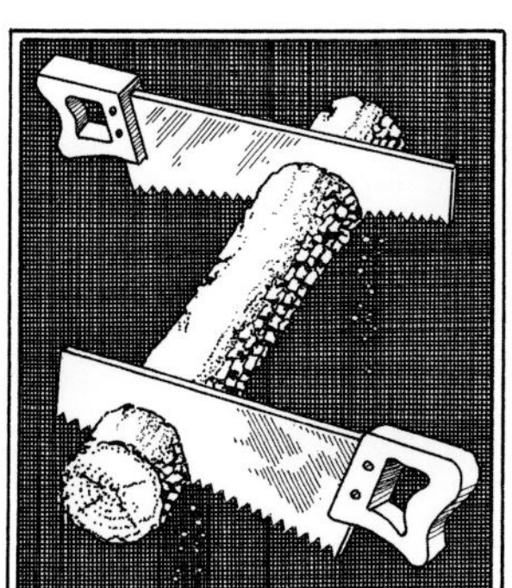

All of these characters and props, games, tricks and mechanisms are carefully deployed to play with our emotions. There is much wit and some belly laughs, a little lust and quite a large dose of gloom and pessimism. There are beautiful drawings and clever notions (not always combined successfully). As with any good artist's world it is inhabitable, atmospheric, not always cheerful, questioning, sometimes exquisite and best of all funny. I have a note of a telephone conversation dating from my being asked to write about *Seven Secret Alphabets*. It simply reads: "Tony said 'The thing I like most in life is laughing'" and "He could be morose at times. An autodidact". These alphabets clearly describe him perfectly.

Notes

1. George Melly, 'Sign and portents', *The Guardian*, 30 November 1972
2. Edward Lathem, *Interviews with Robert Frost*, Holt, Rinehart and Winston, New York, 1966
3. Marcel Jean, letter to A.E., 19 July 1978
4. Les Coleman, letter to the author, n.d.
5. John McConnell, quoted in McAlhone & Stuart, *A Smile in the Mind*, Phaidon, 1996

The letters illustrating this essay have been chosen by the author from all seven alphabets.

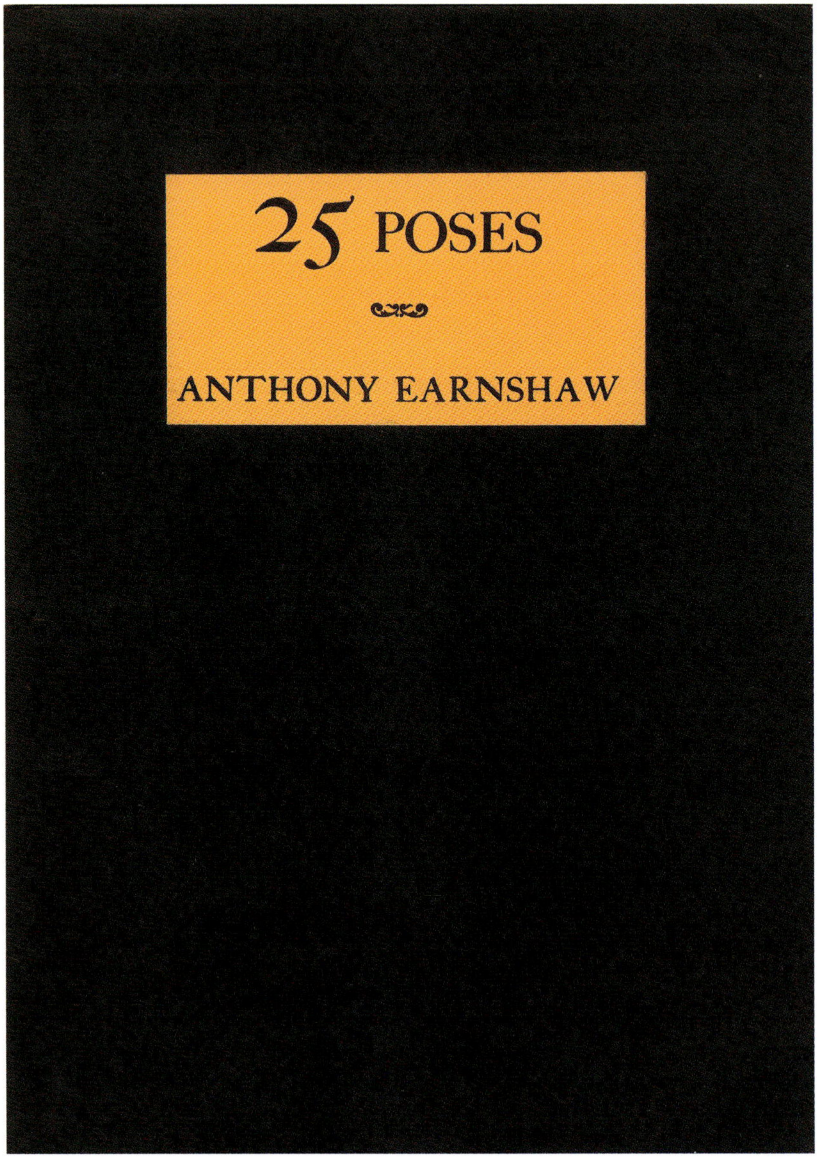

Front cover, *25 Poses*, 1973

Paul Hammond

On *25 Poses*

25 Poses is a book of Earnshaw drawings that Michael Randle and the artist published with the aid of a grant in 1973, in an edition of ninety signed copies. The book needs identifying, since it never appears in the bibliographies. It has never been reprinted and the images have not previously appeared in the literature on the artist.

25 Poses has fifty-six pages. It is offset printed in black ink on stiff matte paper, signal yellow in colour and measuring 20 x 25.5 cm, and perfect bound in black matte card of the same weight as the sheets within. The front cover bears a 12.2 x 6.3 cm printed label on yellow paper which reads "25 POSES / ANTHONY EARNSHAW", the title and author's name being separated by a small ornamental vignette. The typeface and the vignette are reminiscent of those on the label stuck on the front of the clothbound first edition of *Musrum* (1968). The twenty-five images in *25 Poses* appear on the recto of each page; that is, on the right hand side of each double-page spread; the verso facing page is, therefore, blank.

25 Poses is an inscrutable and austere tome, since aside from the cover label and the title page—which has a black-bordered, same-sized version of that label plus the following information: "Published and Printed by A Earnshaw and Michael Randle at Westbank Bradford England 1973"—it contains no text, no introduction, no page numbers, not even captions to the drawings (although each of these has a word, or words, within it). Like Tony, Mike Randle—who is famous today for his long history as a peace campaigner and as an enabler of Soviet spy George Blake's escape to the USSR in 1966—was at the time a teacher at Bradford College of Art. The book itself was printed on a small litho machine in Michael and Anne Randle's basement, the binding being undertaken by a local printer. As for distribution, most copies were sold to friends, with a few making it into bookshops in Bradford, Leeds and London.

25 Poses is a book of hand-drawn pseudo-engravings. Each 'engraving' is a serial variation on a naked male or female statue atop a circular, drum-like plinth in shallow space. The space is similar to the one described by those big hanging 'scoops' of blank paper where horizontal floor and vertical wall pass seamlessly from one to the other. It was using such a system that the Baileys and Avedons photographed their subjects in the 1960s. The unadorned backdrop before which Earnshaw's plinth stands receives the strong shadow of the figure in front of it. (Perhaps we are in a museum by night, whistling in the dark, being led from one statue to the next, letting the conspiratorial guide illuminate each figure with his powerful torch beam). Nineteen of the poses are of a full-bodied male nude standing in a spread-eagled position, as if waiting to be frisked—or executed—his eyes closed. Of the five female nudes, two are full-figure, and headless; two are half-figure, from the waist down, and one is all but absent altogether, save her legs. There is a single image of an almost entire woman—she is amputated at the knee—superimposed on, and occluding, the torso and head of the standard male. She, too, has her eyes closed.

25 Poses has twenty-five plinths that bear the suggestion of an incised title—often an abstract, but sometimes a concrete, noun—that resonates with the surprising allegorical additions or subtractions borne by the statue. The titles are, in order of appearance: Shame, Clothing, Pride, Secrets, Masturbation, Transvestism, Voyeurism, Exhibitionism, Christianity, Irreverence, Sainthood, Perversity, Censorship, Cowardice, Love, St. Sebastian, St. Sebastian's Wife, Marriage, Adultery, Politics, Art, Jehovah, Violence, Shadows and Liberty. Two or three of these titles might have appeared on the plinths of Victorian statuary, the kind of high-minded civic sculpture you find in the public squares of Leeds and Bradford—but most are too sardonic to even contemplate. As Ian Breakwell once put it: "If erected (there's no other word) [these statues] would give our moral guardians apoplexy."[1] At other times they allude to the drives the repressive Victorians did most to express.

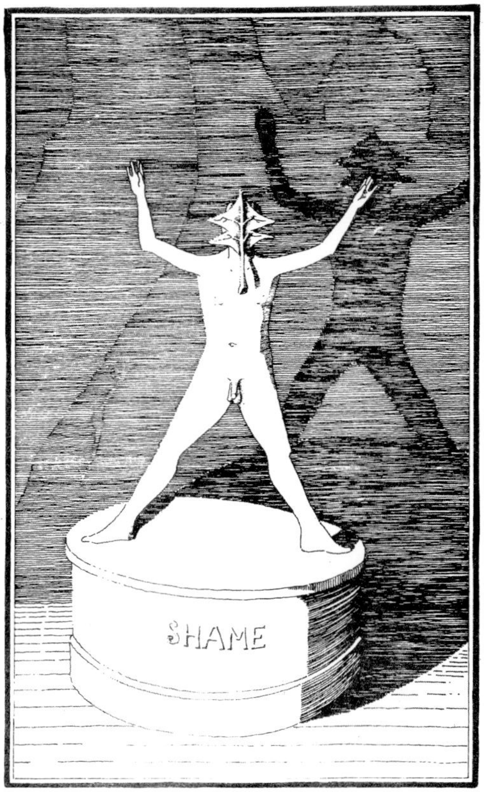

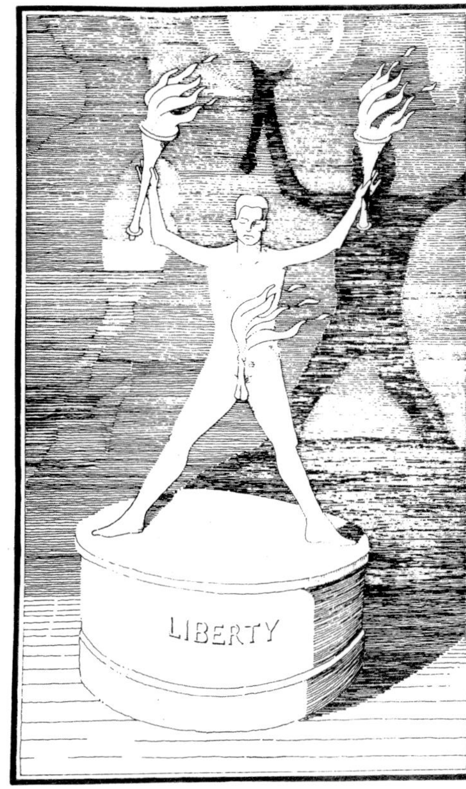

25 Poses contains twenty-five jokes at the expense—both credit and debit—of the penis. Tony called it a book of "dirty drawings". I think you could say the thrust is phallocentric, at once triumphalist, defiant and quizzical. Earnshaw was forty-nine when he drew these images with a hard-on. Les Coleman has pointed out that in the early seventies there were a number of cartoonists publishing humorous drawings about the penis. He cites himself, as well as the cartoonists Topor, Siné, Tetsu and Willem, to whom we might add the artists Patrick Hughes and Marcel Mariën. A few years after the publication of *25 Poses* Hughes and I wrote *Upon the Pun*,[2] which contained many penile *double-entendres* in visual form. Dicks were in the air then.

25 Poses is a work of *umoralism*, in the Jacques Vaché sense. It uses blasphemy and eroticism and enigma to take the rise out of conventional morality.

25 Poses opens with shame and closes with liberty. Although

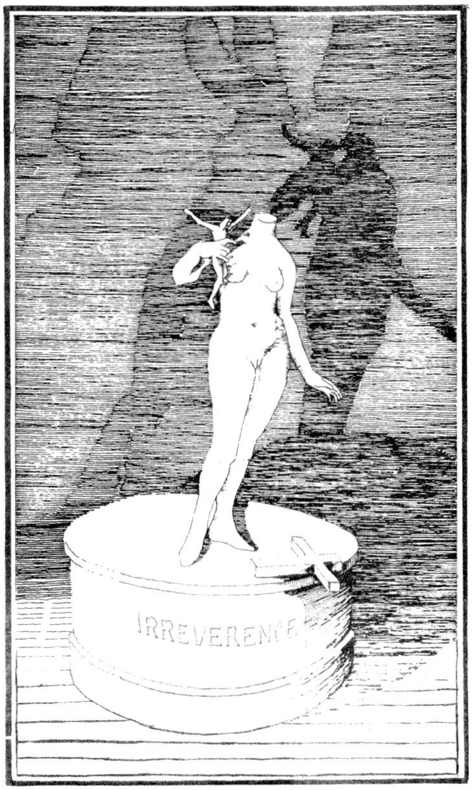

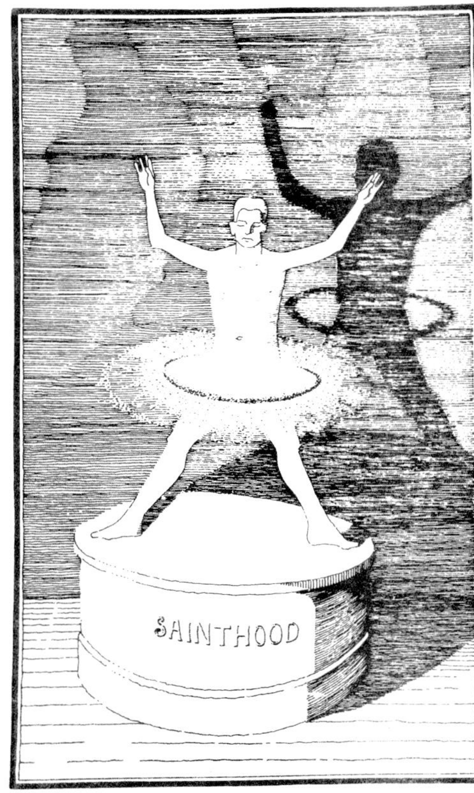

the book's argument is far from being a straight one—it is serpentine at times—the shift from the first to the second of these two categories can be said to frame it. In 'Shame', the male statue has a detumescent cock and his facial features—and thus all possibility of vision—are hidden by a curiously shaped leaf; a fig leaf, perhaps, displaced upwards from the genital region. In 'Liberty', the man's cock is tumescent and emits flames from the glans; moreover, he has a flaming torch in each hand. Freedom is tantamount to ardour and arson—it is conflagration that brings light. In an alternative version of 'Liberty'—I shall return to the drawings Tony reworked or discarded—the same torch-bearer stands on a plinth engraved with the word 'Surrealism'.

Between shame and liberty, there is many an allegory to do with moral abjection and transcendence.

It is not my intention to give a verbal résumé of every one of the twenty-five poses, but I will pause over one or two more. In 'Irreverence', an acephalous statue of a naked woman—a "*femme*

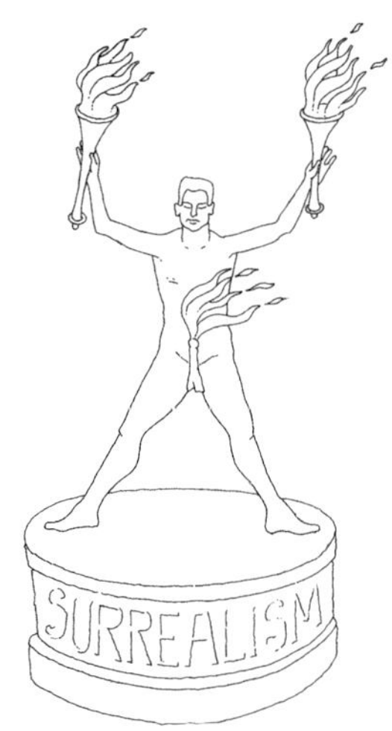

Surrealism, previously unpublished drawing, c.1972

100 tétes"—with shaved pudenda clutches a Corpus Christi to her breast, while at her feet there lies the cross. In a (blind? unthinking?) gesture of defiance and lust she has plucked the doll-like Jesus from the crucifix. (His extended arms echo the stance of the male statue dominating most of *25 Poses*). What you do not immediately notice is her little finger hooked delicately around the Son of God's erect micro-penis. She has conferred a human carnality on him. Is it because they never get an erection that all godheads lay down the law about sexual repression? In 'Irreverence' Earnshaw joins *fin de siècle* artists like Felicien Rops and Martin van Maele in a splendid *mélange* of sex and religion that harks back to the Marquis de Sade.

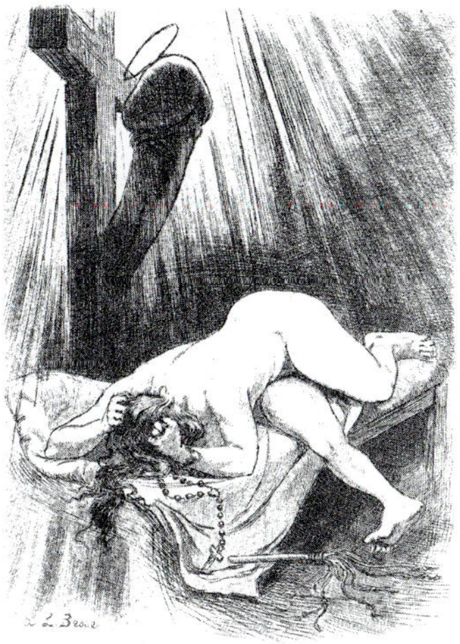

Martin van Maele, from his suite of etchings *La Grande Danse macabre des vifs* (c.1907–8).

In 'Sainthood', the male statue's halo has increased in diameter and slipped down, hoopla-style, to encircle his pelvic region. (Floating there, it has something of the hula hoop about it). Moreover, the dazzle of this displaced halo obliterates the figure's penis. The hint is that sainthood is emasculating; or that only the emasculated can be saints.

The following is not a binding statement, but I would draw attention to an image by one of Earnshaw's favourite artists, Marcel Mariën. The Belgian surrealist's iconoclastic re-working of the logo of Leslie Charteris' famous character Simon Templar, a.k.a. 'The Saint', is on the back cover of *Crystal Blinkers*, the Mariën collection published in 1973 by Tony's great friend, John Lyle. In the Mariën, the saint's halo, which now does double duty as a vagina, hovers at the end of the matchstick-man's erect member.

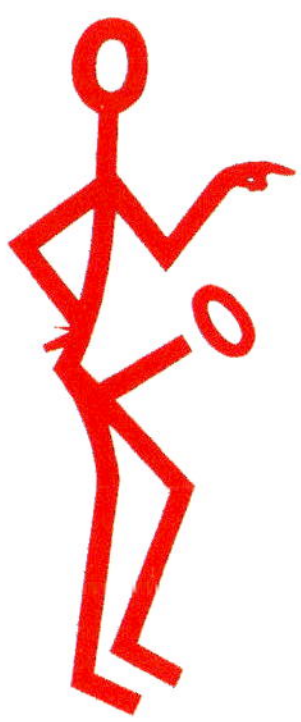

Marcel Mariën, Le Pécheur endurci (The Hardened Sinner), 1973

Earnshaw did a close variation of his own drawing—and, in passing, of Mariën's visual gag—in 'Perversity', which comes after 'Sainthood' in the book. In it, an effulgent, miniaturised halo rings the statue's boner. In what is perhaps a joke told against himself, the artist is suggesting that to treat the erect penis as if it were a holy thing, something sacrosanct, is tantamount to perversity.

I will end this brief tour on an illustration that surely *is* a statement of personal belief: standing on a plinth incised with the word 'Politics', our Joe Soap, whose facial features are forever minimal, conventionally handsome, has had them wiped altogether. But not just that—his cock and balls have gone

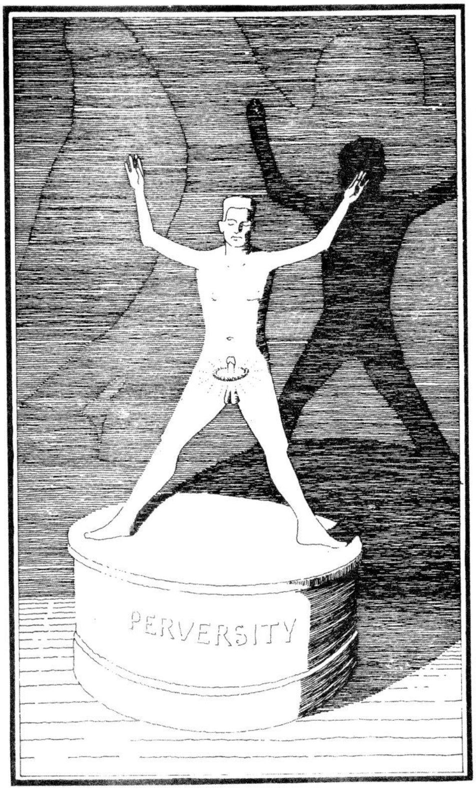

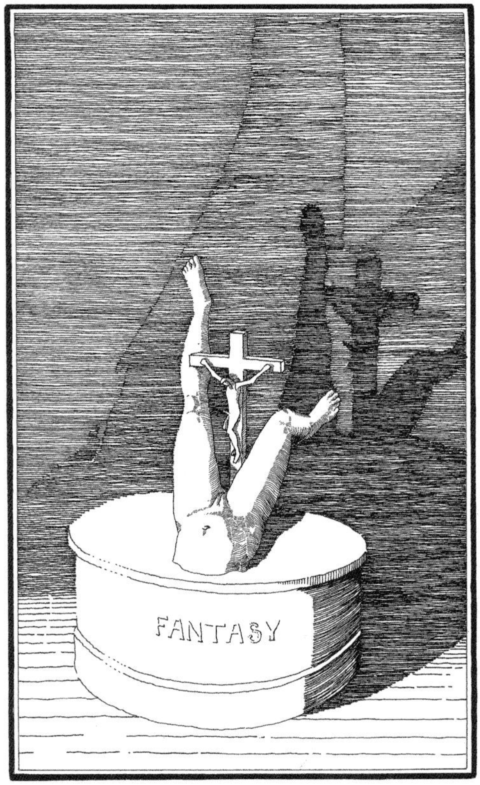

too. You do not have to be Paracelsus to divine that Earnshaw is insinuating that politics—politics under actually existing democracy—is a sham and lobotomises and emasculates the individual, and therefore the mass. (Another reading would be that political power is faceless and impotent in the face of the implacability of capitalism).

There are things to be said about the way Earnshaw drew these heraldic illustrations. I would guess he used tracing paper to repeatedly put down the linear paradigm of the circular plinth and the male lay figure, who appears curiously two-dimensional, like a cardboard cut-out that is not "all there," aside from a bit of tentative hatching on his left groin, left flank and left cheek and neck. (Are not such plinths an important iconographic element in a primal source of figurative Surrealism, *pittura metafisica*? cf. de Chirico's 'The Disquieting Muses' of 1916). In this ploy of tracing—which also applied to the female statue, of course—Earnshaw remained true to the

Leeds College of Art aesthetic that was in place by the mid-sixties. By this I mean the impersonal 'colouring-book' style that subverted the *passé* system of 'existential' volumetric drawing from the live model. In short, the pencil or scratch-nib pen had given way to the uniform-line Rotring rapidograph dear to technical draughtsmen. Practitioners of this 'anti-artistic' style in Leeds were Patrick Hughes, Trevor Winkfield, Glen Baxter, Les Coleman and Jeff Edwards, among others.

And Anthony Earnshaw, except that Earnshaw only kicked things off with his traced templates, assembling the figures and part-figures from them in Identikit style, before going on to flesh things out with his hand-drawn, horizontal hatching system. This system, which was already in use in *Wintersol*, was employed in *25 Poses* to suggest the perspectively gradated ground surface and the uniform wall plane, the shadow on one side of the drum-like stand and the figure, plus the shadows cast by said figure. I say shadows, because Earnshaw had the umbral shadow cast a further, penumbral shadow, perhaps in order to fragment, and thus control, what would have been a rather long line to ink in by hand. (A previously unpublished drawing, 'Fantasy' [p.74], illustrates this well). In the darkest areas the closely spaced nervy lines sometimes coalesce into black blips and smudges, adding interest to what might have been relatively large areas of uniformity. I suspect that coining and inking in the hatching system was a source of pleasure for the artist, on account of its potential for contrived accident. Aside from the aura of Victorianism that often suffuses Earnshaw's language, both visual and written, I take the hatching *per sé* to be an homage to one of Earnshaw's lifelong heroes, William Blake. Did he, as I do, have a fascination for Blake's etchings from 1797 for Edward Young's *Night Thoughts*? [3]

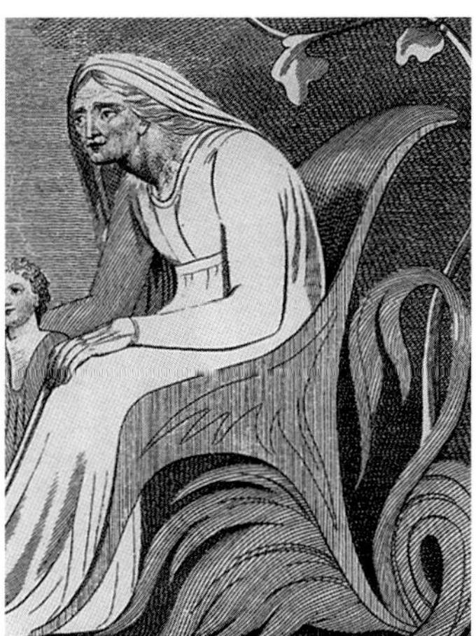

William Blake (detail), Edward Young, *Night Thoughts*, 1797

25 Poses was assembled, edited, from a total of fifty or so drawings. Some of these were alternative versions of the images which found their way into the book, the difference being a change of detail or simply the substitution of one inscription-cum-title by a second ('Desire' by 'Transvestism', or 'Surrealism' by 'Liberty', say). In yet others the statue on the plinth gave way to something non-human: a Godzilla dinosaur, 'War' or a smoking factory chimney, 'Freud'. This quintessential

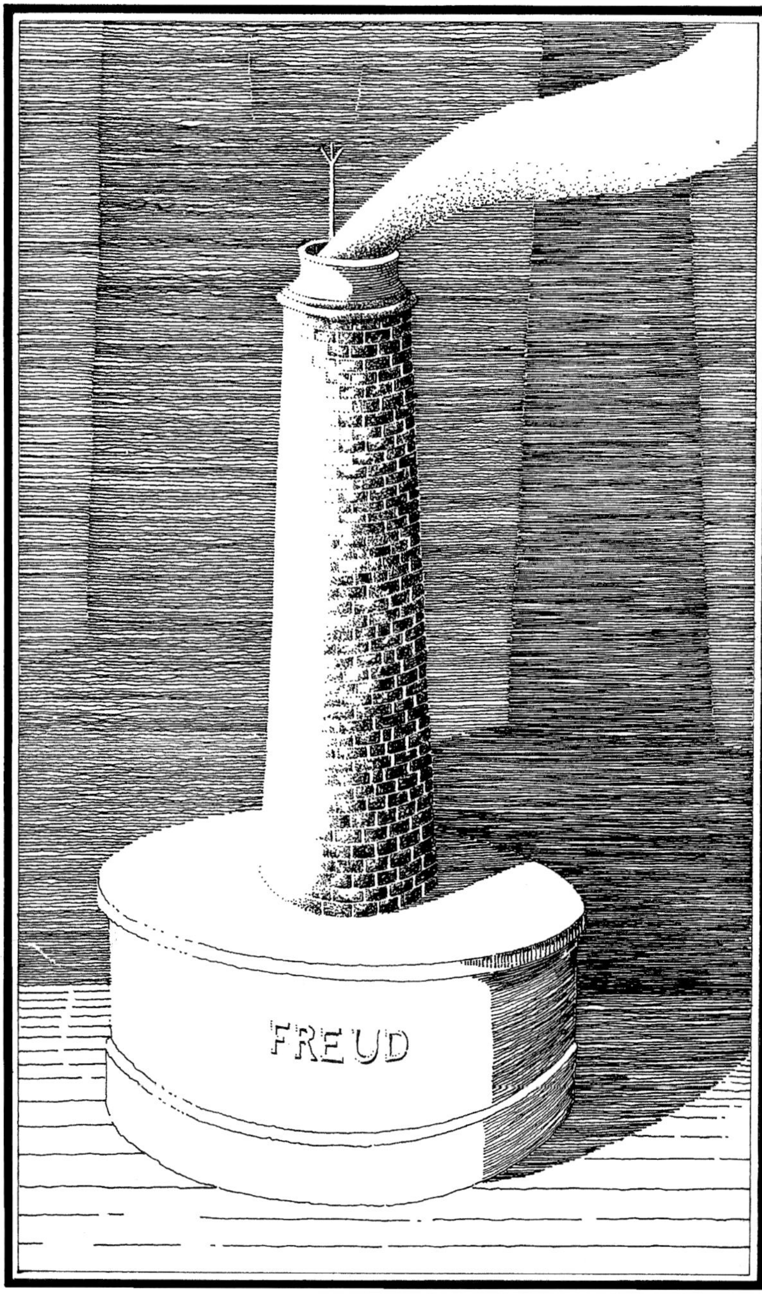

Freud, previously unpublished drawing, c.1972

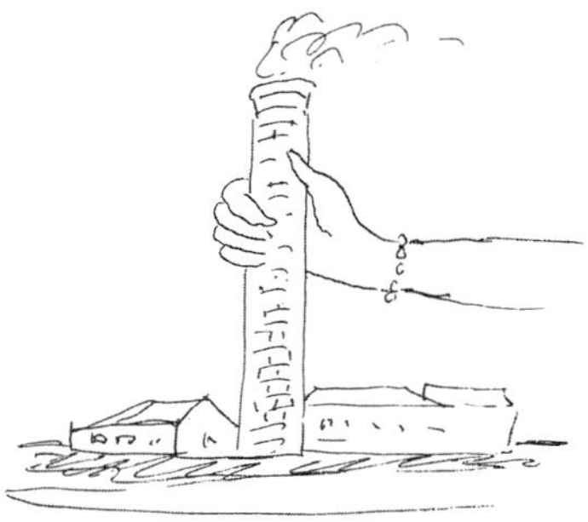

René Magritte, untitled drawing, n.d.

Earnshavian signifier—as no end of Tony's social-realist drawings demonstrate—was perhaps set to one side for the obviousness of its connotations—let's face it, Magritte had made something like the same point many years before—but viewed from a different angle, the drawing hints at how this Wokker-surrealist eroticised the industrial landscape he inhabited.

The very idea of a sequence of poses suggests the notion of a *poseur*, a dirty word in the northern working-class-made-good artist's vocabulary that evokes the perceived inauthenticity and pretentiousness of the bourgeois London artworld, thought to be teeming with poseurs. (I remember such us-and-them superiority being expressed by a Leeds artist when he pissed on the floor at an opening at the Angela Flower's Gallery in the late 1970s). I cite this by way of saying that a further stratum of humour in Earnshaw's book may involve this sort of generalised class-conscious disdain.

And then again, there is the very pose of the nude protagonists, so stiff and motionless—hieratic, even. I cannot help thinking of how, in days of yore, nudity could be displayed in the theatre, as long as the (female) objects of the public's gaze do not move on the top of their podia. Cue the 'living statues' of the Windmill Theatre. And another theatre, Leeds City Varieties, where Earnshaw, the onlooker of a stripper standing amidst her divested clothing, called out for her to "Put 'em back on!"

Notes

1. Ian Breakwell, 'Tomes from the Tomb', *City Limits*, 5 January 1989
2. Patrick Hughes & Paul Hammond, *Upon the Pun: Dual Meanings in Words and Pictures*, W. H. Allen, London, 1978
3. Robert Essick & Jenijoy La Belle (editors), *Night Thoughts or The Complaint and the Consolation*, illustrated by William Blake, text by Edward Young, Dover Publications, New York, 1975

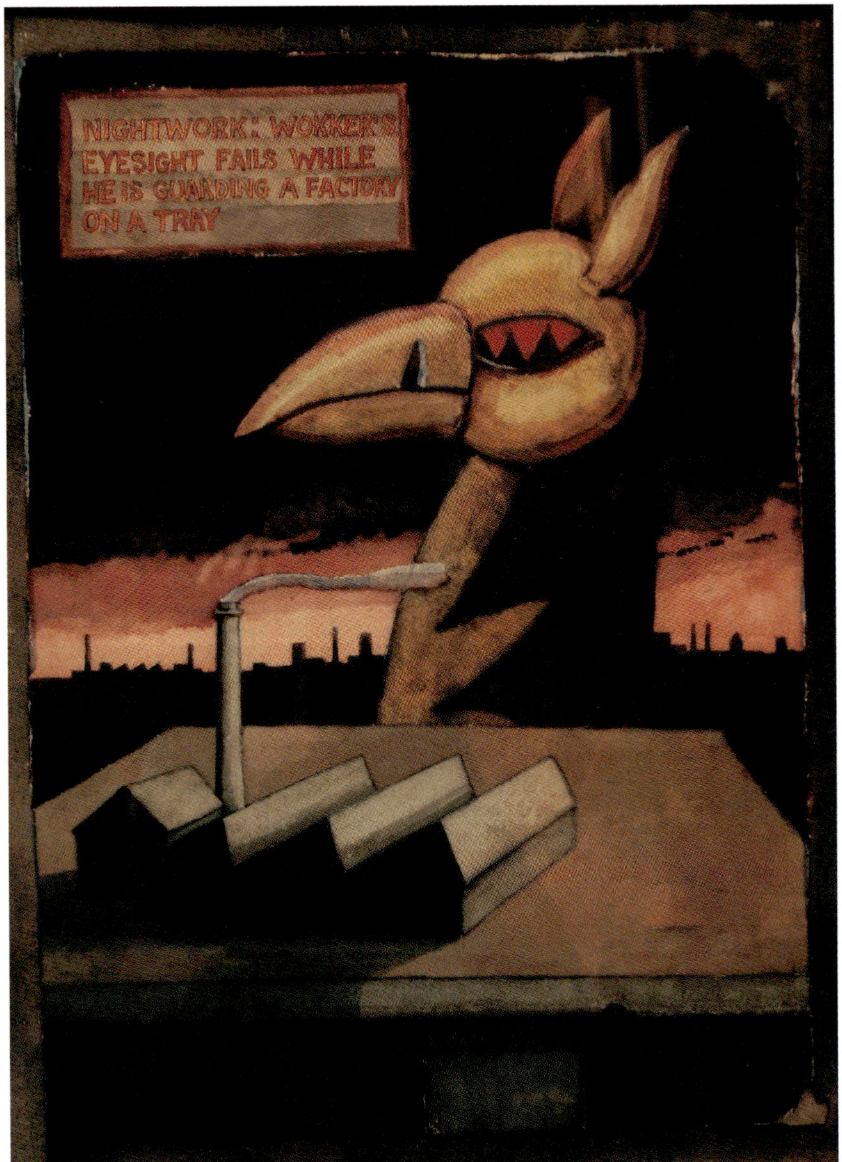

Nightwork: Wokker's Eyesight Fails While He is Guarding a Factory on a Tray, 1974

Roger Sabin

Wokker's World

"A mischief-making innocent abroad, Wokker shares many characteristics with Earnshaw's own personality." [1]

—Ian Breakwell

The strip 'Wokker' was originally the work of two men, both with writing and drawing skills, but who had little or no interest in the wider comics world. 'Wokker' thus remains impossible to categorise within the orthodoxy. When it seems that every kind of cartooning has been classified—'mainstream', 'underground', 'alternative'—and even the more *outré* experiments have been retrieved from obscurity and celebrated (in books like Dan Nadel's *Art Out of Time* and Peter Maresca's *Forgotten Fantasies: Sunday Comics 1900–1915*), 'Wokker' simply does not fit. No comics history has ever mentioned it.

The strip, created by Eric Thacker (1923–1997) and Anthony Earnshaw, was best-known at the time of its appearance in the *Times Educational Supplement* between 1971–72. Though it would later make sporadic appearances elsewhere, 'Wokker' was not part of a subculture that could be identified—like underground comix that sprang from the counter-culture of the 1960s. Instead, it came from a creative wellspring linked to postwar jazz, anarchism and Surrealism. This milieu was populated by a small group of 'bohemians' of differing class and background in the UK. Among their number were Wokker's creators, artist Patrick Hughes, anarchist and art critic Arthur Moyes and jazz-man and surrealist champion George Melly. The latter also scripted 'Flook', the *Daily Mail* comic strip, casting an irreverent eye over the 1960s. Although they came to know each other, they were too dispersed to be called something as coherent as a subculture. Possibly they were a proto-subculture—though this would be a label they would doubtless have rejected, in the same way they rejected all labels as a matter of course.

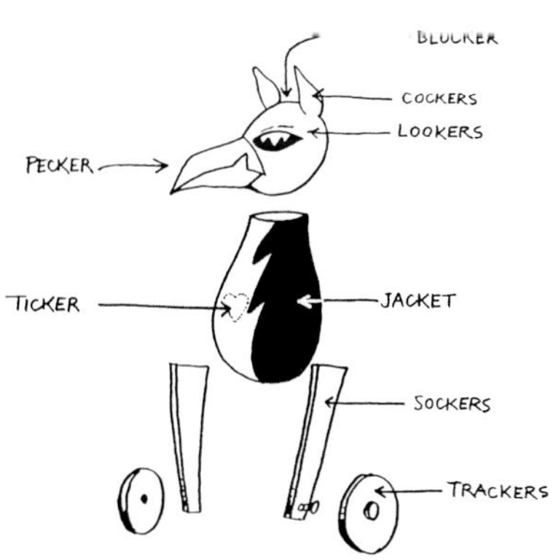

Eric Thacker, Explosion, n.d.

Wokker was originally the brainchild of Thacker, a sometime Methodist minister, jazz authority and occasional poet. He was also a friend of Anthony Earnshaw. The character made his debut in 1966 "as a long, thin, ill-nourished figure with thin black legs, spoked-wheels and a head with a crest atop: at the time Wokker was quite deaf… he had no ears".[2] As he evolved, so would Earnshaw add a pair of ears, plus wooden legs and wheels. The name was borrowed from a poem by Thacker that attempted to capture the sound of a drummer hitting the rim of a drum: "Wok, Wok, Wok…" Both men would write the strip

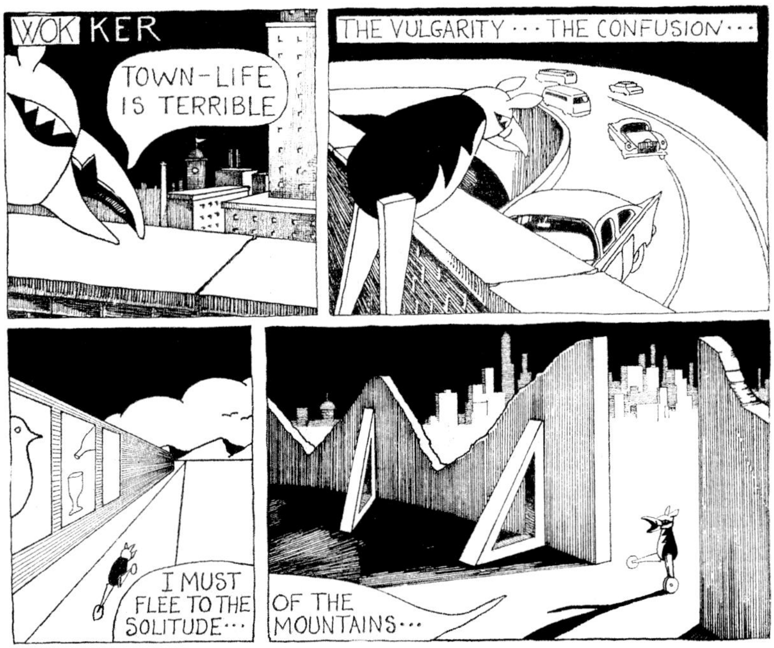

Times Educational Supplement, 8 October 1971

in its early days, but Thacker lost interest over time: when it was clear that no success—commercial or otherwise—would be forthcoming, he declared the creation "a dead duck".[3] However, Earnshaw remained undeterred and continued on his own.

Wokker, an evil-looking wooden bird, trundles around on wheels. In spite of his puppet-like appearance he is definitely not a toy to be played with. His identity is never fixed: he is more at home in the city than the countryside, though inhabiting all manner of surroundings, with a dislocated sense of time and place. He often takes the persona of a helpless innocent, while at other times that of a surly mischief-maker. His temper is fearsome, his wit urbane and often cutting, and his attitude generally is that of a cantankerous curmudgeon. His adventures are (typically) five-panel journeys into graphic delirium that set their own logical, or illogical boundaries. "In some respects he represents a ventriloquist's doll, acting as a mouthpiece for his two masters."[4] But this does not stop him shouting "WOKKIT!" if he does not get his own way. "Thacker was also aware that 'voc' was an Old English word meaning voice. The original name for his creation was Wokbird which it seems reasonable to interpret as voicebird. The female persona of Wokbird was abandoned early on making Wokker the first comic strip character to change gender."[5]

'Wokker' was always more of an experimental comic, and for this reason never aligned itself with comics culture. The mid-1960s and early 1970s were the days of underground comix, and publications such as *International Times* and *Oz*, reflecting the liberal ideology of drug-taking, and so-called 'free love'. 'Wokker' was a very different prospect. The strip's often angry edge and refusal to adhere to anything resembling a plot, curtailed its potential appeal to this market, and despite the occasional appearance of mushrooms in the stories it was never psychedelic.

There were occasionally similarities with some counter-cultural comics. Their more inventive panel transitions and experimental layouts being reminiscent of the kind of thing American underground cartoonists Art Spiegelman and Victor Moscoso were attempting. It is also known that Earnshaw was familiar with Bill Griffith's 'Zippy the Pinhead' character who travels through a nonsensical world spouting *non sequiturs*.

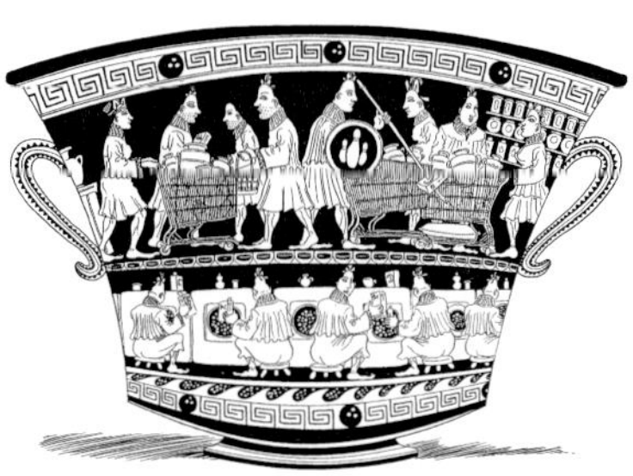

Bill Griffith, *The Zippy Calendar*, 1990

'Wokker' was unique; the narratives combined Surrealism and absurdity in equal measure—in one strip Wokker decides that 'Pataphysics is "obviously THE science!"[p.82]—but still manages to retain an ineffable Englishness. George Melly reflected that, "It saddens me that the strip appeared in print for only a comparatively brief moment. The trouble perhaps, as Patrick Hughes once suggested, is that you cannot, unless you are of a masochistic, even suicidal tendency, imagine cuddling Wokker."[6]

Hughes was right. Wokker was far from 'cute' and certainly

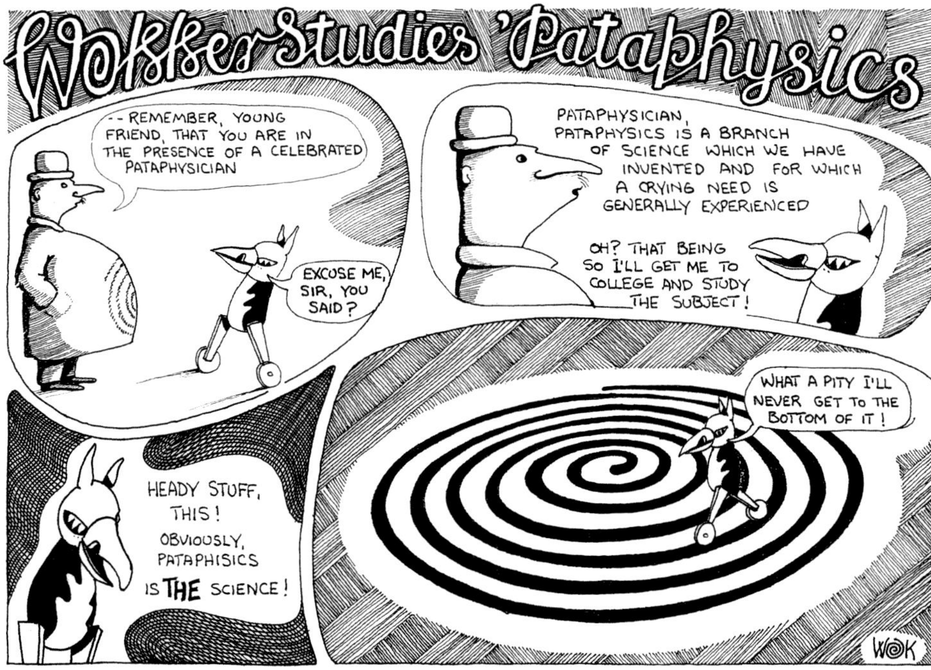

Eight Wokker Postcards, 2003

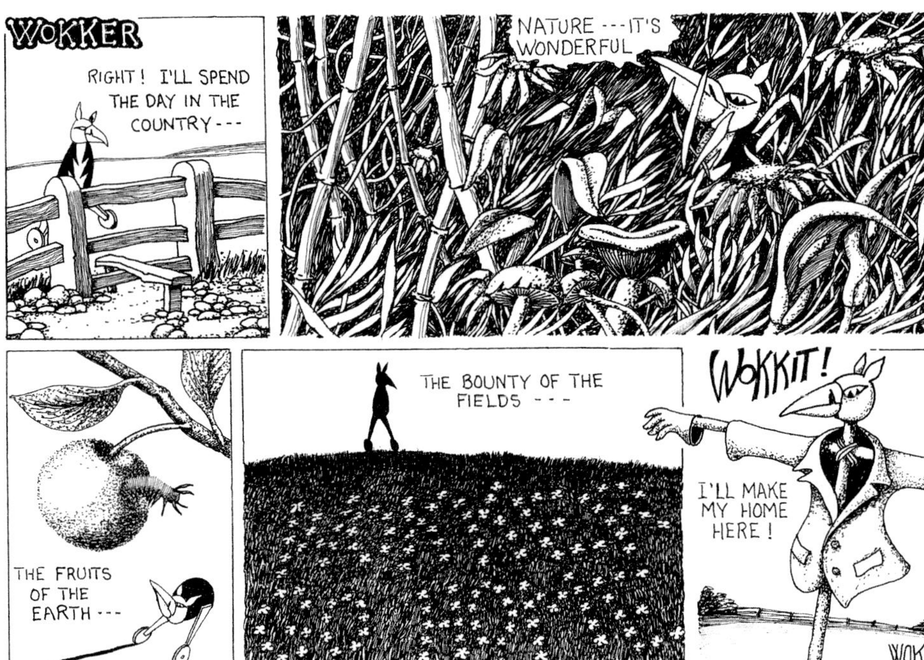

Eight Wokker Postcards, 2003

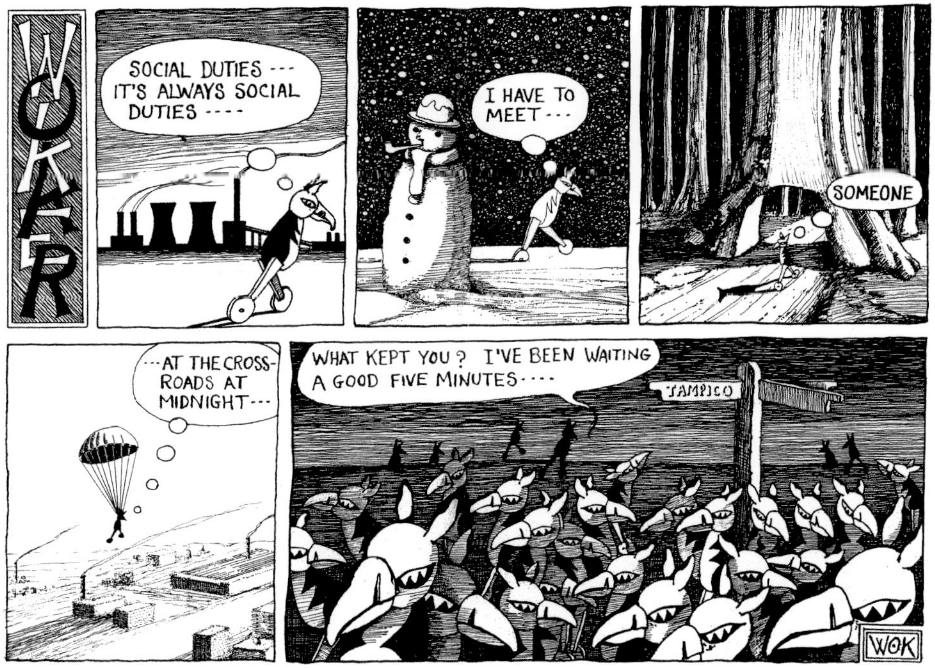

Eight Wokker Postcards, 2003

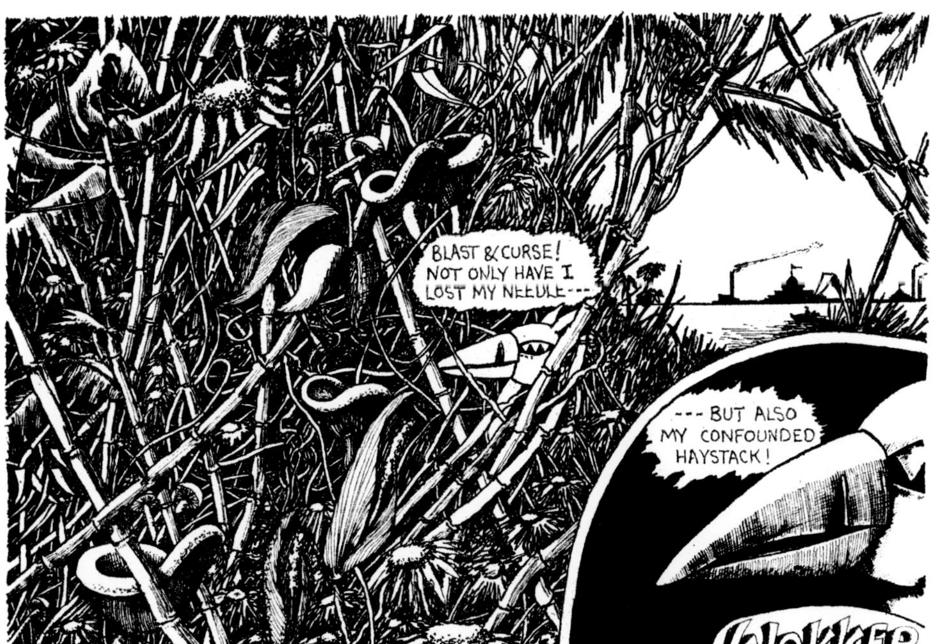

Times Educational Supplement, 1 September 1972

did not invite being cuddled. But he was not an unsympathetic character, and the stories always have a bleak if not black sense of humour. This was underscored by elements of social satire and outbursts against class exploitation (Wokker as "wokking class hero"). It was no accident that some strips had industrial backgrounds featuring cranes and smokestack factories, given Earnshaw's early working life. The artist's complicated feelings about his early life remained with him, and remembering his childhood he wrote: "Ever-present were the metallic clatter and dull booms from the works of steelmasters… and acrid smells from the plumes of coloured smoke…"[7]

Their satire was occasionally complemented by more spiritual content. Thacker's religious beliefs surfaced with the appearance of a recurring character known simply as the 'Evil Sperrit' [sic], and in one unpublished story, Wokker appears with a halo above his head[p.87]. For Thacker, the character's existential angst evidently had a focus that was not always in tune with Surrealism or anarchy—though this aspect of the strip was undeveloped. Earnshaw, for his part, was an atheist, but was tolerant, even interested, in his friend's views.

There was subtlety and innovation in 'Wokker'—both verbal and graphic—and a willingness to play with narrative and to examine the nature of the comic strip itself. Several examples draw attention to the nature of their construction: one ends with Wokker wondering how the story will conclude, while

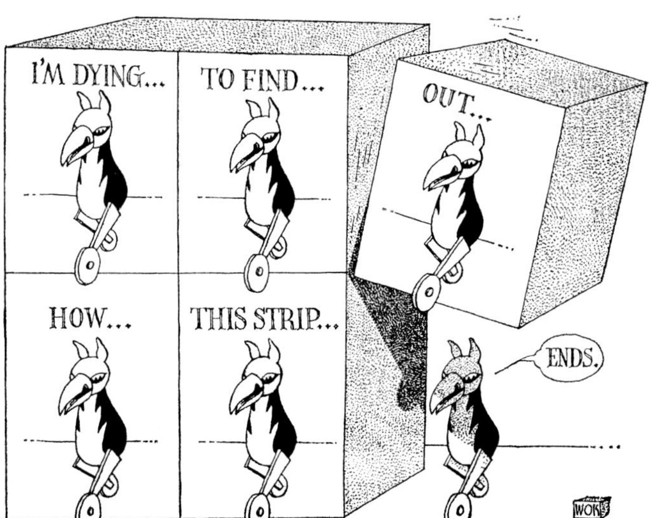

Eric Thacker, *Times Educational Supplement*, 24 March 1972

about to be crushed by a falling panel above him. Although they might appear to be plotless they are at the same time highly structured—there is not a wasted syllable or line. Possibly this was a reflection of the kind of jazz that both Thacker and Earnshaw loved.

It is clear that the two men instinctively understood what would become known as the 'language of comics', in spite of their lack of interest in the artform. There are parallels with a history of left-field cartoonists stretching back to the origins of the form. An early example being the inventive work of Gustave Verbeek's (1867–1937) 'The Upside-Downs of Little Lady Lovekins and Old Man Muffaroo'. Verbeek devised his strips in such a way that six panels became twelve by turning them upside down. He used the first "six panels to set up the 'plot' for his heroine, the ever-adventurous but essentially feminine Little Lady Lovekins and would have six more to enable her side-kick, Old Man Muffaroo to save the day."[8] Another strip that has some similarities to 'Wokker' is George Herriman's (1880–1944) 'Krazy Kat', in which the background scenes change from panel to panel. As for his construction, Wokker is made up like a simple wooden assembly kit devoid of facial expression, yet he exhibits emotional depth, and this too is something which echoes previous comics even if Wokker's unmoving features were in contrast to the Disney tradition of anthropomorphised inanimate objects.

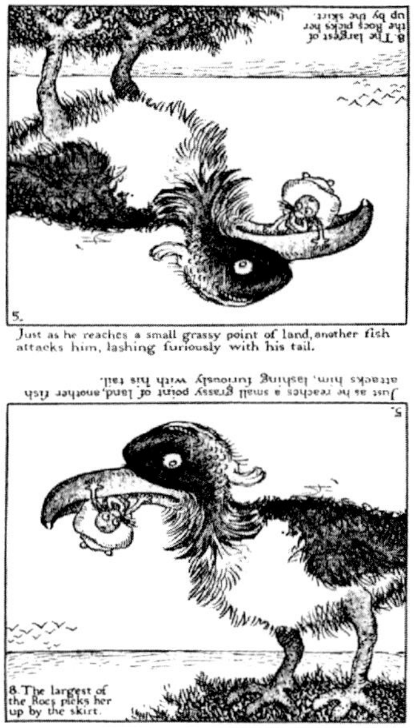

Gustave Verbeek, two views of a panel from 'A Fish Story', c.1904

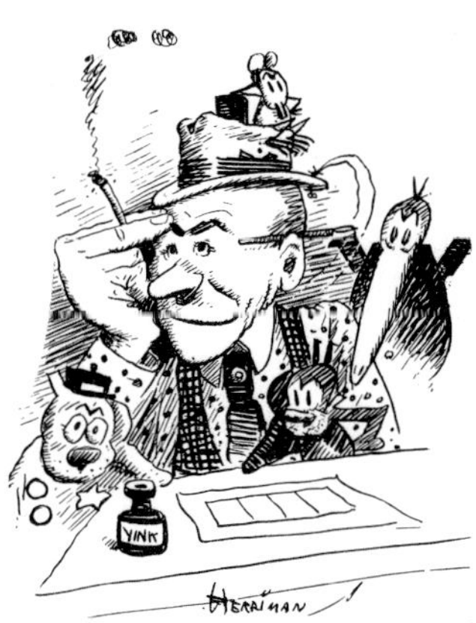

George Herriman, Self-caricature, n.d.

For all the imaginative skill involved in creating 'Wokker', the idea of locating him in a history of the comic strip is a pointless undertaking. Earnshaw and Thacker were artists of a different hue, and always occupied a place that was an alternative-to-the-alternative. Fine artists that have similarly dabbled in creating strips include Pablo Picasso, Lionel Feininger and Ad Reinhard: for an entertaining survey of "the unholy marriage of art and comics" see Craig Yoe's book *Arf Museum* (2006).

In 1970, twenty 'Wokker' strips were exhibited at the ICA in London. They were presented unframed and "thumb-tacked to a screen",[9] as part of a larger exhibition 'Comics' based on strips produced by fine artists, at the invitation of George Melly. Four years later Earnshaw produced a watercolour painting of Wokker, titled 'Nightwork: Wokker's Eyesight Fails While He is

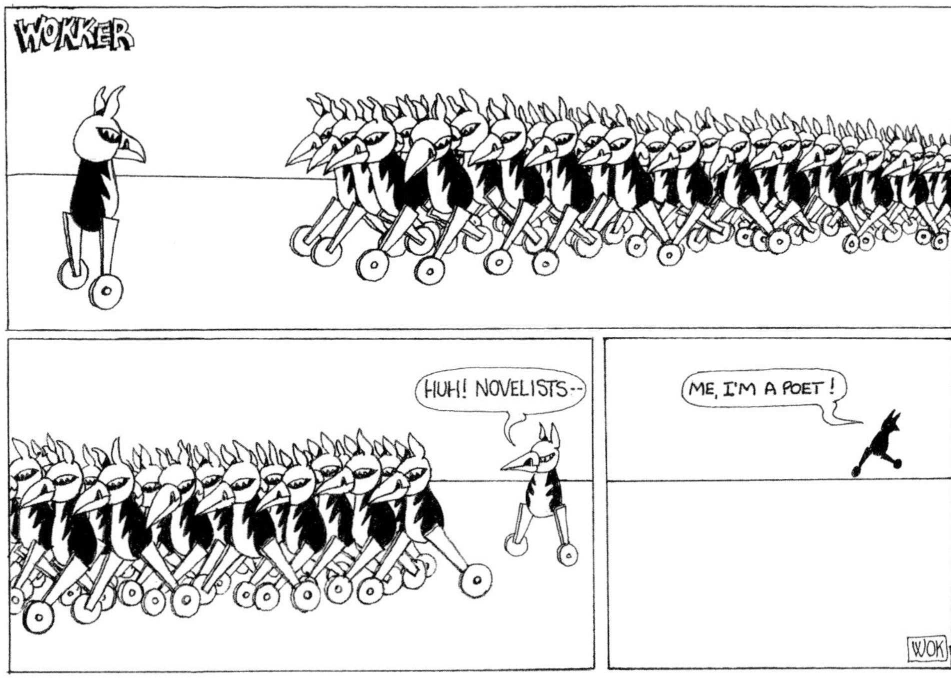

Previously unpublished drawing, n.d.

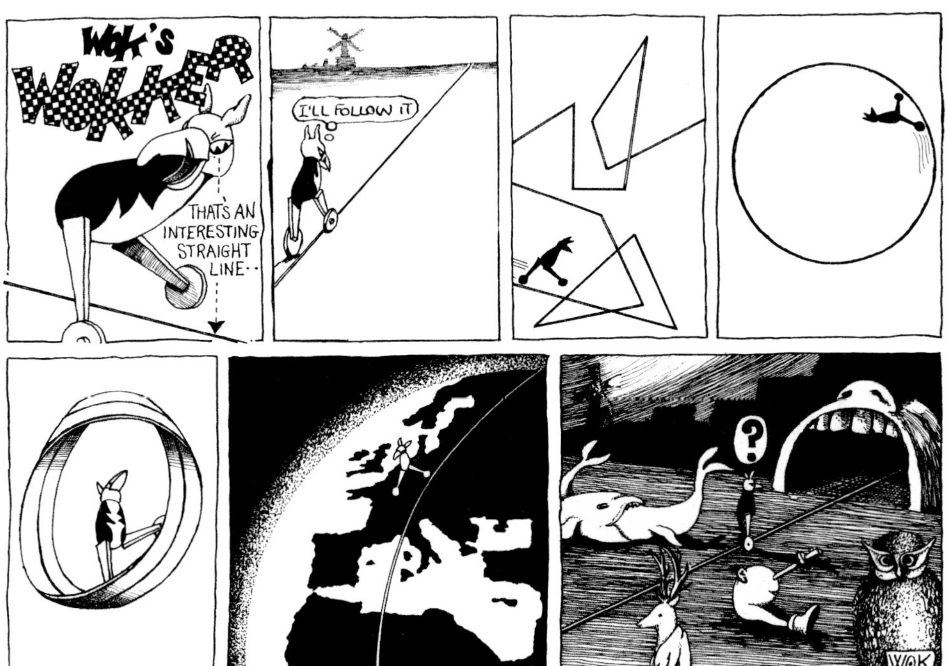

Previously unpublished drawing, n.d.

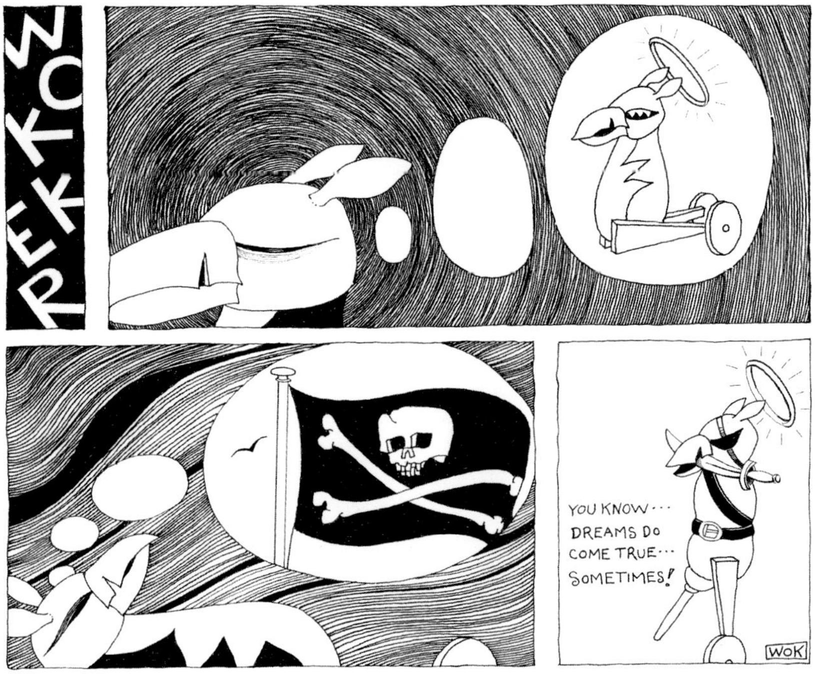

Previously unpublished drawing, n.d.

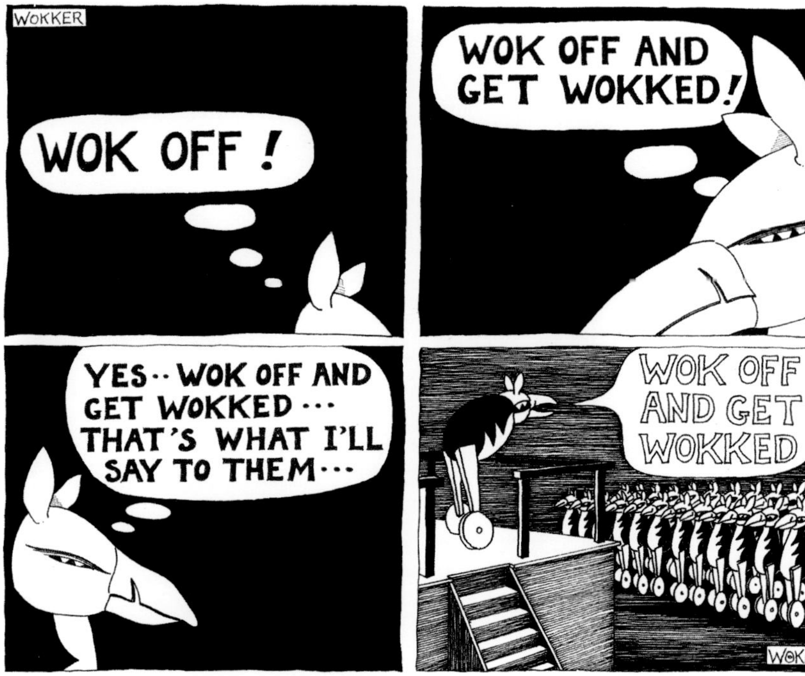

Previously unpublished drawing, n.d.

Guarding a Factory on a Tray' and in 1988, Dean Clough Gallery, Halifax put on a show of 'Wokker' original artwork.

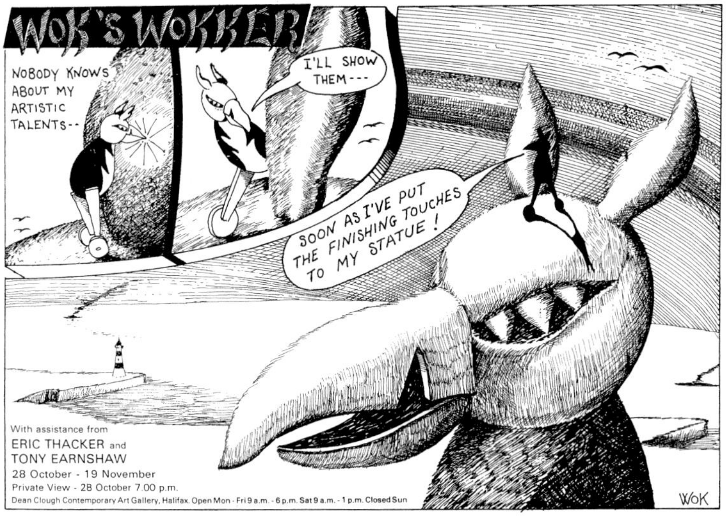

Private View card, Dean Clough Gallery, Halifax, 1988

Although it was true that Earnshaw and Thacker welcomed exposure, be it in a gallery or in print, there was always a sense that 'Wokker' was a private joke between themselves. Correspondence that has survived between the two men reveals that their relationship could sometimes be an intense and almost hermetically sealed world—as can often be the case when friends have known each other for so long (they met when they were teenagers). For example, in the letters, the references to 'Wokker' sometimes become so abstract that the language and sketches descends into nonsense (could this be a reflection of both men's love of jazz and the invented language of Slim Gaillard? Or perhaps a homage to the automatic writing encouraged by Breton?). There are Christmas cards, postcards and decorated envelopes, all with versions of 'Wokker', many largely incomprehensible. What is interesting about this more private material is how loose and spontaneous it is—in contrast to the carefully drawn published work. Evidently, it was here that the improvisation took place, and Wokker clearly kept his creators amused for decades: "The Wok-strip became a game we played to keep deadly boredom at bay."[10]

It is clear from the correspondence that 'Wokker' fed from and into other projects that the two men were dreaming up, in particular their pictorial 'irregular' novel *Musrum*. This, again, was an enterprise that took years to come to fruition, eventually being published in 1968. In the letters dated prior to the publication, the surreal aspects of the book sometimes fed from jokes and thoughts concerning 'Wokker', and sometimes it was the other way round: at one point, the title for the strip was 'Musrum's Wokker'. Other projects discussed by the two men in the correspondence similarly made their way into the strips, such as illustrated letter-forms: "Huh! What kind of a cartoon strip is this…", enquires an angry Wokker in one example, as he surveys a massive spelling-out of WOKKER, "…where the hero takes a back seat to his own name!"

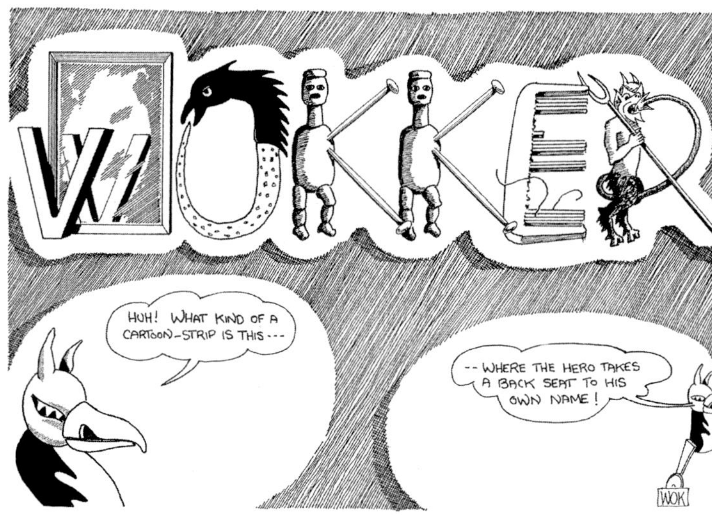

Previously unpublished drawing, n.d.

It appeared that a supportive editor at the *Times Educational Supplement* kept the strip alive—much in the same way that William Randolph Hearst had championed 'Krazy Kat'—though Wokker's vulnerability was highlighted when a reader wrote in to complain that it was "incomprehensible", and it was dropped soon after. Though the tenureship was short-lived, one year, 'Wokker' did acquire a small following, and was remembered fondly enough to be resuscitated in three publications thereafter: first in Jeff Nuttall's fanzine *Knuckleduster Funnies* (1985–86); in a national satirical magazine *The Truth* (1987–89); and finally in the Chelsea Arts Club magazine *The Whistler Journal* (1995–99). Artist Ian Breakwell, writing in *City Limits* in 1989, described 'Wokker' as "the most original cartoon creation since Mickey Mouse".[11]

It has been interesting to watch how the vagaries of cultural theory have changed in recent years, to the point where the strip might be labelled 'postmodernist'. Earnshaw and Thacker would probably have shuddered at the term, and no doubt considered it less useful as an analytical tool than 'Pataphysics. But if postmodernism is defined, following Lyotard and Jameson, as involving shifting identities, a sense of irony, a de-centred view of the world, unstable relationships, and confusions of time and space, then the *raison d'être* of 'Wokker' might well apply. But then so would much surrealist painting, not to mention comic strips like the aforementioned 'Krazy Kat' and 'Zippy'.

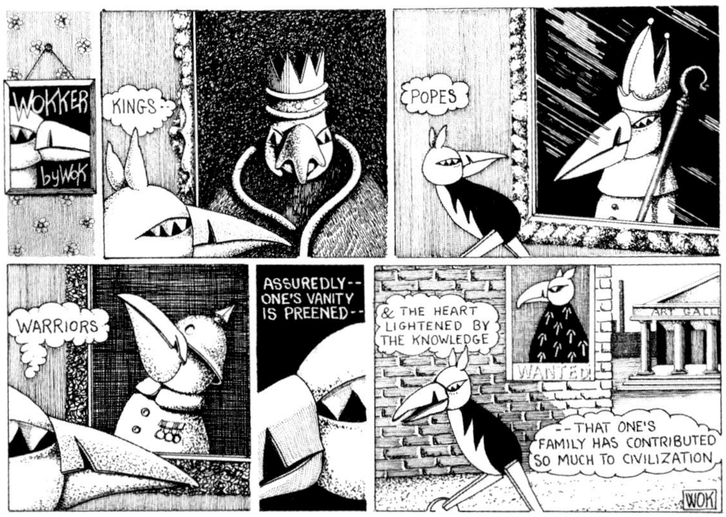

Previously unpublished drawing, n.d.

It has been said that vagueness is postmodernism's Achilles' heel, and its detractors complain that it is a label that can be applied too glibly—"mumbo jumbo", according to Francis Wheen.[12] While it is arguable that other ideas associated with postmodernism might possibly be construed in 'Wokker' stories, we should be wary of fitting any theory to the artwork.

Other ways of assessing 'Wokker' have recently become possible. For example, we might look back on him as being symbolic of the flowering of a hitherto-ignored cultural underground. The rise of 'subcultural studies' in the 1980s and 90s gave rise to books about the mod, punk and rave movements, while subsequent academic work has sought to identify precursors going back to the 19th century. It has become apparent that the 1940s saw a coming together of enthusiasts for

Surrealism, jazz and poetry in a loose-knit alternative culture. George McKay has drawn attention to the connections between this culture, anarchism and the push towards Aldermaston in his book *Circular Breathing* (2005). But as we have seen, there was no 'uniform' uniting these individuals, and no common subcultural politics.

'Wokker' remains nigh-on impossible to pigeon-hole. Which is just as his creators would have wanted.

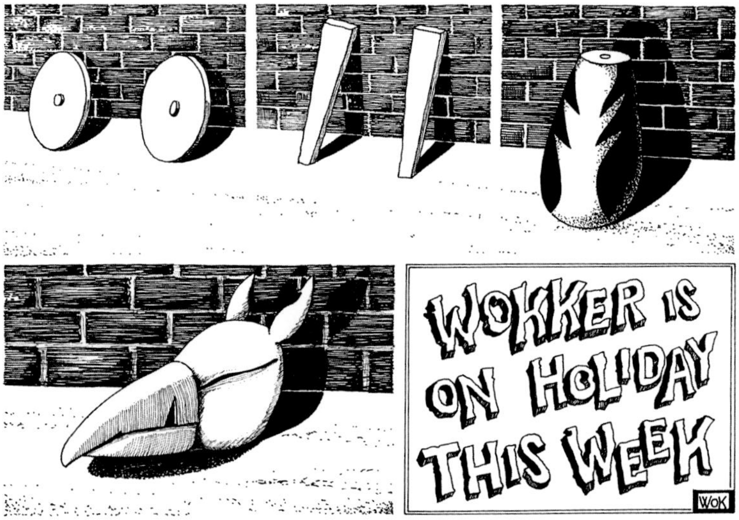

Times Educational Supplement, 11 August 1972

Notes

1. Ian Breakwell, 'Tomes from the Tomb', *City Limits*, 5–12 January 1989
2. Les Coleman in conversation with the author.
3. Anthony Earnshaw, 'A Short History of Wokker', *The Whistler* no.10, Spring 1996
4. *Ibid.*
5. Coleman, *op.cit.*
6. George Melly, 'Anthony Earnshaw', *A View from Back o' Town*, Leeds City Art Gallery, 1987
7. Anthony Earnshaw, 'Autobiographical Sketch', *Ibid.*
8. Frank Dickens, 'The Upside Down World of Gustave Verbeek', *Linus*, May 1970
9. Anthony Earnshaw, 'Tony Earnshaw Introduces Wokker to the Good People of Halifax', unpublished, 1988
10. *Ibid.*
11. Breakwell, *op.cit.*
12. Francis Wheen, *How Mumbo-Jumbo Conquered the World: A Short History of Modern Delusions,* Harper Perennial, 2004

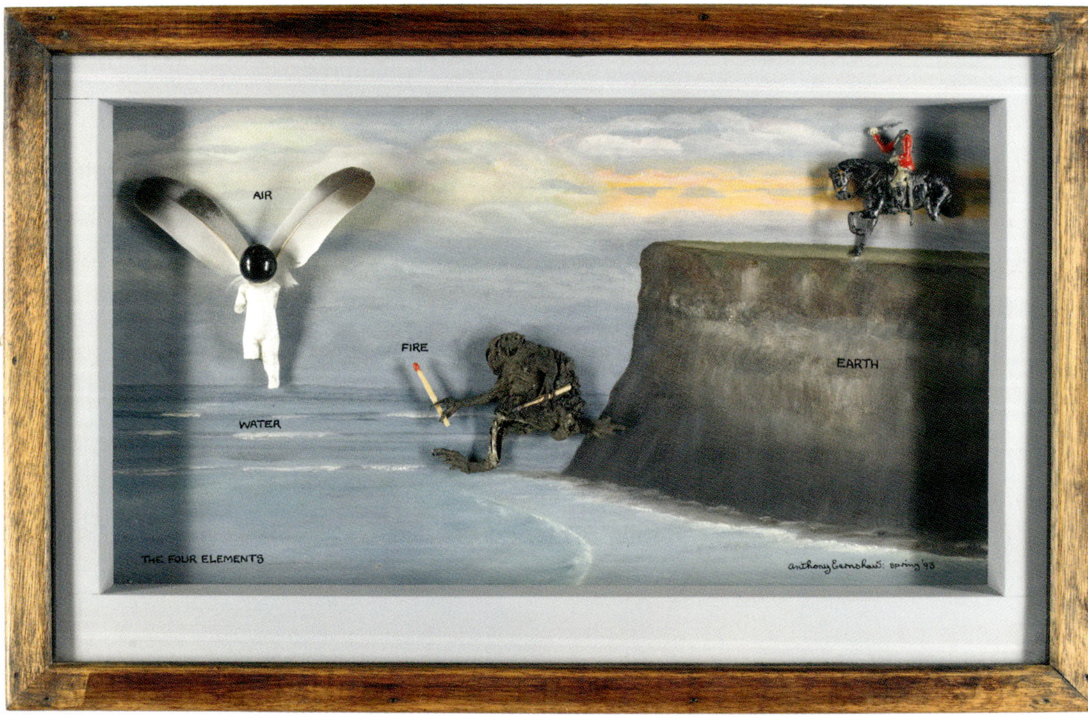

The Four Elements, 1993

The 'Spirit of the Air' came from the back garden, the china doll with one leg, both arms & its head missing came from the back garden of the house in London where my good friend Patrick Hughes was squatting(!) with his girlfriend of that time some twelve or so years ago. Gail & I were there for a long weekend; after lunch on the Sunday Patrick, all of a sudden announced "We're going to dig the garden…" In due time, I armed with a spade, exhumed the doll. To go on, the black head—*bête noire*—is an artificial cherry from one of those bunches of cherries one can buy from one's local haberdasher. The feathers, meanwhile, are gulls' feathers, picked up from the streets of Saltburn. The wonderful cavalry officer, alas his head has been shot off & his brave mount—legs blown off in battle (Mons?), was found in the grass in the garden of my old pal Liz Berry's house at Horsforth, Leeds. I picked up the petrified frog from the roadside while out on my bike in Eskdale; he has nice hands, don't you think? As for the 'background', a view of Hunt Cliff and the sea at Saltburn. Gail bought it for its frame from Shelley's junk shop, here in Emerald Street. I cut a slice off the bottom… which I enclose. You will note it was painted by one G. D. Harrison.

—*A.E.*

James Heartfield and Patrick Hughes

His Subjects Are Our Objects

Anthony Earnshaw puts things together in his boxes. Things—like footprints, Mickey Mice, toy animals, wrenches and everything else—have meanings. Meanings usually come from an object's function for human beings. Some things, like Sellotape for instance, do not have a lot of meaning invested in them. Others are more profound, like the footprint or shoe that stands for the person. Others, like the crucifix, have rather too much symbolism for Earnshaw (which is why lazy art students like to wedge them in dirt, or put them upside down). Things have a meaning which arises from their use. Earnshaw ponders the meaning of the one, and the other, then sets them against themselves. He teases the meaning out of everyday things, so that a spirit-level and a high-heeled shoe, for instance, could grapple with one another, making a small drama in a box. Putting two things together can bring out their own meanings, but also suggest a third, as when you add blue to yellow to get green.

There are two words we often use as if they were the same, object and thing. Their meaning is subtly different. The Latin word object, comes from *object*, thrown before, a thing thrown or put before the mind. It suggests something that has been thought about and put to human purpose, selected or re-moulded for use. It takes the imprint of one of mankind's many needs. The word 'thing' does not have quite the same meaning (strangely it comes from the Old English for 'assembly', but has come to mean an entity with its own existence). The thing in itself, the philosopher Kant says, always withholds some part of itself that is irreducible to human understanding.

But the thing as object stands in relation to a subject, a person, who, by putting the thing to use or contemplation makes it more than the thing it is, now a thing-for-us, an object. When we put things to use, make them into objects, we invest them with meaning. The offered flower stands for love and lust. The string of pearls stands for feminine elegance. The human meanings invested in these objects were grist to Earnshaw's mill, a hidden resource that lingered in his objects, a slumbering power waiting to be aroused.

In a time of mass production, the objects around us carry an intentional imprint, and are further away from their natural origins, like factory-made goods rather than harvested fruit or handicrafts. Earnshaw's things are often the detritus of industrial civilization. He felt an affection for the stuff tossed to one side by the consumer society.

Earnshaw elicits feelings of humour, affection, horror, triumph, melancholy, pity and revenge from these objects. He finds rich ideas, some ghostly, others razor-sharp. How do these sentiments and ideas get into the objects? The much-lauded thinkers of Earnshaw's youth, Karl Marx and Sigmund Freud, were interested in the way that people invested extra meaning into objects. They knew from the explorer Charles de Brosses' book *On the Cult of the Fetish Gods* (1760) of the primitive 'fetish' object, the totem pole or idol that, though made by men, was invested with godly power as if *it* had made them. So it was with modern goods or commodities, said Karl Marx. In the act of exchange, the comparison of my bag of corn with yours of nails, the relations between men assume the fantastic form of relations between things. Slaving away to fill the supermarket shelves, those industrial goods that were made by us have taken us over, said Marx, who called this the 'fetishism of commodities'. The psycho-analyst Sigmund Freud treated patients whose own emotional desires had become misplaced from the ordinary object of affection, the parent, nurse or uncle, on to some associated object, the fur coat, rubber apron or shoes—sexual fetishism. The cultural critic Walter Benjamin drew attention to the way that the surrealists created new meanings by juxtaposing different things, taking advantage of their fetishistic meanings.

Latterly some thinkers, like Bill Brown and Bruno Latour, have protested that in our rush to uncover the human meaning behind the object we have forgotten to dwell on the things themselves—and that is certainly a feeling Earnshaw would have understood. Earnshaw knew that many people had theorised the relations between things. He wrote about his own work using Walter Benjamin's ideas of juxtaposition. But Earnshaw's work was not theoretical, but practical and artistic. Wherever these meanings were coming from, he teased them out, drawing them from the most everyday things to arrest our attention.

In European art history, big pictures with people in, religious or classical allegories, are the most prestigious work. Painters who struggled to cope with many life-models took to the 'still life', painting things instead of people, and were pleased to find much meaning in them. The suggestion of the fleeting quality of life and the intimation of mortality could be seen in the bowl of fruit that would have rotted away by the time you saw the painting. Fine materials or flowers could stand for vanity. Another treatment of things in the early Renaissance was the 'cabinet of curiosities' that enquiring noblemen kept. These were collections of extraordinary things, like the narwhal's horn, a snake's skeleton, as well as man-made curiosities, lenses and distorting mirrors. The intent was both scientific and playful, so the cabinets could include *vexatious objects* like gloves with no opening, such that however much you struggled with them, you could not put them on. The surrealists, who inspired Earnshaw, admired the cabinet of curiosities, and Man Ray and Marcel Mariën put unlike things together to make curiosities of their own.

Earnshaw was happy to find a way of making his art come alive by using real things and getting people to look at them. The electricity was in the air instead of in the paint. The viewer completes the pictures by seeing meaning in the relations between things. Tony made brand-new relations between things. The boxes contain the space, isolating the objects from any other things in the room, to focus on the relations that Earnshaw has set up, whereas Méret Oppenheim's 'Object', Man Ray's assemblages or Nancy Fouts' objects stand alone and unbound. Sometimes Earnshaw uses printed 'scraps', from the Victorian hobby of découpage, the pasting of printed decorations into scrapbooks, which was the common man's pastime long before art students re-discovered it in the collage work of Cubists and Dadaists.

Ever the craftsman, Earnshaw was proud that he made his own boxes and mocked the artist Joseph Cornell (1903–1972) for using found boxes to put his found objects in. Tony considered Cornell's work an exercise in vague sentiments of melancholy rather than the stark dramatics of his surreal encounters. He was in art, as in life, a *bricoleur* who loved to make things out of things *ad hoc*.

Anthony Earnshaw's boxes are his apotheosis. Though he was at first nervous about the reaction of his 'comrades' to his boxes—he thought we might think them trivial or easy—this work came to represent his finest hour. A big part of the Earnshaw aesthetic is to be varied, not to be trapped into repetition, including as it does drawings, cartoons, novels, paintings, aphorisms, alphabets. But the boxes are the best. They are Earnshaw *par excellence*: playful, naughty, learned, sexy, utterly unexpected and different to anything else. Earnshavian wit in conversation has been lost to us since his death, but it lives on in the sparks he generates between disparate objects in his boxes. The subject of Earnshaw is our tricky subject, and it has been hard to be objective about his skittery creations. His curious cabinets are at the same time, and in the best way, both subjective and objective.

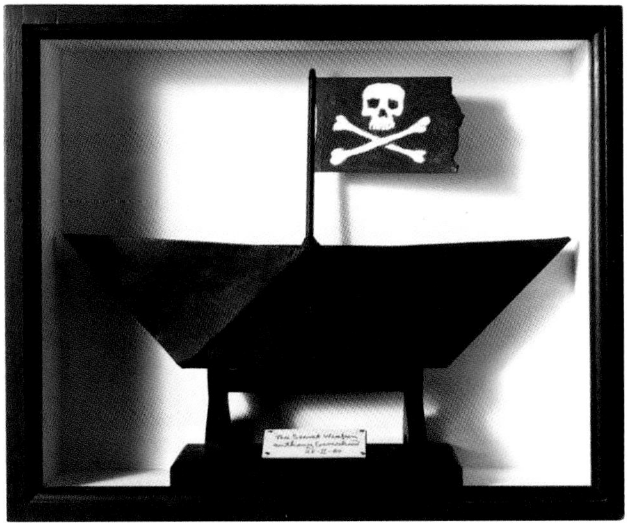

The Secret Weapon, 1980

The Secret Weapon is a boat made of tar paper, used for roofing. This paper boat carries the Jolly Roger of the outlaw—Earnshaw's flag—not the Union Jack. A child's paper boat is usually white, Earnshaw's is black, the colour of anarchism. Historian Peter Linebaugh said that the pirates were the first revolutionary proletariat. It brings to mind the Brecht/Weill song Pirate Jenny, who dreams of rebellion against her masters: "And a ship, a black freighter / With a skull on its masthead / Will be coming in". Looking at his own suburban house, Tony once said, to Ian Breakwell's horror, "it would be nice to tar that roof".

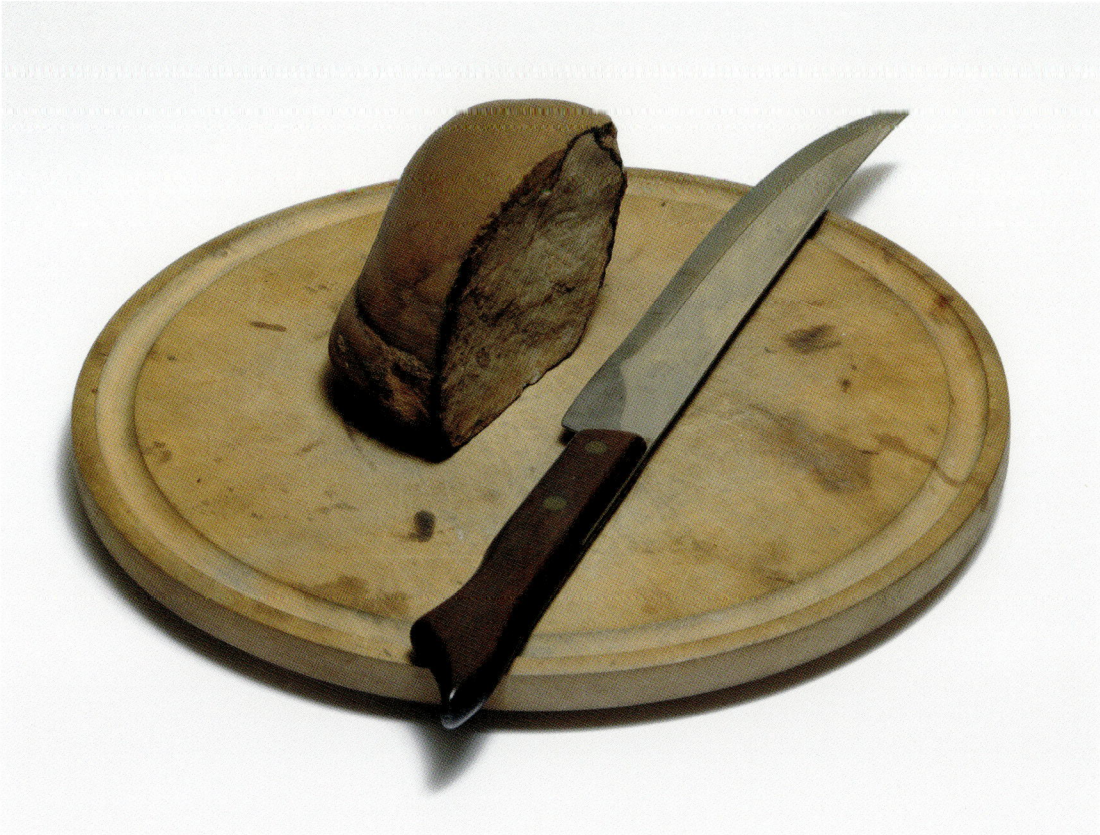

Raider's Bread, 1979

In a letter to Paul Hammond Tony wrote: "When at Lyle's place the other week we went for a walk across a stretch of heathland. I made a wonderful find: a stone, or rather half a stone, it looks so exactly like a brown bread cob, cut in half, the right shape, the right colour, the right markings, even the cut side looks right… a bit 'toasted'. I've put it on a bread board with a bread knife alongside… it fools everyone, everyone who's seen it is taken in—HA HA!" The quality of unyielding, geological stone is so different to sustaining, oven-made bread, that it is an oxymoron, where the quality of the stone contradicts absolutely the nature of the bread. When he puts it on the bread board with its knife he makes the chance similarity into a deliberate provocation.

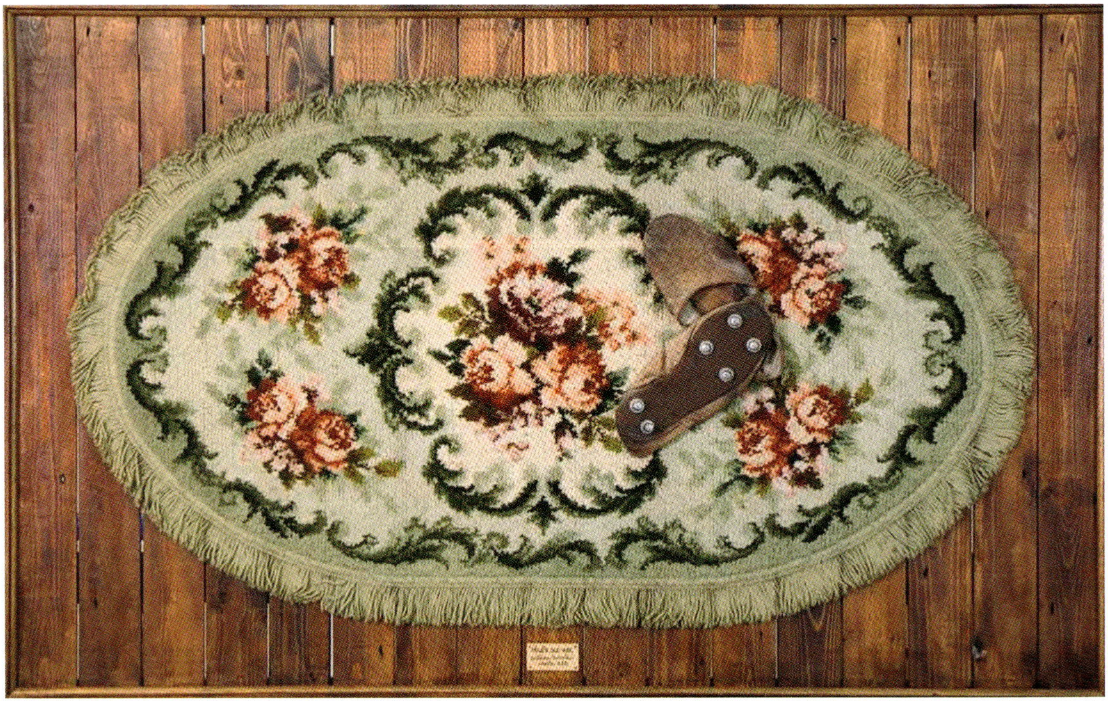

Pelé's Old Age, 1979

Pelé—Edison Arantes do Nascimento—was a footballing star of the 1970s who rose from the backstreets of Brazil. Earnshaw imagines Pelé's retirement, with football studs on his slippers, the lively youth echoed in the pacific old age—a companion piece to 'The Hungry Infant' [p.107]. Pelé, though, lived on to enjoy an active retirement.

God Creating Eve, 1997

Michelangelo's painting on the ceiling of the Sistine Chapel has God giving life to Adam in the touch of his outstretched hand. Here God debases himself in adoration before the dominatrix Eve. She, naked and so innocent in the Bible story, is dressed here sinfully with a high heel, conflating the creation with the Fall. There is an echo of Jesus washing Mary Magdalene's feet. The parts are spares from showroom dummies, approximations of the human form to hang clothes on. Earnshaw makes them stand for this emblematic relation of God to Woman.

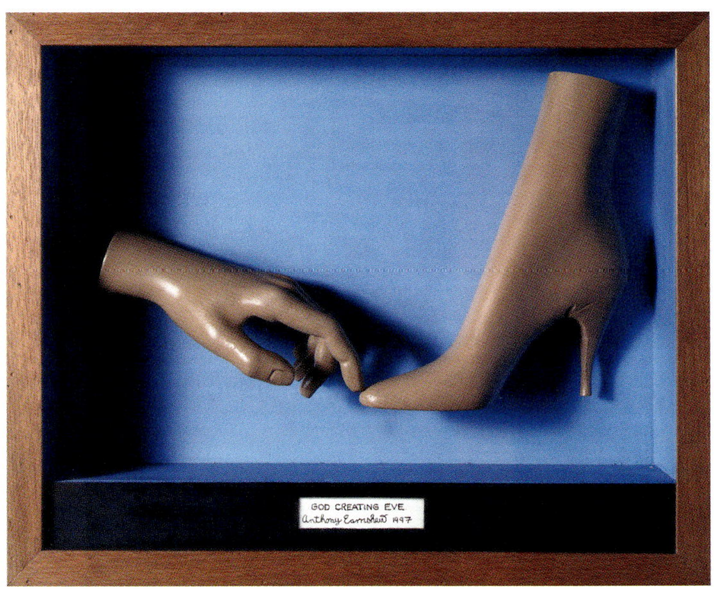

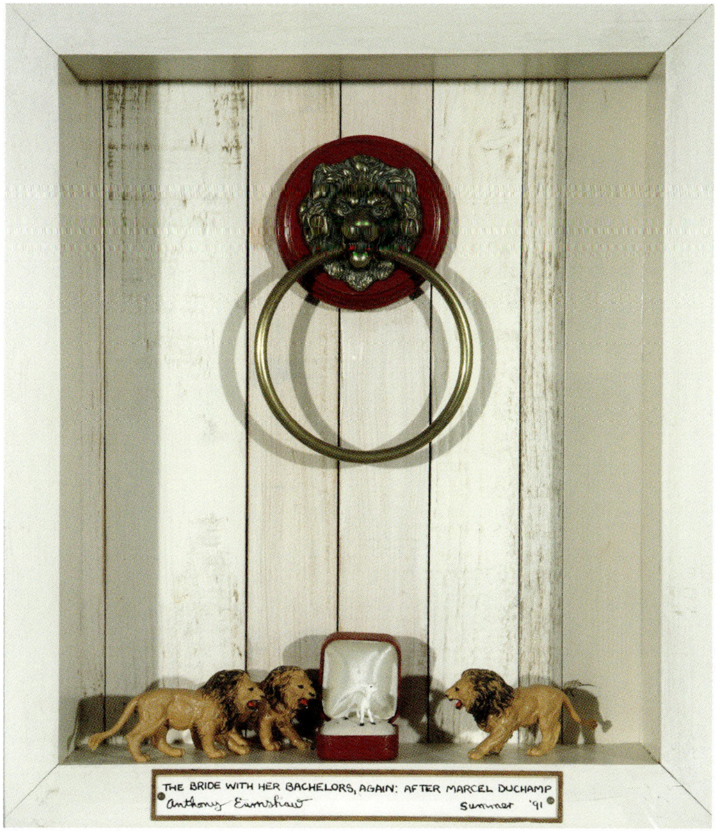

The Bride With Her Bachelors, Again: after Marcel Duchamp, 1991

In Marcel Duchamp's 1923 painting on glass 'The Bride Stripped Bare By Her Bachelors, Even' the positioning of the nine bachelors was decided by chance, Duchamp firing matchsticks at the glass from a toy gun. Here the bride is a sacrificial lamb, offered up in the presentation box for an engagement ring, encircled by lions—a Bluebeard image—although these lions are plastic toys. Above them, the folk motif that so charmed Earnshaw, the knocker placed in the mouth of a ravenous beast. This circular knocker echoes the missing engagement ring, and says 'enter here'—but this door will not open and the glazing stops you knocking.

Weary and Bewildered: The Spirit of the Century Meets the Angel of Death, 1996

Earnshaw makes a chimera—a grotesque monster formed of the parts of various animals. Or perhaps it is Dr Doolittle's Pushmi-Pullyu which had a head at either end: a symbol for not knowing where you are going. It is held up by a cowboy, who is also painted grey with two feathers for wings. The weary spirit at the end of the 20th century was dominated by a struggle between Communists and Capitalists, both deluded according to Earnshaw's anarchistic ideal of freedom. The Angel of Death is perhaps threatening and liberating.

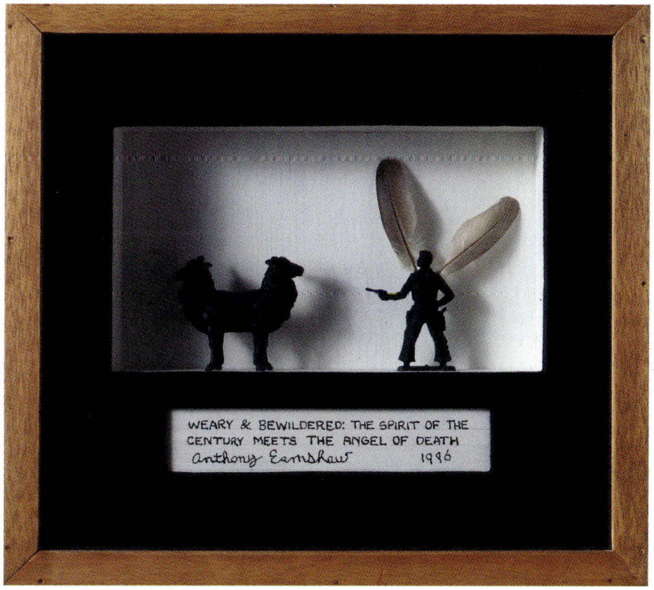

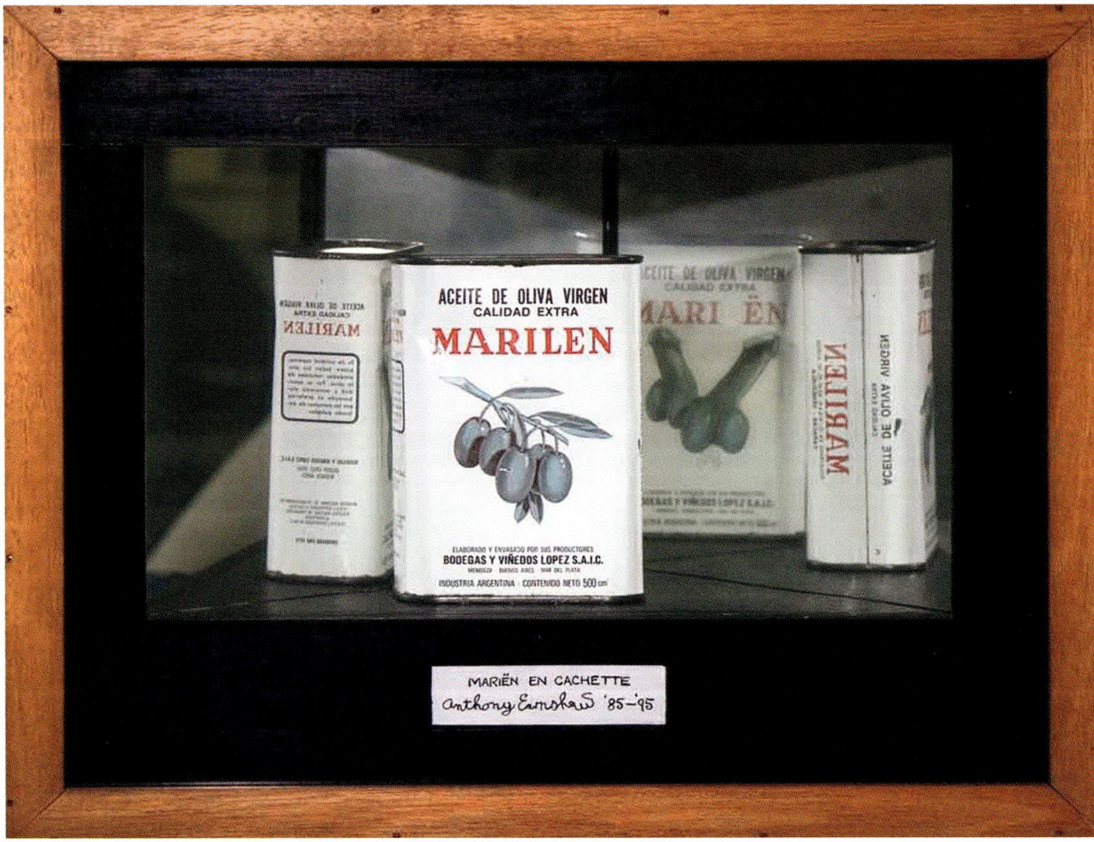

Mariën en Cachette, 1985–95

Anthony Earnshaw, Patrick Hughes and Les Coleman met up with their surrealist hero Marcel Mariën in Brussels, and this is Tony's tribute. The olives printed on this oil tin reminded him of dangling bollocks—on the reverse side he has painted a pair of stiff, green cocks. Having altered one side of the 'Marilen' olive oil tin to read *Mariën*, Earnshaw gave the empty tin to the surrealist. It is an affectionate tribute: himself and Mariën as two cocks together. The Belgians like to torture natural products like the cocoa bean, trees or olives into highly cultured goods, like chocolate, pollarded trees and olive oil. They have no olive trees in Yorkshire. The fruit of the olive tree is the regenerative capacity of the bush, like the man's seed. After Mariën's death, his heir, Sarah Whitfield, gave the tin to Patrick Hughes, who asked Earnshaw to build a box that would show the front and the back, with mirrors, which he did, and gave it back, boxed up.

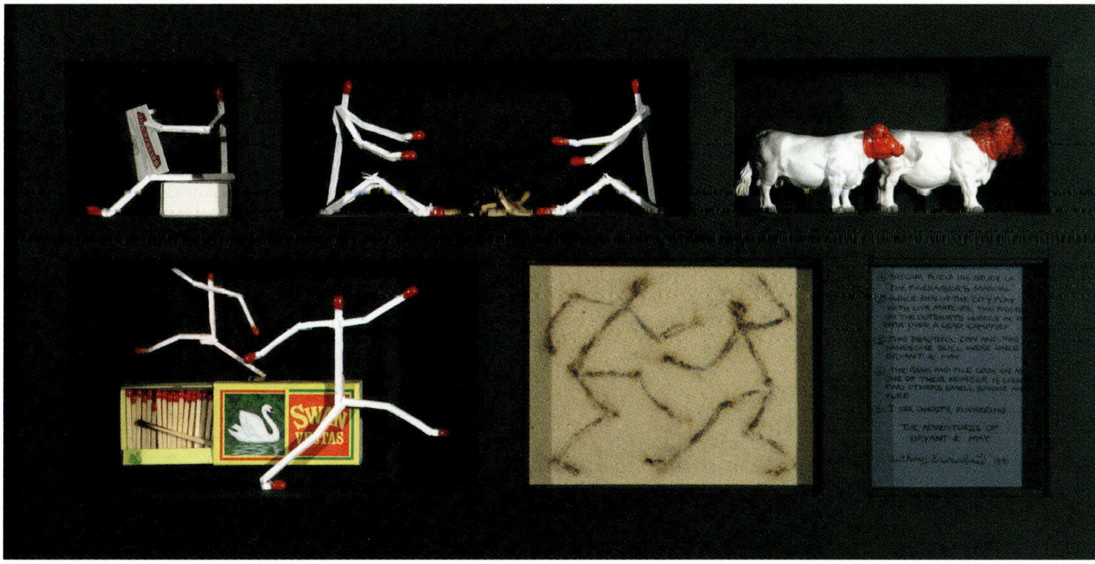

The Adventures of Bryant and May, 1990

Earnshaw was a smoker and valued the inspiration—the rush of ideas—that came with a sharp inhalation of nicotine. Smokers often play games with matches. The figures in L.S. Lowry's paintings of northern working class-life are often derided as 'matchstick men' and here Earnshaw's matches take on a life of their own. They 'study the fire raisers manual', the legend tells us, or huddle over a campfire, and two smelling fire flee "while the rank and file look on as one of their number is spent". They leave burnt traces. The Quakers Francis May and William Bryant set up a model match factory in Bow. But to keep their profits high Bryant and May used white phosphorus, which rotted the jawbones of the matchgirls: who struck for better conditions in 1888.

Delilah's Tools, 1979

Earnshaw painted the heavy drill bit noticing that its spirals echoed the patterns of a barber's pole—itself a schematic representation of flesh and blood from the days when barbers were also surgeons. Delilah emasculated Samson when she cut his hair. Here the drill bit's colours threaten violence. It is Delilah's malevolent phallus: "Screw You!" she says. Circular and linear motion meet in the spiral, the action is solidified in a drill bit.

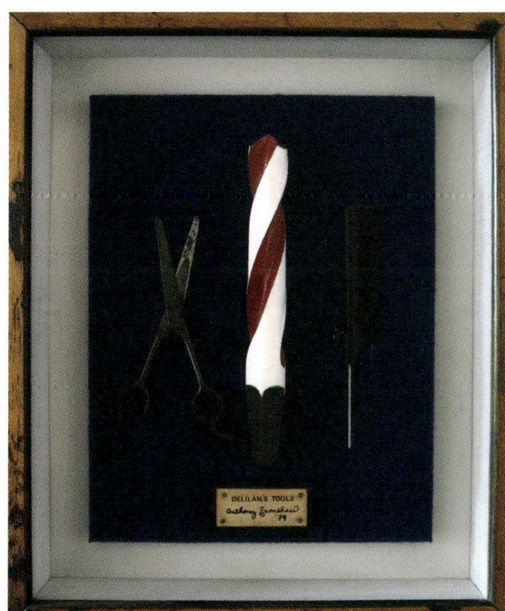

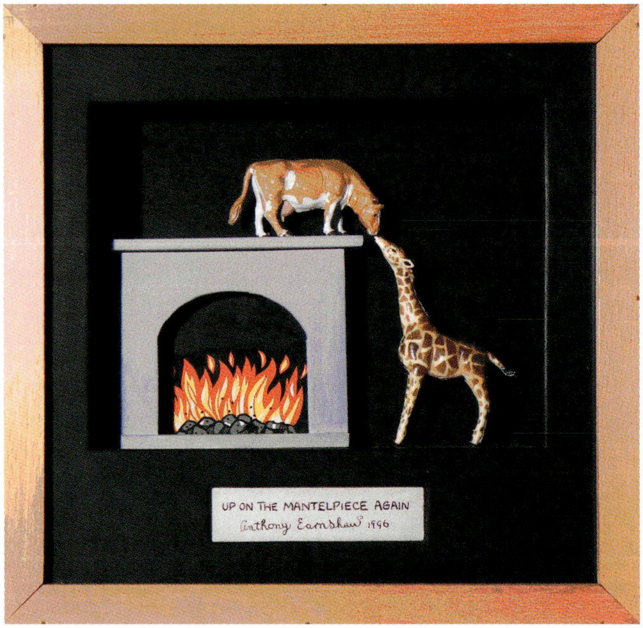

Up On the Mantelpiece Again, 1996

This piece was Earnshaw's contribution to a collective show at Angela Flowers Gallery on the theme of 'Sex'. The beauty of the work is in its simplicity. The improbable meeting of the cow and the giraffe can only take place by putting them on two different levels, so that as she leans down to graze, and he reaches up, their lips kiss. On the mantelpiece is a novel venue for sexual intercourse, as on the kitchen table, or dangling from the chandelier.

In the Canteen at the Headquarters of Doubt (Second version), 1983

The Headquarters of Doubt, a place that Tony liked to imagine, where people did not know what was coming next, the opposite of, say, the Headquarters of ICI. In this assemblage the table is set for someone in a hurry, half of it for breakfast, the other for shaving—the knife being replaced by a cut-throat razor. The first version, which was stolen from an exhibition, included a flick-knife instead of a knife. A third version, with the same title, had a fork headed with barbed wire.

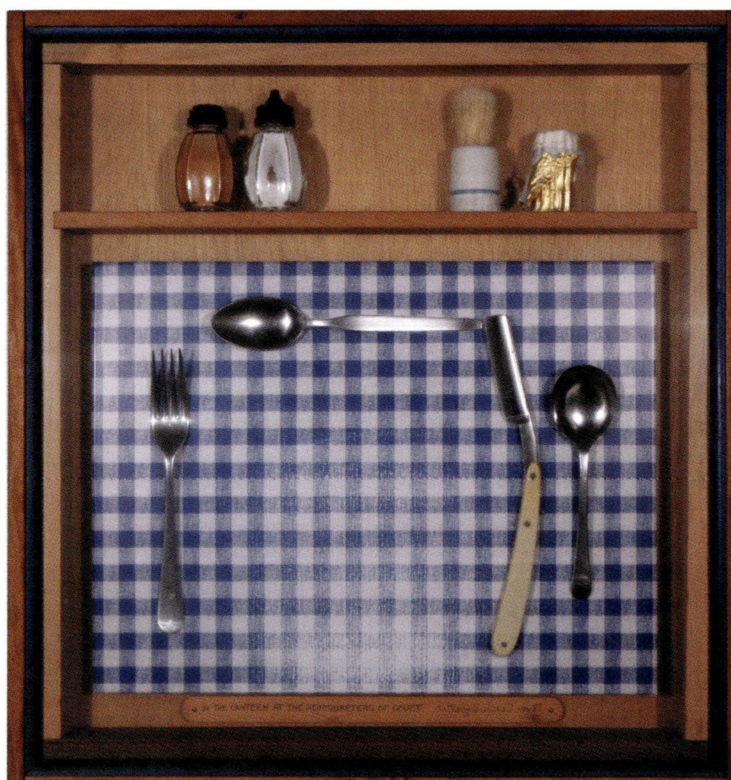

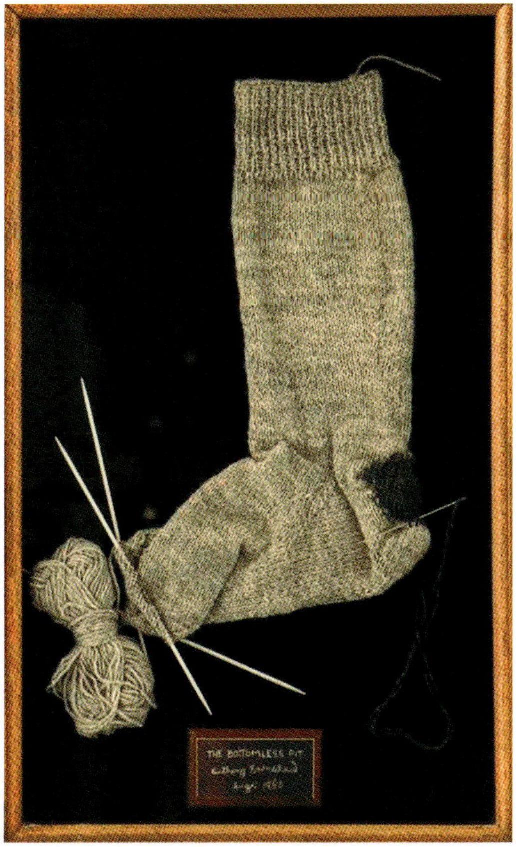

The Bottomless Pit, 1980

This sock is already being darned, though its knitting is not finished yet. The work of mending and knitting clothes speaks of the grind of women's lives in the 1930s, when Earnshaw was growing up. It also stands for rebirth and decay. There is a circular action here, like the painting of the Forth Bridge, it wears out before you have finished it—which can apply to a work of art, if the imaginative leap becomes ordinary before the work is completed.

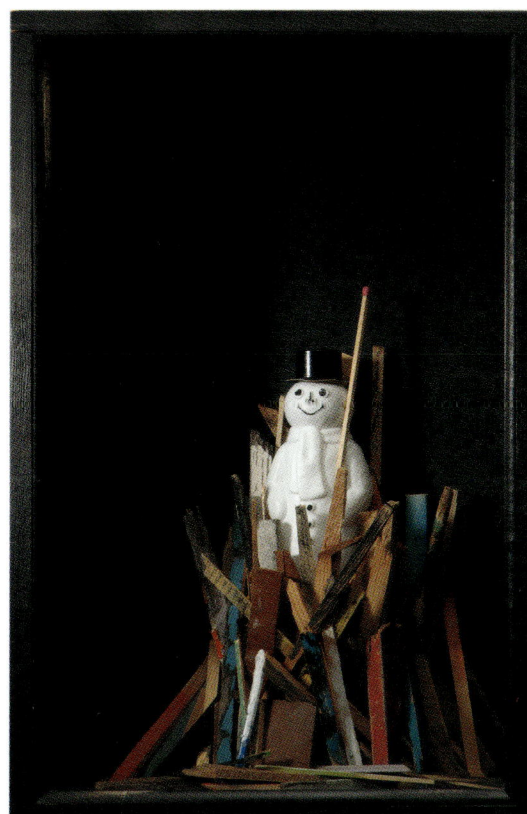

The April Fool, 1978

A Snowman, not a Guy, on a bonfire. This Snowman was originally a plastic container for bath-foam; small bits of waste wood standing in for their larger cousins on the bonfire. November the 5th is celebrated as the day Guy Fawkes went to Parliament to blow it up: the anarchists' slogan was "Vote for Guy Fawkes, the only man to enter parliament with the intention of fulfilling his promise". The event is a contradiction of hot and cold—Earnshaw's drawing of it carried a subtitle: "May his juice put out the flames". H_2O can assume three forms: steam, water, and ice or snow. Earnshaw's assemblage suggests how things change. It is a version of the question what happens when an unstoppable force meets an immovable object—the answer here would not be an inconceivable catastrophe, but a damp squib. The title is another joke—since neither Guy nor Snowman are the April Fool, another personification with its own season.

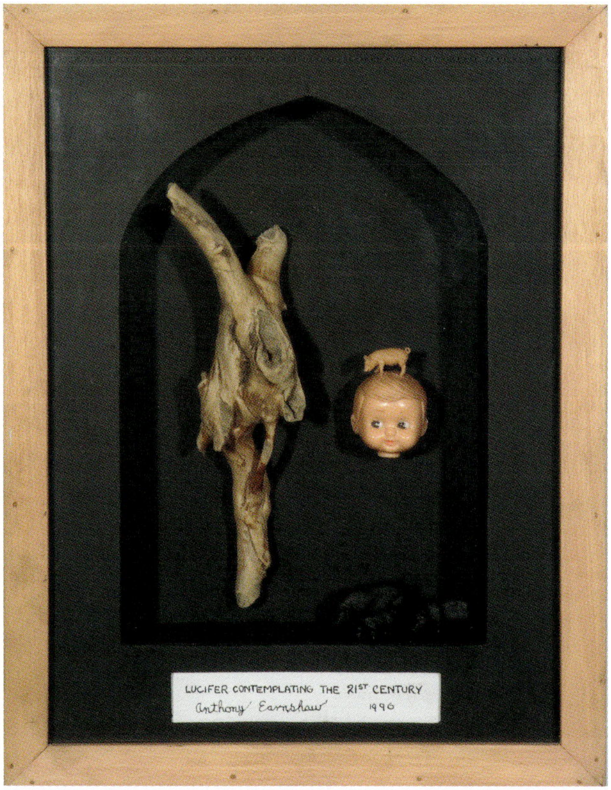

Lucifer Contemplating the 21st Century, 1996

Earnshaw rarely made use of found objects in nature, usually being taken with the odd bits left over from the world of industry. He did find a stone that became 'Raider's Bread', and here he has found a bit of tree root that looks like a Dennis Wheatley-style horned Lucifer and put it in a niche that could have been made for a Madonna. Perhaps the dark pigs are the old century shuffling off, and the innocent-looking child is the new century. Still, the child's cuteness is undermined by a cheeky sideward glance at Lucifer, while the pig on his head says we are all carcasses (pig carcasses often featured in Tony's drawings, perhaps to show the way people were delivered up for slaughter under capitalism).

The Rules Discarded, 1986

Here the play is between pleasure and measure, the mechanical and the natural, work and play. The cocktail is elegant, and, in its own way, so is the micrometer. It really does not matter whether your cocktail cherry is a micron wider or not, it is there to make your cocktail sweeter. But cherries do all vary minutely in size, why not measure them, as a man in his cups might think. Earnshaw is putting unlike things together, finding things that exemplify unlike qualities, as he does in the 'Game With No Rules', where a spanner grips a flower.

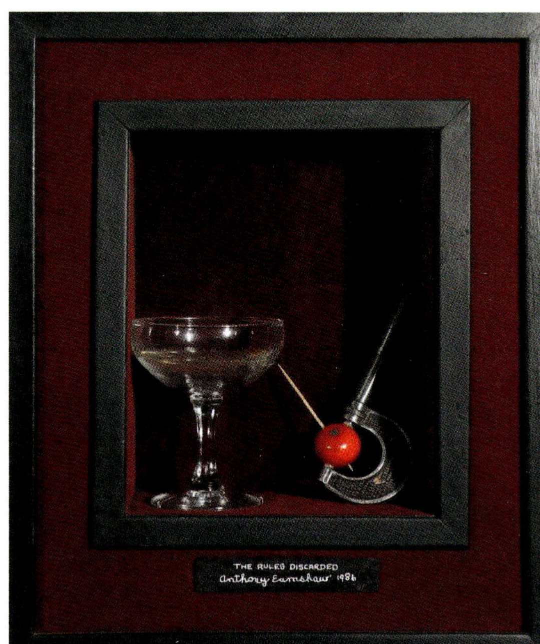

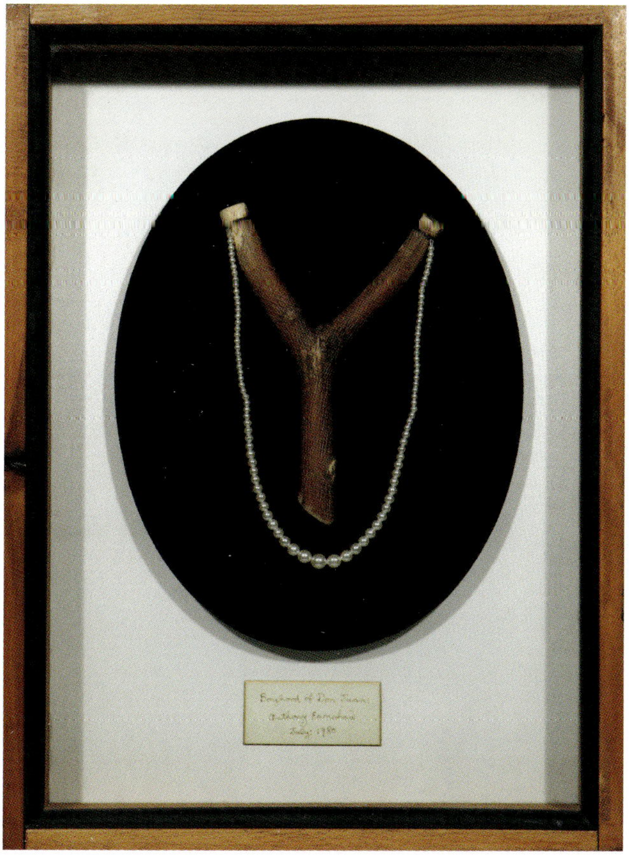

Boyhood of Don Juan, 1980

Boys used to make catapults, when they found the right piece of branching wood, with elastic and a pouch to fire pebbles sometimes at defenceless girls. Earnshaw takes this primitive weapon into the sexual arena. He swaps a pearl necklace for the elastic and puts it on the branching antlers of a stag. Betrayed husbands were said to be wearing the horns of a cuckold, because they could not see what everyone else could. Poetically the female pearls and the male horns are combined in Earnshaw's weapon to suggest the excitement and damage that the catapult of love can cause. It is rather like Cupid's Bow.

Mickey Has Chopped Off Dumbo's Left Ear, 1999

This work re-uses somebody's home-made Mickey Mouse, arming him with a blood-stained axe. In the Disney film 'Dumbo' finds friendship, against the odds, with a mouse, who encourages him to fly with the psychological prop of a magic feather. Earnshaw has turned this schmaltz into open warfare, with a sadistic Mickey justifying the elephant's traditional fear of the mouse.

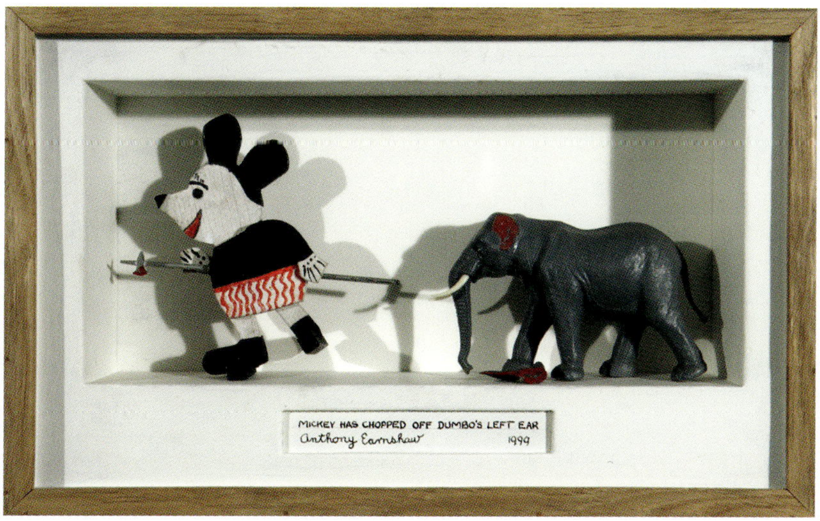

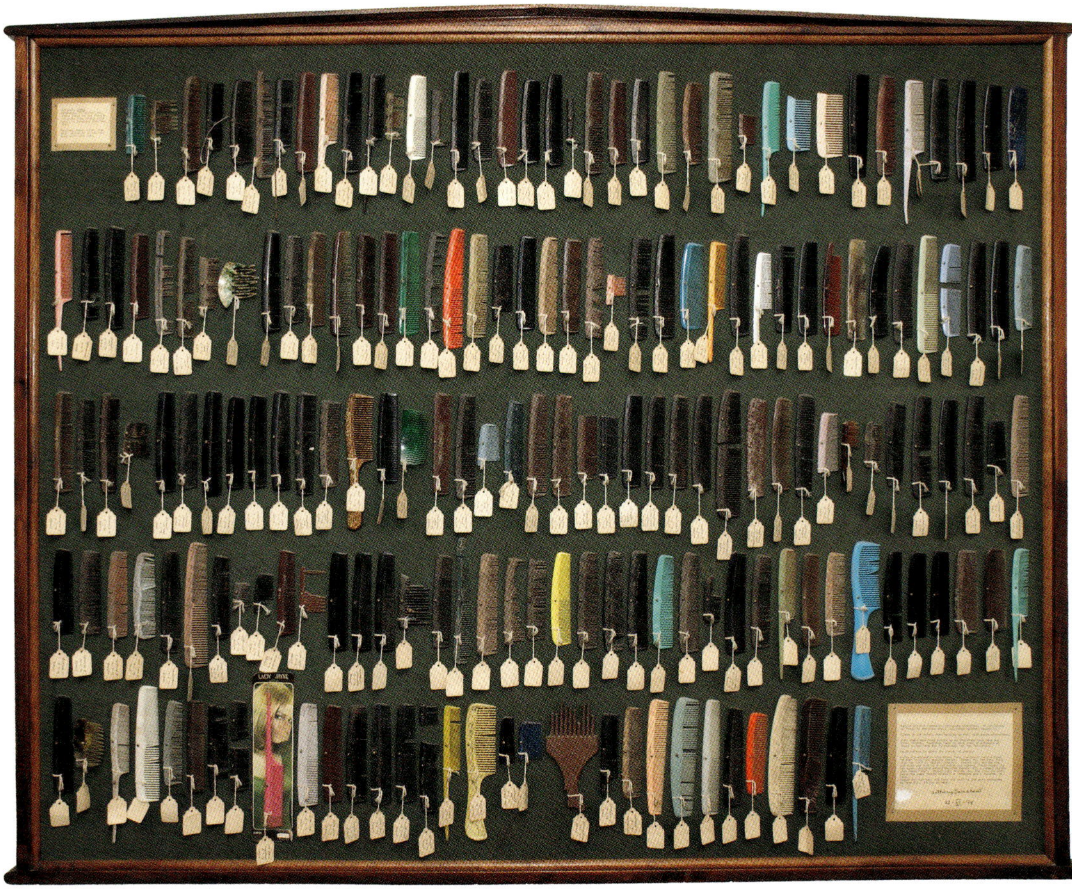

Lost Property, 1979

The collection of combs was brought together as a joke, to make fun of Conceptualism. "I set myself a task for one calendar month to pick up discarded combs from the streets of Leeds no matter where I was. My intention was to date and record where I found them, as one does in an investigation." Most of them were found on his way to work at Leeds Polytechnic, a route many students took: "students are egocentric people and spend a lot of time combing their hair. Combs are everywhere, along with the odd sock, shoe and glove. The lost object interests me. I feel sorry for them. They have been discarded, abandoned and they are alone in the world." The joke was on Earnshaw; he was a much better conceptual artist than those he was guying.

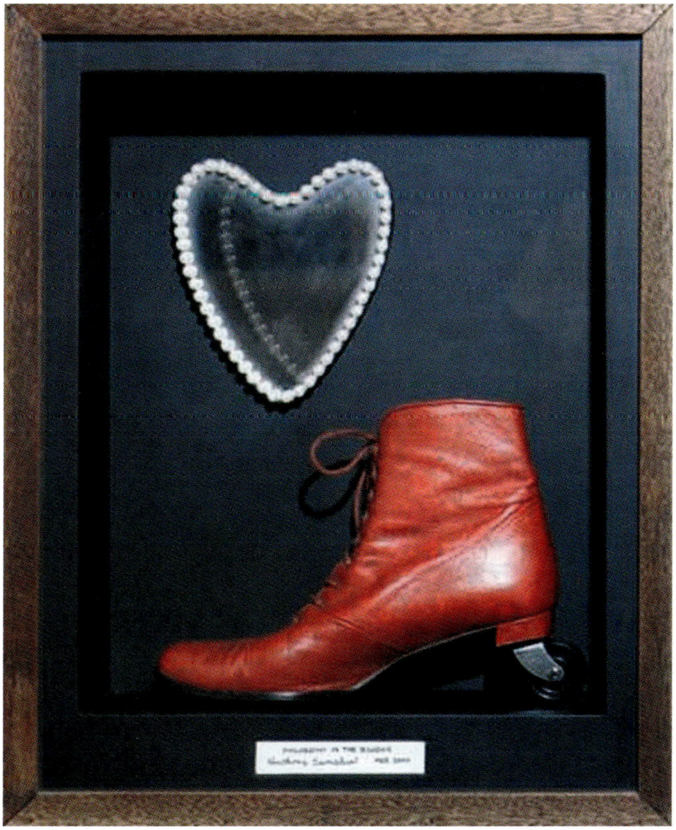

Philosophy in the Boudoir, 2000

This funny work is named after the book by De Sade, or perhaps a painting by Magritte which takes the same title (where a hanging dress retains the image of the breasts that have been in it). This was made for Diane Atkinson, and it is on her own boot that Tony has fixed a wheel where the heel should be—what ought to offer stability is suddenly all too mobile. Tony would have made the mirror by nibbling the glass away with a glass cutter; adding the necklace in a heart shape, as found in a jeweller's shop. The mirror is a short-cut to portraiture.

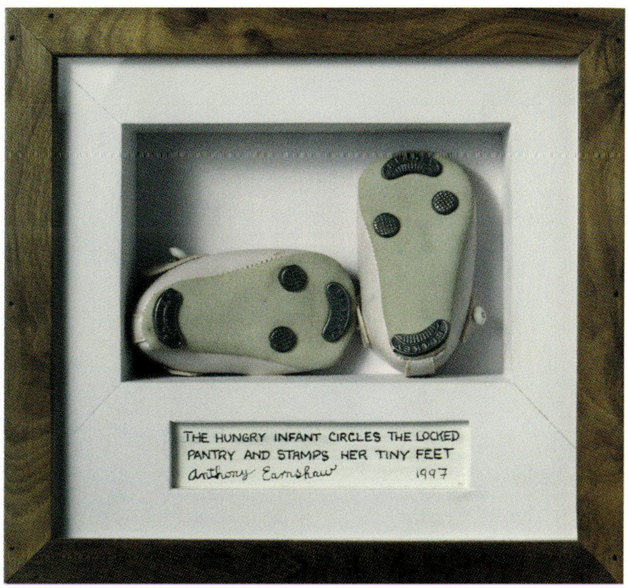

The Hungry Infant Circles the Locked Pantry and Stamps Her Tiny Feet, 1997

These baby shoes have blakeys, or segs, fixed on them, a poor man's reinforcement to get more life out of shoes, which gives this pair a thuggish feel. A child's first shoes do not wear out, because they are usually outgrown before the mite starts walking. There is a contrast between the working world and the innocence of childhood. This child seems overgrown, or maybe old before her time.

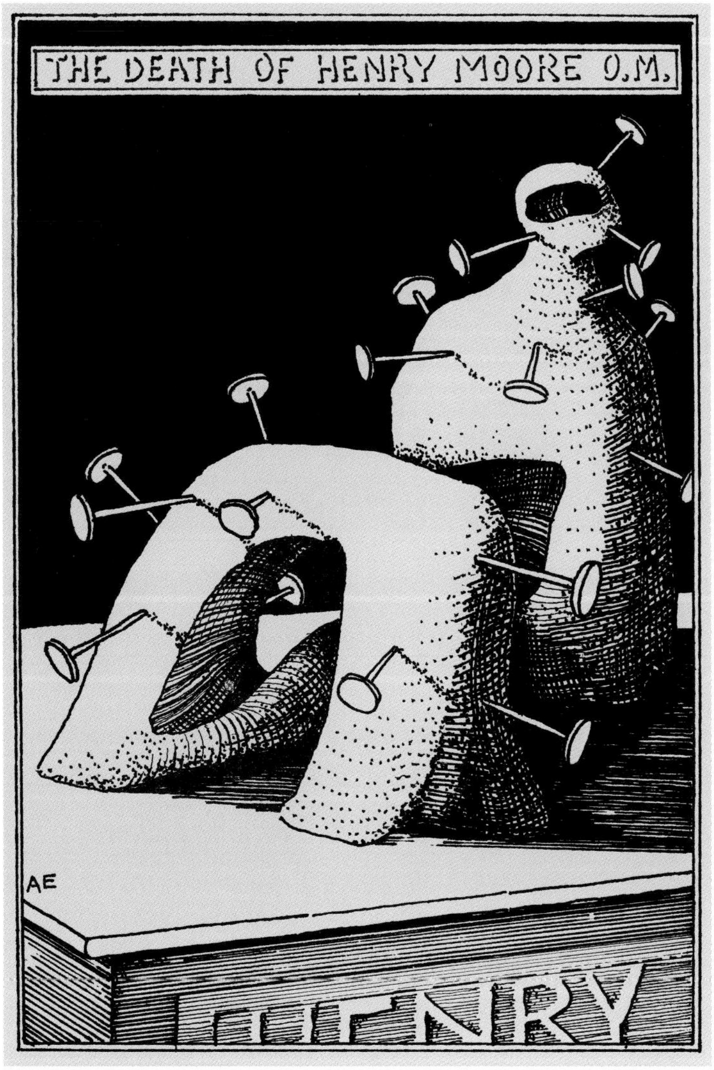

The Death of Henry Moore O.M., 1970

Les Coleman

Poison Pen Drawings

"We laugh, but not at the same time as you."—Marcel Mariën

To appropriate or refer to works by other artists, in either complementary or derogatory fashion, was something Anthony Earnshaw did on occasion. This was partly to debunk a sacrosanct view of art but more importantly to declare where his allegiances lay. Among his various homages to surrealist artists and poets is an amusing crayon drawing based on Man Ray's painting 'Observatory Time—The Lovers', 1932–1934. Ray's image depicts a pair of bright red lips, exaggerated in scale, floating in the sky above a landscape. Although painted, the lips appear as if collaged to give an increased sense of disjuncture. An admirer of Man Ray, Earnshaw's reworked version integrates the lips with a naked female figure while retaining their exaggeration. Dated 1998, Earnshaw's drawing is titled 'Observatory Time For A Second Time (after Man Ray)'.

An earlier work 'The Death of Henry Moore O.M.' by Earnshaw that appeared in the pamphlet *Blue Food* no.2, 1970, presents us with the approximation of a Henry Moore reclining nude sculpture with nails hammered into it, as if it were a voodoo doll. That he should include O.M. in the title is not without significance. Earnshaw concurred with Erik Satie's view about state awards. Satie said, "The disgrace is not accepting the Legion of Honour but to be deemed worthy to receive it in the first place." The drawing, openly speaks of Earnshaw's mistrust of art that places its belief primarily in issues of aesthetics.

In more recent times, roughly speaking the last one hundred and twenty years, esoteric jokes about art have become part of the art world's consciousness. When Marcel Duchamp made his Dadaist gesture to draw a moustache and goatee beard on

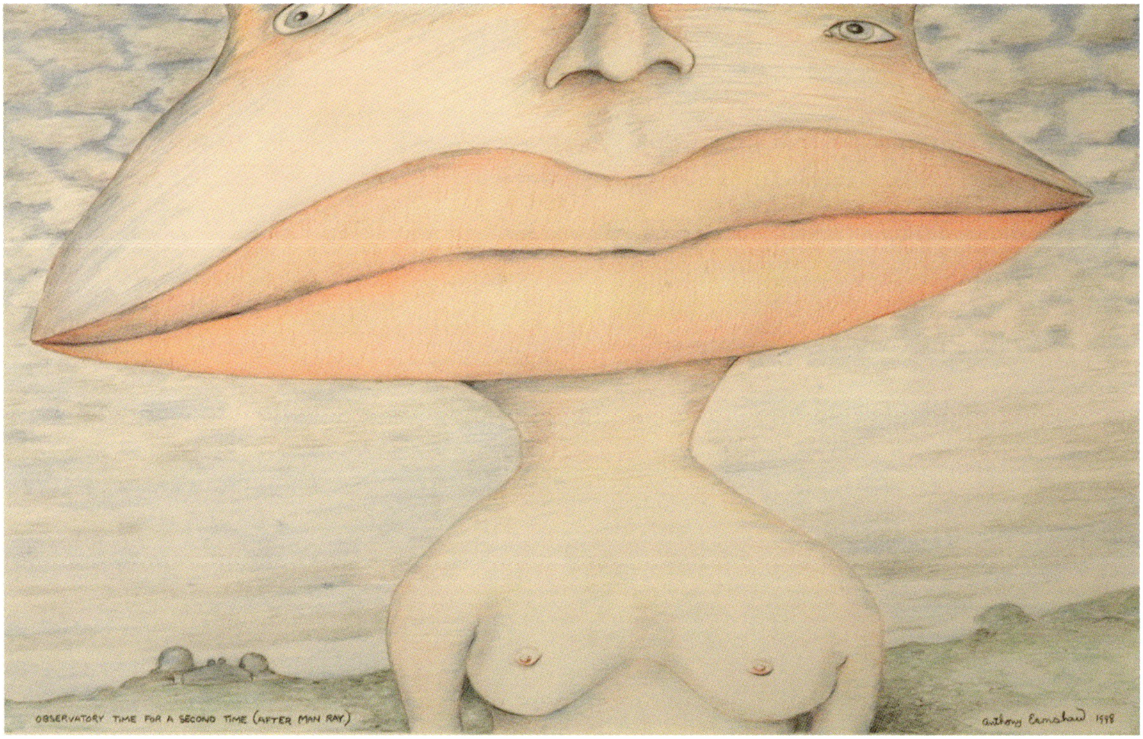

Observatory Time For A Second Time (after Man Ray), 1988

to a reproduction of the 'Mona Lisa', it was originally a piece of light-hearted flippancy. Titled 'L.H.O.O.Q.' (1919), when pronounced phonetically in French it reads "elle a chaud ou cul", translating as "she has a hot arse". It went by virtually unnoticed given that Duchamp showed little interest in exhibiting work at the time. But as Duchamp's star gradually rose so his work was increasingly analyzed under the microscope of the academic world. Today Duchamp's version of the 'Mona Lisa' is regarded as a seminal and radical gesture by the art Establishment it originally set out to ridicule. All this has come about in spite of the fact that the 'originality' of Duchamp's jape was pre-dated by thirty-two years when Sapeck (Eugène Bataille 1853–1891) published in *Le Rire* a pipe-smoking Gioconda "with wreaths of smoke that mocked the halos of Art and Genius".[1]

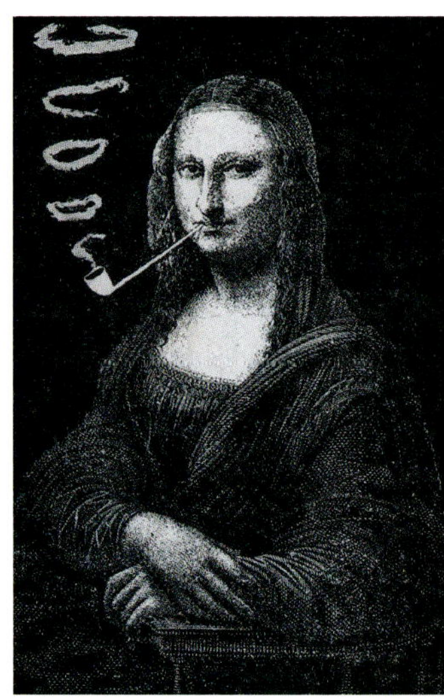

Eugène Bataille (Sapeck), Mona Lisa with a Pipe, 1887

René Magritte made three separate versions of his painting 'Perspective' where he parodies works by David, Gérard and Manet. Magritte made meticulous pastiches of the original paintings but then concealed their subjects in coffins shaped to reflect the pose of the sitters, by then long since dead. Man

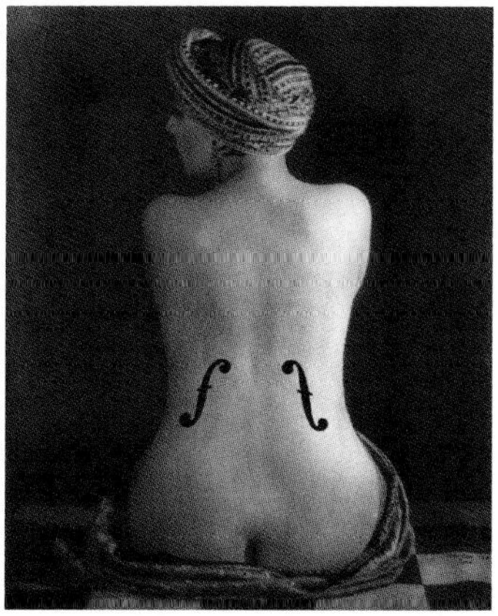

Man Ray, Le Violon d'Ingres, 1924

Ray's 'Le Violin d'Ingres' is a witty reference to Ingres' painting 'The Bather of Valpincoa' (1806). Furthermore Ingres was an accomplished violin player. Belgian surrealist Marcel Mariën poked fun at Duchamp's 'L.H.O.O.Q.', as well as works by Dali and Magritte, while Saul Steinberg made visual jokes about the 'geometric' paintings of Piet Mondrian. Roy Lichtenstein's dull deadpan transcriptions of works by Picasso painted in trademark cartoon-style, are the best known examples where art quotes art to be accepted by the custodians of the 'official' version of Art History.

The various schools of modern art have given cause for countless cartoons to be drawn. So much so that in 1973 the Tate Gallery, London mounted 'A Child of Six Could Do It!', an exhibition devoted to the subject. When art is put on a 'pedastal', to be discussed in overly precious and sometimes pretentious fashion the situation becomes open to satirical attack.

Showing a fanciful relationship between art, patronage, and finance, Earnshaw's drawing 'Trying to catch his patron's eye'

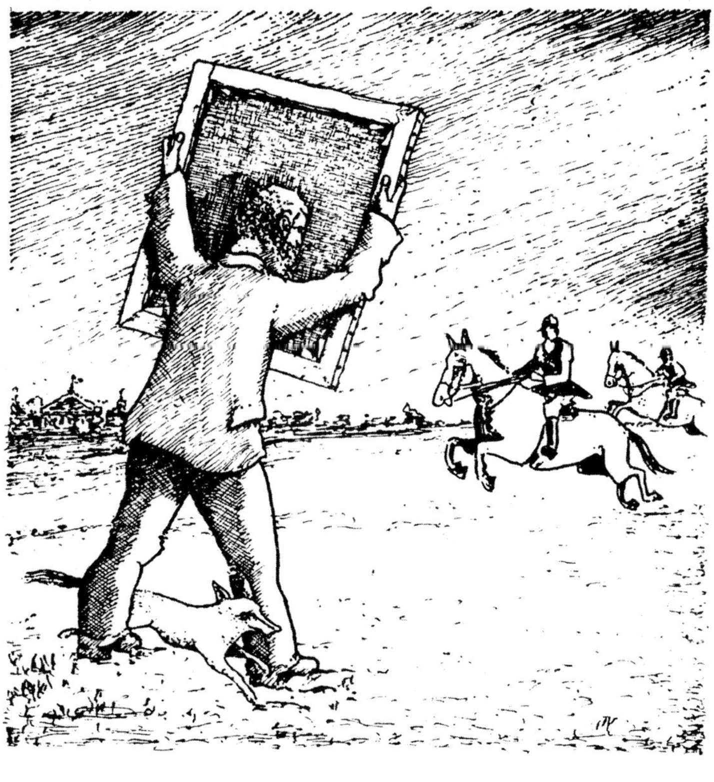

Trying to catch his patron's eye
c.1983–86

there is a strong sense that the scene portrayed is deliberately ridiculous. The choice of timing by the artist to display his latest 'masterpiece' could not be more inappropriate, giving emphasis to the disparity in the relationship between artist and patron. Seeing the back of the canvas only we are made aware that Earnshaw's artist has been cast as the underdog in this scenario as the hunted fox, identifying with the artist, darts between his legs. The drawing is a wonderfully theatrical comment on the English class system.

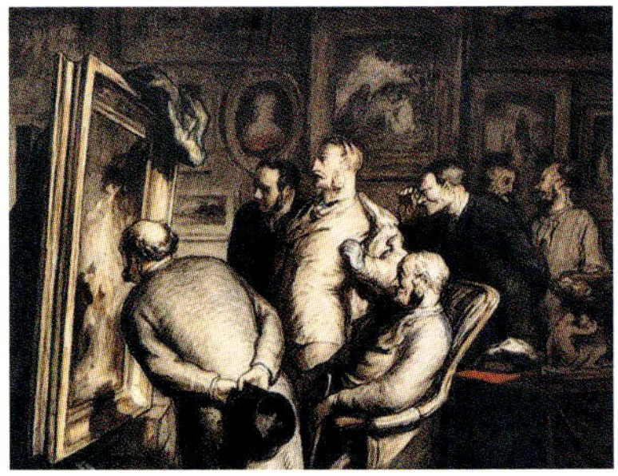

Honoré Daumier, The Critics, 1862

In 'The Critics', a satirical painting by Honoré Daumier (1808–1879), the five 'experts' are the prime focus of our attention whereas the painting they are scrutinising is placed in a secondary role. Looked at askance, the painting is indecipherable to us while the artist whose painting it is has been relegated into the background where he is ignored. It is in the posturing of the connoisseurs that Daumier tells his story. In cartooning parlance they would be described as 'types', similar to the archetypes we encounter in literature.

The graphic arts have a long history of social and political satire, particularly in Britain where we like to pretend we have 'freedom of speech'. As early as Egyptian times dissatisfaction with prevailing social conditions would be expressed in the form of a reversed order. By inverting 'reality' a disjointed sense of the familiar is created, as seen in a papyrus of an antelope and lion (circa 1,000 BC) playing draughts. The idea of animals acting out of character and imitating man enjoyed great popularity in medieval times as a way of giving expression to human behaviour. Inanimate objects would come to life to wreak revenge on mankind, as seen in Karl Stauber's (1815–1902) drawing.

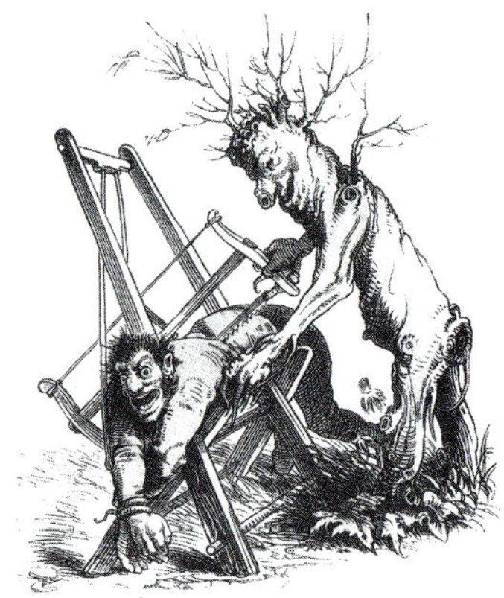

Karl Stauber, The tree-trunk saws up the wood-cutter, 1851

Satirical commentators often compare and contrast antithetical positions to praise one and damn the other. This technique is used to present moral arguments that invite the audience to identify with the good and eschew the bad. It is the job of social commentators to communicate views which the majority have chosen to ignore or do not wish to acknowledge. Such criticism historically has excluded itself from the walls of galleries, preferring to use flyers, illustrated broadsheets and other forms of popular printing as a way of disseminating ideas. It was for this reason that William Hogarth (1697–1764) would produce his moralising narratives 'The Rake's Progress' and 'Marriage-à-la-Mode' not only as paintings but also as editions of popular engravings. In his lifetime, with a few notable exceptions, Hogarth's paintings were rarely collected. It was Hogarth's opinion that no man was so ill-qualified to form an honest judgement about painting as the connoisseur whose dogmatic views would be based on the manner of earlier masters and showing no interest in addressing satire or the topical. Hogarth's subjects were chosen to be accessible to a broad public rather than an elite audience. 'The Politician' shows Hogarth breaking with the tradition of art as flattery. His use of a derisory humour was in opposition to the attitude that High Art was incompatible with a comic sensibility. The snobbery of so-called High Art was founded on the assumed prerogative that humorous content represented Low Art and therefore was not to be taken 'seriously'. It is possible to regard Giuseppe Arcimboldo's (1587–1593) punning portraits as an exception but although he gained court recognition during his lifetime his paintings were then ignored for the next four hundred years.

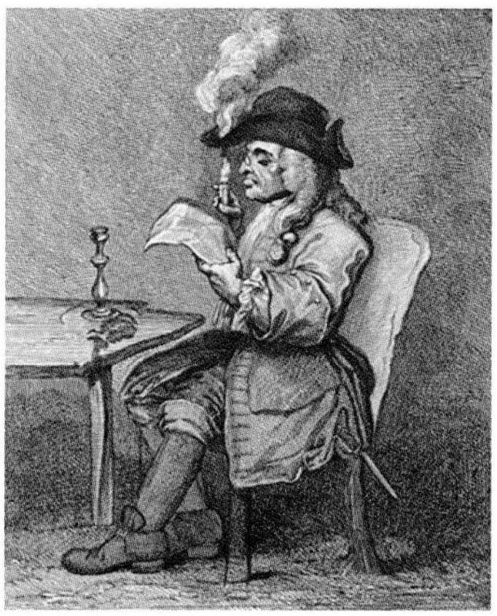

William Hogarth, The Politician, published posthumously 1773

In the introduction to *The Cartoonist's Progress* exhibition catalogue, political cartoonist Steve Bell points out how, "Hogarth's legacy is still very much alive and kicking, whereas the 'History Painting' which ruled supreme in his day (and to which he aspired) is now as dead as a stuffed shark".[2] The corollary to Bell's observation is how social commentators will never be timeless; rather they are defined by the particularity of historical circumstance. Social commentary also represents the antithesis of academic traditions which are endorsed and supported by the Establishment. For creative imagination to focus on the follies and injustice of human nature a combination of mischievousness, resentment and anger is required—qualities that were all part of Earnshaw's persona.

To quote Earnshaw from an interview published in 1987: "In '45, when I was in my early twenties, I saw at the cinema newsreel shots of Belsen, those disgraceful and disturbing scenes that were flashed on British Movietone News. A few months later the Americans dropped their atom bombs on Hiroshima and Nagasaki, scenes of devastation that they produced, civilians with their eyes melted and flesh fried, came on the screen. It was then I thought 'so much for government of every colour and kind' and became an armchair anarchist."[3]

Opposite: Adapted postcards, sent to Les Coleman, 1985–87

In 1983 Earnshaw embarked on a series of drawings that he likened to social-realism. These drawings would stop, just as suddenly as they had begun, three years later. He felt he had nothing more to say on the matter. This was typical of Earnshaw's creative life, subscribing to Duchamp's belief that repetition was an imaginative cul-de-sac. At the time of their making these mordant drawings appeared in issues of *Camouflage*, a low budget surrealist journal edited by Jimmy Gladiator in Paris, and the anarchist publication *Freedom* to which Earnshaw was a life-long subscriber. Two years after the drawings had ceased Gladiator printed all forty-nine drawings to become *Camouflage* no.19 with the title 'Aspects des Bas-Quartiers'. Translated as 'Back o' Town Blues', taken from a 1930s recording by Louis Armstrong, Earnshaw described the title as a metaphor for "that place where society's misfits set up camp and liberty triumphs over necessity".[4] These uncompromising drawings reveal the frustration Earnshaw felt towards an entrenched and impoverished class structure and the restriction that authority presented.

The first drawing in this collection shows a labourer standing in profile, a pickaxe over his shoulder with an industrial landscape of factory buildings and chimneys in the background. Attached to the pickaxe is a balloon on a string. According to the caption below, the man is 'Looking for a Carnival'. Despite the implication of work and play being tied together there are no celebrations in sight. Given the desolation of the scene the drawing suggests that the search will be fruitless and that revelry is not to be part of the labourer's life. It is a drawing about despair. In 1984 I published 'Looking for a Carnival' as a postcard. This provided an opportunity for Earnshaw to make changes to his own drawing. To alter images, find new relationships for objects, was second nature for him. To sieze on the unexpected was Earnshaw's natural way to view the world and his work was a way of sharing his musing with others.

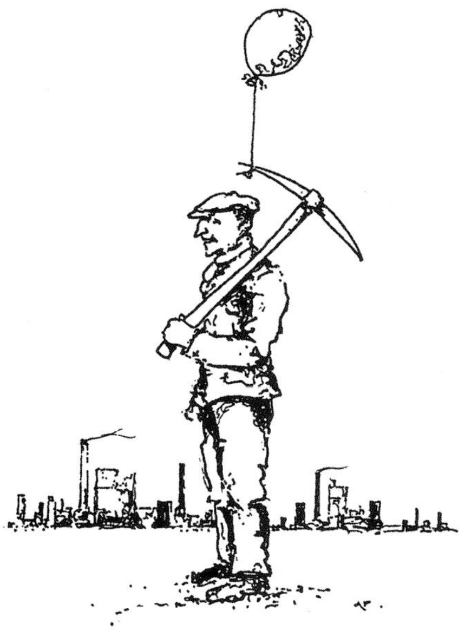

Looking for a Carnival, c.1983

In another drawing Earnshaw's political candidate is portrayed as an incompetent, unable to deal with the simplest

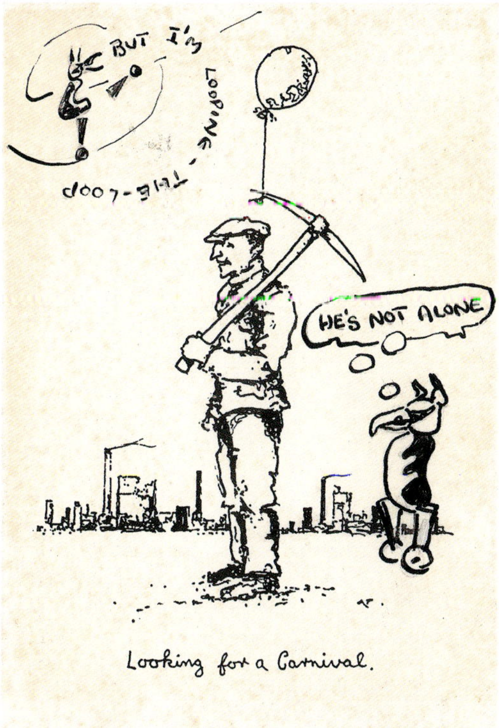
BUT I'M LOOPING - THE - LOOP
HE'S NOT ALONE
Looking for a Carnival.

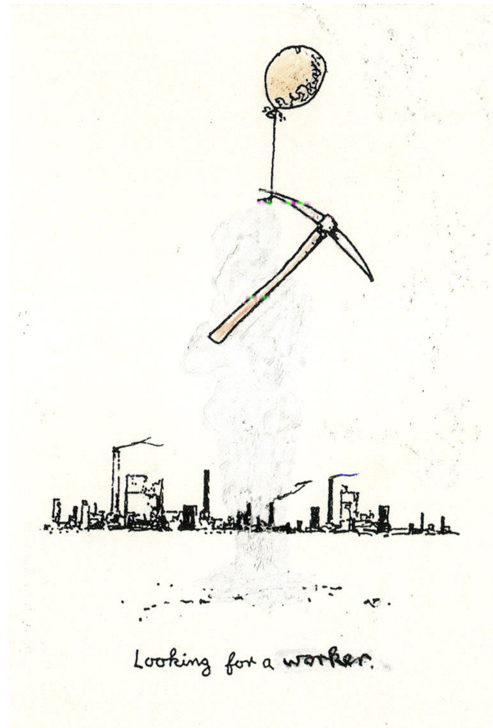
Looking for a worker.

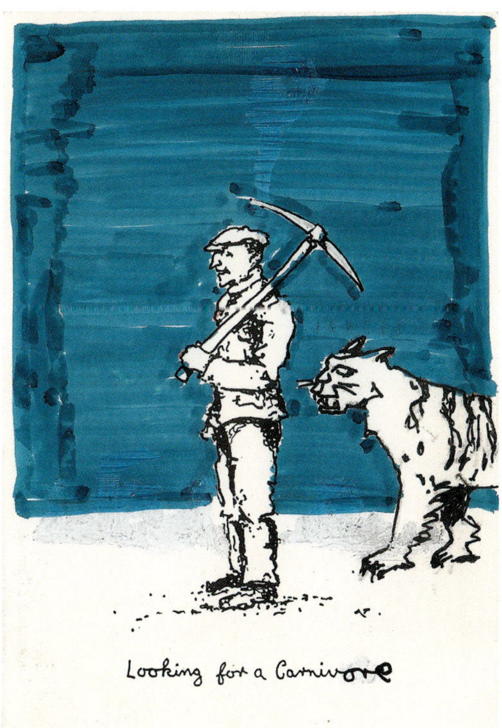
Looking for a Carnivore

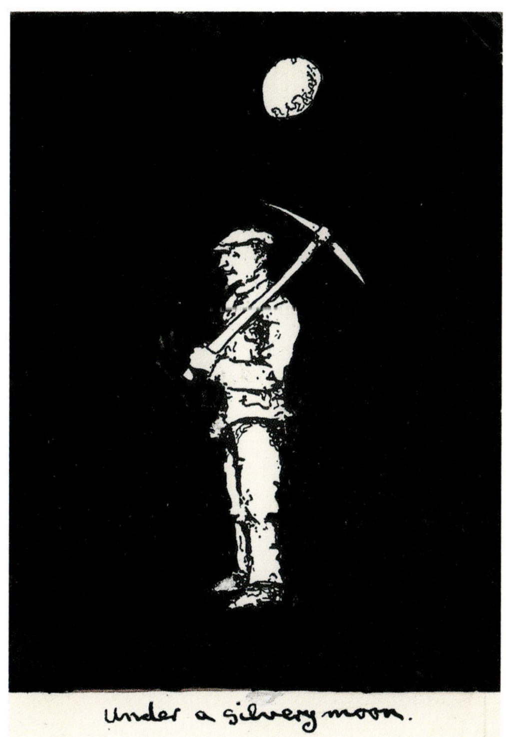
Under a silvery moon.

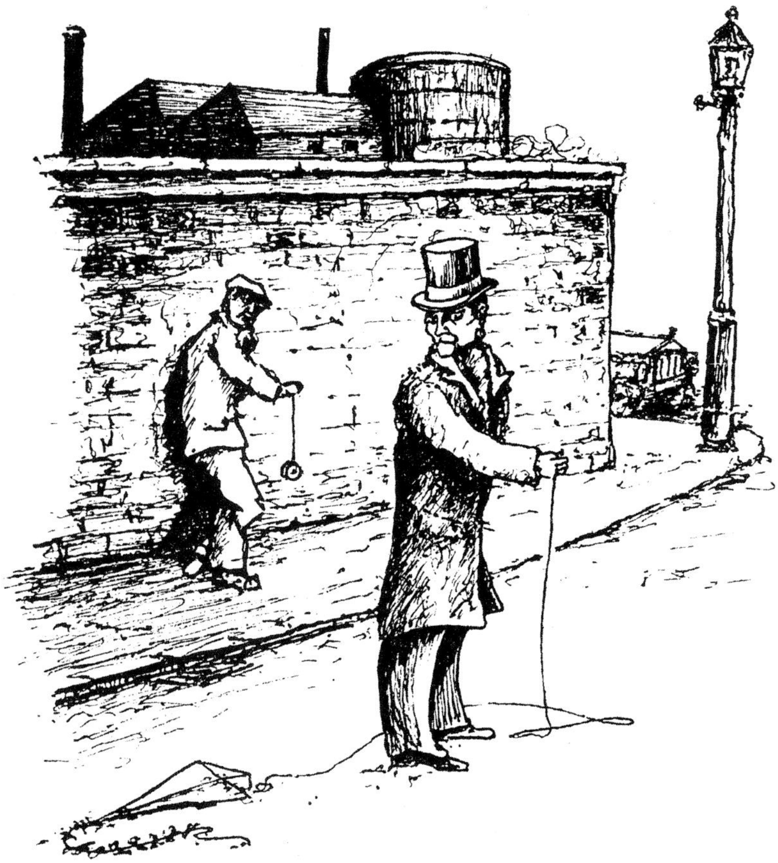

Many parliamentary candidates believe a kite is a yo-yo, c. 1983–86

task. In 'Many parliamentary candidates believe a kite is a yo-yo' we see a factory worker playing with a yo-yo while the top-hatted candidate is incapable of flying his kite. Round the corner a Rolls Royce is parked. The fact that he is wealthy does not exclude the possibility of him being an ignoramus. It should be mentioned that the top hat, denoting wealth, was a symbol of class-distinction commonly used by cartoonists. To what degree the repetitive action of a yo yo is used to reflect the nature of the workaday world in contrast to a kite's dancing movement as a metaphor for the 'promise' of "a better, brighter Britain"[5] could be mere conjecture on my behalf.

Published in 1807, 'Letters from England' was written by the poet Robert Southey (1774–1843) in spite of the authorship being credited to a fictionalised Spanish nobleman with the name Don Manuel Alvarez Espiella. Southey was known for his forthright, and often critical opinions, of English society: "The members of parliament being rich, and associating wholly with the rich, they have no knowledge of the real state of the great body for whom they are to legislate, and little sympathy for distresses which they have never felt: a legislature composed wholly of the rich is therefore liable to lay the public burthens oppressively upon the inferior ranks."

One hundred and eighty years later Earnshaw's drawing makes a similar observation begging the question: Do our managers know what they are managing? Earnshaw regarded his Social Realist drawings as his "first attempt at making a criticism of English society as it actually is, with all its misery, mediocrity, and meanness".[6]

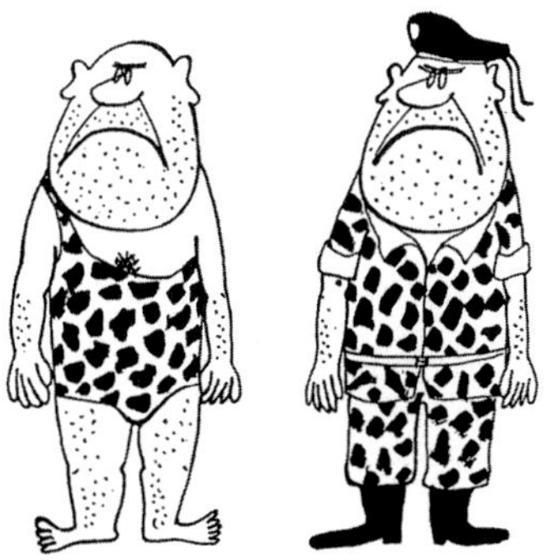

Siné, 1961

A drawing by the French cartoonist Siné (Maurice Sinet, b.1928) from 1961 suggests that as our history develops so will our awareness. But he presents the idea of 'progress' as misleading by portraying his soldier as a contemporary caveman.

In one of Earnshaw's drawings set in an engineering workshop the boss's son is seen in the foreground clutching a child's teddy bear. Due to his protected upbringing he has never had to confront his place in society and so drifts, as if in a cocoon. Why should he need to know what a 25mm twist drill is used for? Surely that is someone else's job. It would appear Earnshaw saw himself living in a world of mediocre values implemented and run by fools. One critic described his drawings as 'bitter'. Earnshaw who "was born, doubtless bawling and kicking" responded, "I'm *still* bawling and kicking".[7]

Writing to a friend in France at the time of the collection's publication Earnshaw felt it necessary to speak out against his detractors."Yes, I'm chuffed with *Aspects des Bas Quartiers,* even though some of my friends who have seen it are light-heartedly critical, they say my view of the working-class is starry-eyed, old fashioned, out of date… but I think the people of the world who have nothing but themselves, whom they sell to the people who own the means of production still obtains."[8] To use flat-caps and top hats, factory chimneys and the Houses of Parliament, rats and sheep as symbols might appear outdated but we still live in a world of the 'haves and have-nots' as defined by capitalism. The fact that these drawings cover the period 1983–1986 might

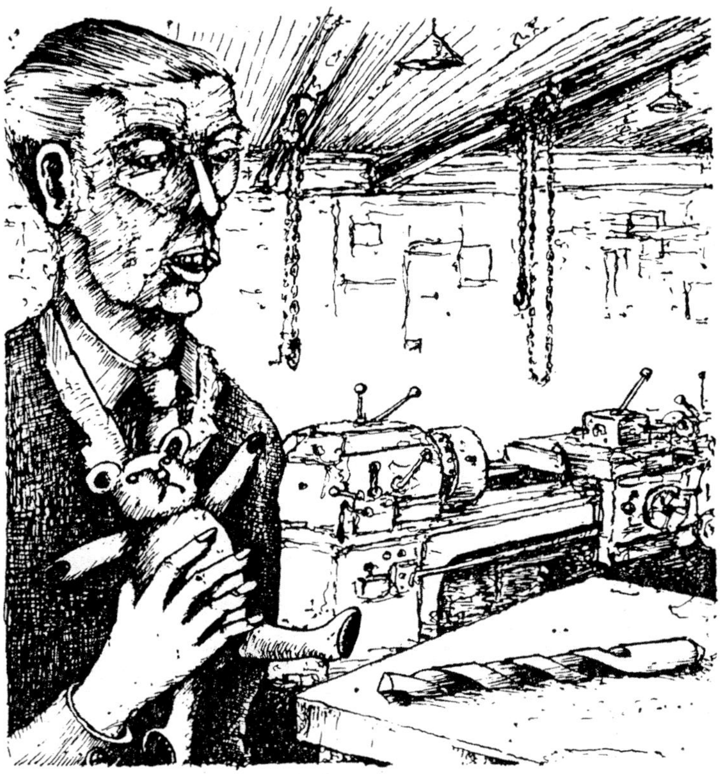

With his teddy in a grip of steel, the boss's son eyes a 25mm twist drill and plumbs the puddle of his brain to fathom what purpose it serves. c. 1983–86

suggest they were, in part, a reaction to the increasingly divisive government policies being introduced in Britain at the time, as material acquisitiveness became the harbinger of a new philistinism. It was Earnshaw's belief that "humour stems from the spirit of *liberty*; it colours *necessity*, and makes sure *banality* doesn't get the upper hand".[9]

Two rats confront each other in a stand-off over a lump of cheese. 'One of these rats is a politician' suggests that an ordinary rat is preferable to a political rat but in looking at the drawing it is impossible to tell which is which. Unlike political caricaturists such as James Gillray, David Low and Steve Bell, Earnshaw never directed his enmity towards specific politicians.

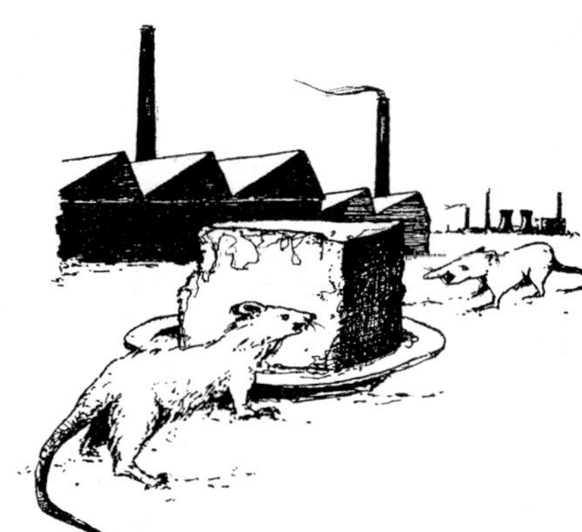

One of these rats is a politician, c. 1983–86

A scene at Earnshaw's Conservative Club depicts a table where two pigs' heads sit on plates, with apples stuffed into their jaws with their back turned on a 'common' pork pie. The drawing, titled 'Snubbing a vulgar pork pie, at the Conservative Club', is Earnshaw's comment on the English class system, and how this is reinforced within party politics. In the municipal art gallery the pictures on show are painted versions of what we expect to encounter in an abattoir. Two gallery-goers have dropped in after doing a morning's shopping, their baskets full of pig's heads. Underneath the drawing it reads 'They don't know much about art but they know what they like', the philistine's excuse to avoid having to formulate an opinion.

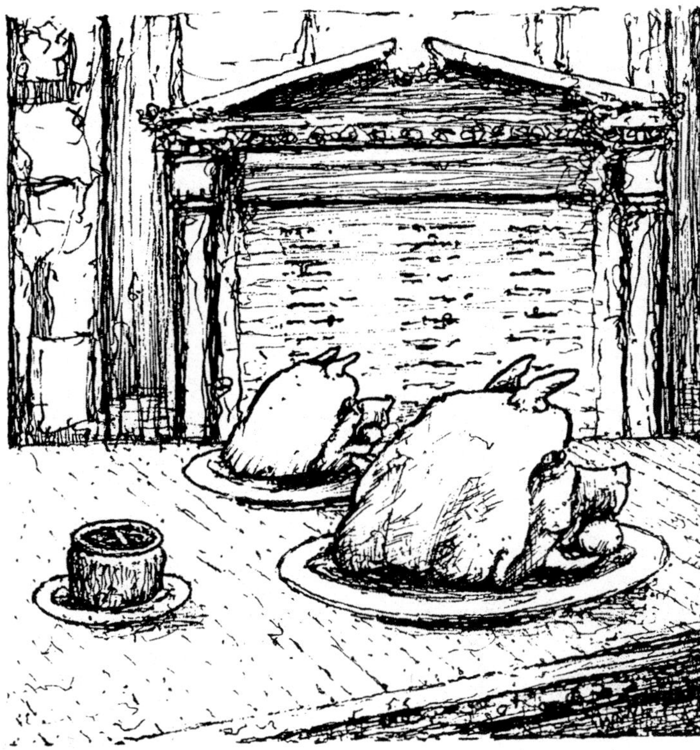

Snubbing a vulgar pork pie, at the Conservative Club, c.1983–86

Earnshaw described himself as "not really a political animal, for me anarchism is as much an intuitive as an intellectual matter, it provides me with an attitude to life—even a way of life—as indeed does my love of Surrealism".[10] Although essentially disinterested in the British political landscape, fascism in the guise of nationalism, is something he would want to resist. He made his views on the far-right quite clear in a drawing that refers to the National Front party [p.120].

Making 'daft' suggestions either in conversations or in letters was characteristic of Tony. After a visit to the Botanic Gardens in Edinburgh he wrote to Paul Hammond: "One glasshouse houses a jungle at the centre of which stands a tree one hundred

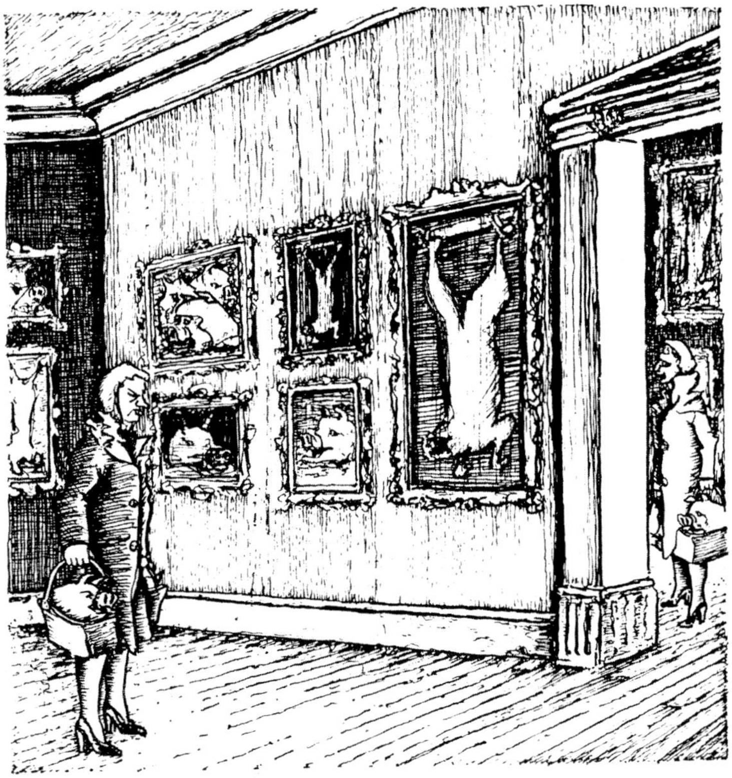

They don't know much about art but they know what they like, c. 1983–86

and fifty years old; all the glasshouses housing various kinds of jungles are amusing! All they need is a few snakes, butterflies and native villagers to make them complete. One houses cactus (cactii?)—rattle-snakes needed there, perhaps with one or two cowboys for good measure." In 'playing silly' he knew full well that his ideas were outside the bounds of possibility but nevertheless he would encourage others to join him in his speculative day-dreaming. His love of science fiction stemmed from the way it would transport him out of the humdrum world of necessity to some *other* place.

An aphorism from Earnshaw's collection *Flick Knives & Forks* reads: "Up with Stalactites! Down with Stalagmites!" In this combination of contradictory sloganising Earnshaw turns the idea of 'for' and 'against' on its head. Like a haiku by Basho we are left to marvel at such simple and direct poetry. Earnshaw's restless mind never stopped conjuring up the unexpected. In a letter to his friend the illustrator Tony Blundell, he wrote: "Friday night bodes well, plenty to talk over, plenty of laughs—

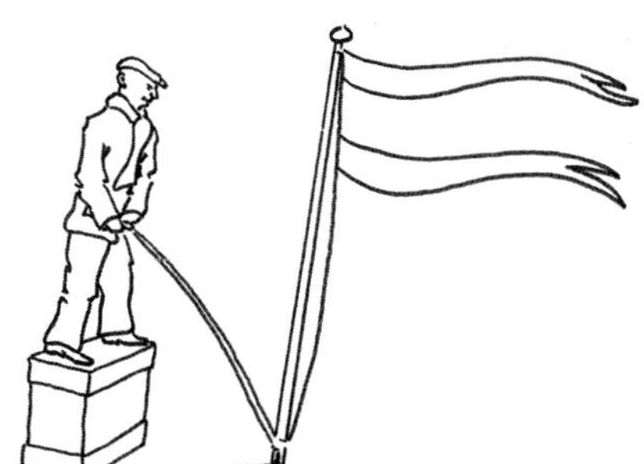

Ever willing to help, our artist, A.E., has redesigned the NF trademark, 1980

my favourite activity, laughing."[11] Earnshaw loved to tell the joke of a condemned man going to the gallows on a Monday morning and declaring, "What a way to start the week!"

Notes

1. Daniel Grojnowski, 'Hydropathes and Company', *The Spirit of Montmartre,* Jane Voornees, Zimmerli Art Museum, 1996
2. Steve Bell, *The Cartoonist's Progress,* Gardner Centre, University of Sussex, 1997
3. Patrick Hughes, 'Earnshaw', *Art Line*, April/May 1987
4. Michael Howard MP, 2005
5. Anthony Earnshaw, *Aspects des Bas-Quartiers*, Camouflage no.19, Paris, 1988
6. Patrick Hughes, *op. cit*
7. Anthony Earnshaw, *A View From Back o' Town',* Leeds City Art Gallery, 1987
8. Letter to Marie-Odile Gain d'Enquin, 31 May 1988
9. Anthony Earnshaw, 'Tony Earnshaw Introduces Wokker to the Good People of Halifax', unpublished, 1988
10. Letter to Frances Earnshaw, 27 January 1994
11. Letter to Tony Blundell, 24 September 1980

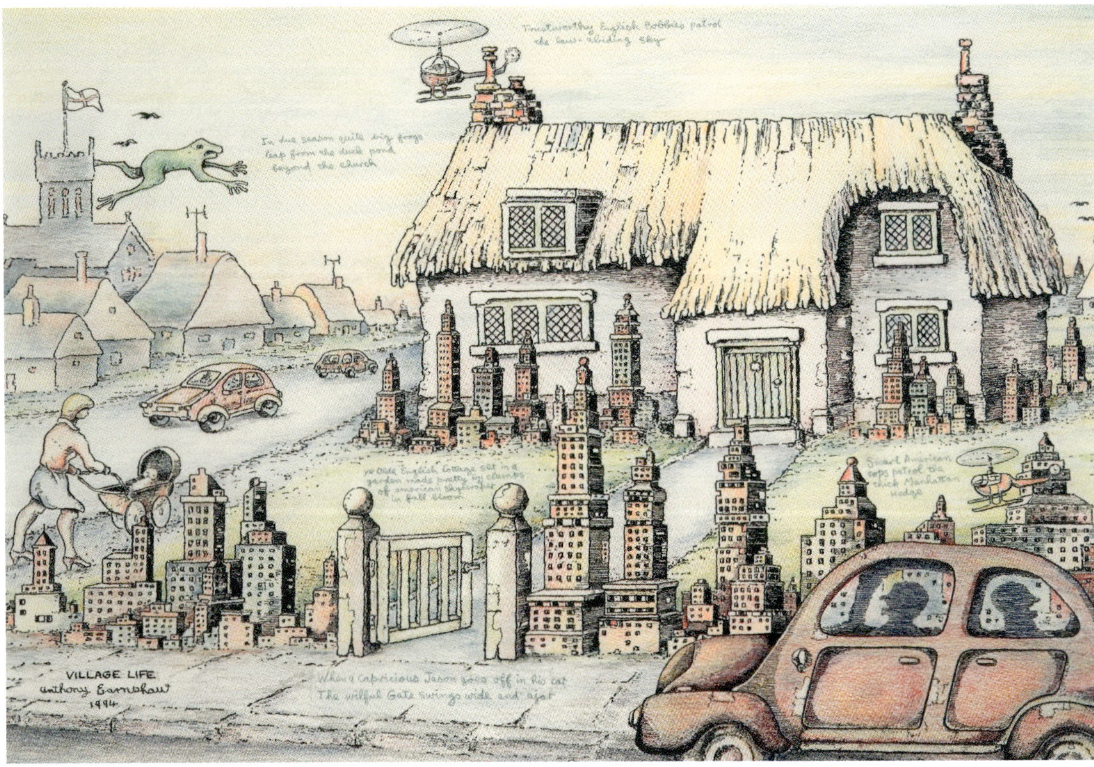

Village Life, 1994

Chris Vine

A Cottage in the City

"If I had lots of money I would buy up Lewis's Department Store on the Headrow in the middle of Leeds. I would have it demolished and flatten the land to make a big field. In the middle of this, I'd build a small old-fashioned farm cottage with leaded windows and a thatched roof. Around the edge of the field there would be a fence to keep animals in—cows, pigs, chickens—and a five-bar gate facing directly into the main shopping street. Every morning, after eating a leisurely breakfast, and feeding the animals, I'd walk down the path and lean casually on the gate. While chewing a long piece of tasty grass, I'd greet all the laden shoppers going past, with a chirpy 'Good morning' and 'Another fine day again?'"

In 1967 Tony Earnshaw taught drawing for a day a week at Bradford Art College. It was during one of the early sessions that Earnshaw told us the story above. As a group we realised that with Tony teaching us it was not going to be a conventional drawing class. For the following year and a half we enjoyed the fruits of his self-education.

We saw the final drawings completed for 'Musrum', the early beginnings of 'Wintersol' and 'collaborated' with the likes of Alfred Jarry, Paul Klee and Jorge Luis Borges via Tony Earnshaw.

In 1997 Tony Earnshaw exhibited his boxes at Gallery M, in London—'Lucifer Contemplating the 21st Century & Other Boxes' and at Belloc-Lowndes Fine Art Gallery in Chicago—'I Only Want To Help'. Dean Clough Gallery exhibited his later drawings from November of the same year to the following January. This exhibition 'Because I Felt Like It' comprised nearly forty crayon, ink and wash drawings which were completed between 1985 and 1997.

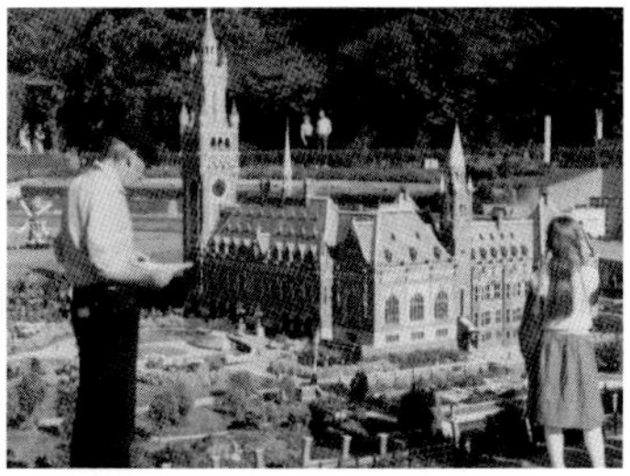

A.E. visiting Madurodam Model Village, c.1980

Although Earnshaw's output is often exhibited separately as assemblages, drawings or published work, the drawings can be seen as part of a whole genus, as John Slyce describes it, "centred on the expression of poetic conspiracies".[1]

As accomplices in these conspiracies, Earnshaw enrols his 'A' list of heroes, villains and innocent bystanders—Mickey Mouse, God, Fidel Castro, Père Ubu, Fay Wray, Leonardo, Lucifer, Man Ray, King Kong, Adam and Eve, cats, dogs, fairies, cows, lions and frogs. All play their part in small acts of defiance.

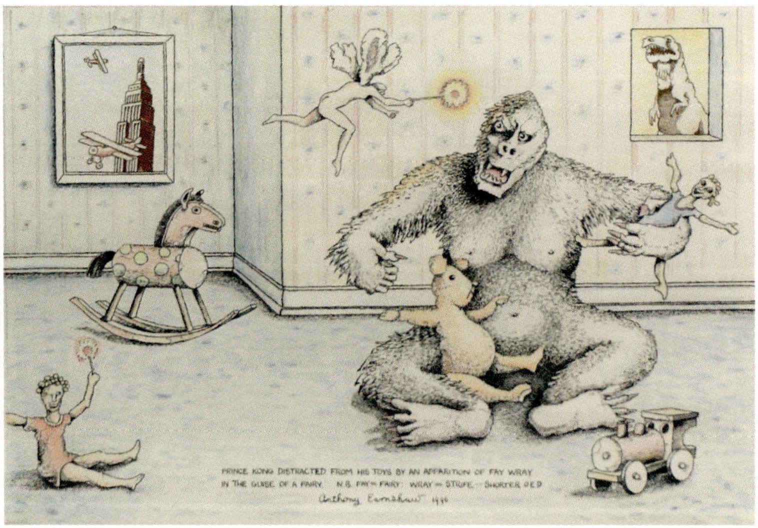

Prince Kong Distracted From His Toys by an Apparition of Fay Wray in the Guise of a Fairy, 1996

'Village Life' [p.122] at first glance, depicts a typical rural village scene—a picturesque country cottage with a thatched roof, leaded windows and ornamental brick chimney stacks. The garden lawn is bordered by a series of model buildings. From the front door a path leads down to a rustic wooden gate. A car drives past—maybe on its way to the little parish church round the corner with its charming bell tower? A flag flutters gently in the warmth of the afternoon sun; an English idyll.

But there is something not quite right with the garden. It is as though the model buildings, unlike the cottage, have moved forward in time to reflect contemporary urban development. But the appearance of the buildings has nothing to do with England. Instead they have given way to skyscrapers, office blocks and residential tower blocks in the architectural style of a present-day Manhattan. This headlong development has had its social consequences—police helicopters whirl overhead patrolling the streets for signs of a breakdown in law and order, civil disobedience and inevitable vigilantism. The surveillance costs of this miniature cityscape have spiralled out of control. Earnshaw presents an idealised image of village life and then undermines it by leading us down a garden path to an urban dystopia.

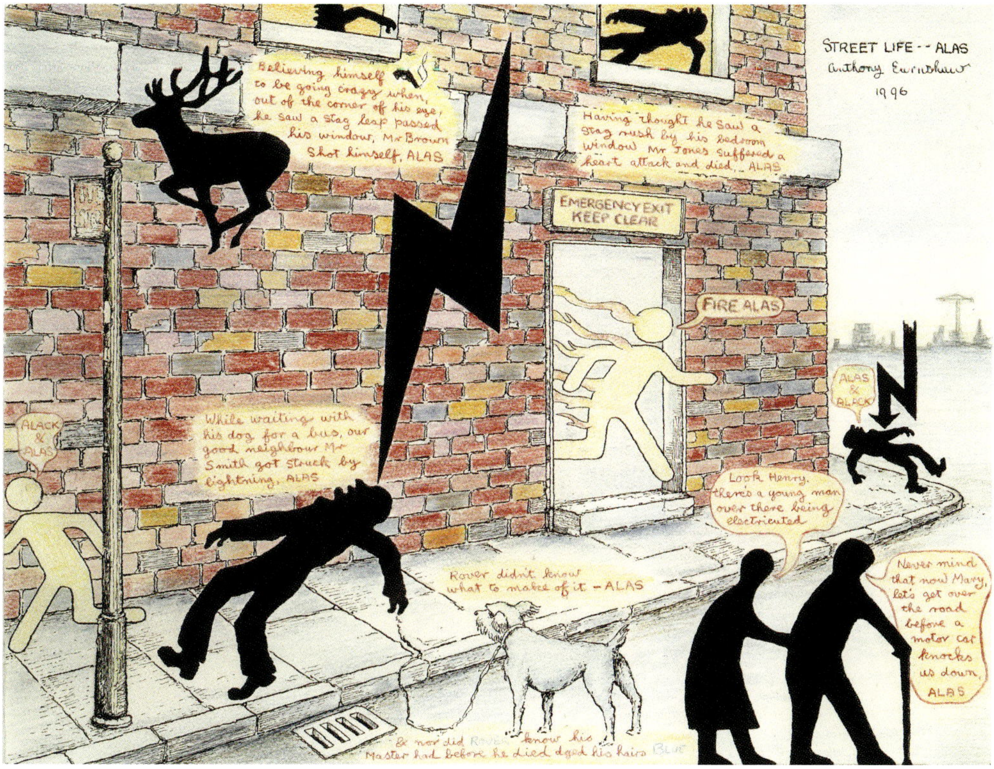

Earnshaw's companion piece to 'Village Life' is 'Street Life—Alas' where the 'characters' are all familiar symbols taken from public warning signs. Suffering a variety of hazards, they are repositioned to create a bizarre scenario of predicted calamities. These silhouettes simultaneously enact their unfortunate fates. The scene of this accident black spot is a brick building on a street corner where, by chance, the victims are struck by lightning, electrocuted by overhead wires, shot while distracted by passing wildlife and burned alive. And if that is not enough by way of coincidence and bad luck, there is another accident waiting to happen as an elderly couple, oblivious to any approaching traffic carefully cross the street. A black comedy melodrama of foreseen mishaps—ALAS.

Street Life—Alas, 1996

“From now on NO BUTTONS on either shirt, trousers nor jacket. Thank you very much… OR ELSE!” warns the police helicopter to a hapless car being driven past a road sign displaying a large button with a red line across it. In ‘No Buttons’ the landscape is strewn with abandoned threaded needles and

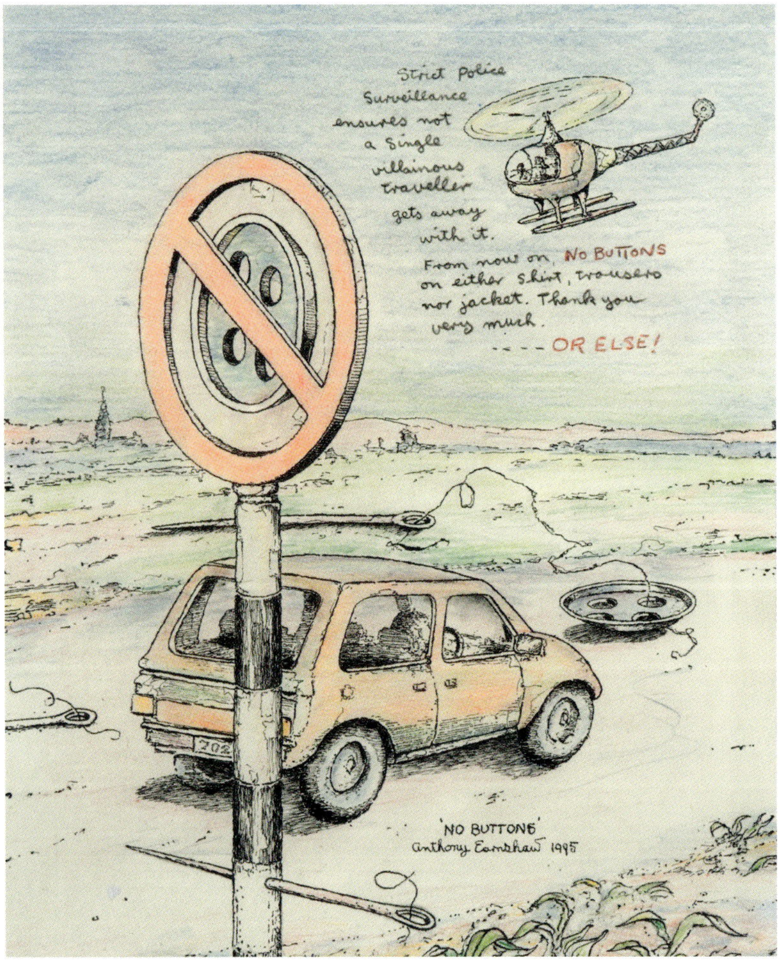

No Buttons, 1995

buttons where previous would-be button-wearing criminals have had to discard their incriminating evidence. “Strict police surveillance ensures not a single villainous traveller gets away with it.” Earnshaw’s analogy of random discrimination.

Several years before Tony drew ‘No Buttons’ he sent a letter to the local Bradford newspaper about the newly introduced council policy of trying to drive away starlings from the city centre. Every night the birds were bombarded with bird distress calls amplified through loudspeakers to get them to move on.

Earnshaw's use of helicopters is a recurring image to denote the presence of surveillance. In 'Gentlemen & Workers With Red Balloons' top-hatted, booted and tailcoated young gentlemen hold red balloons and watch over the workers. One, in turn,

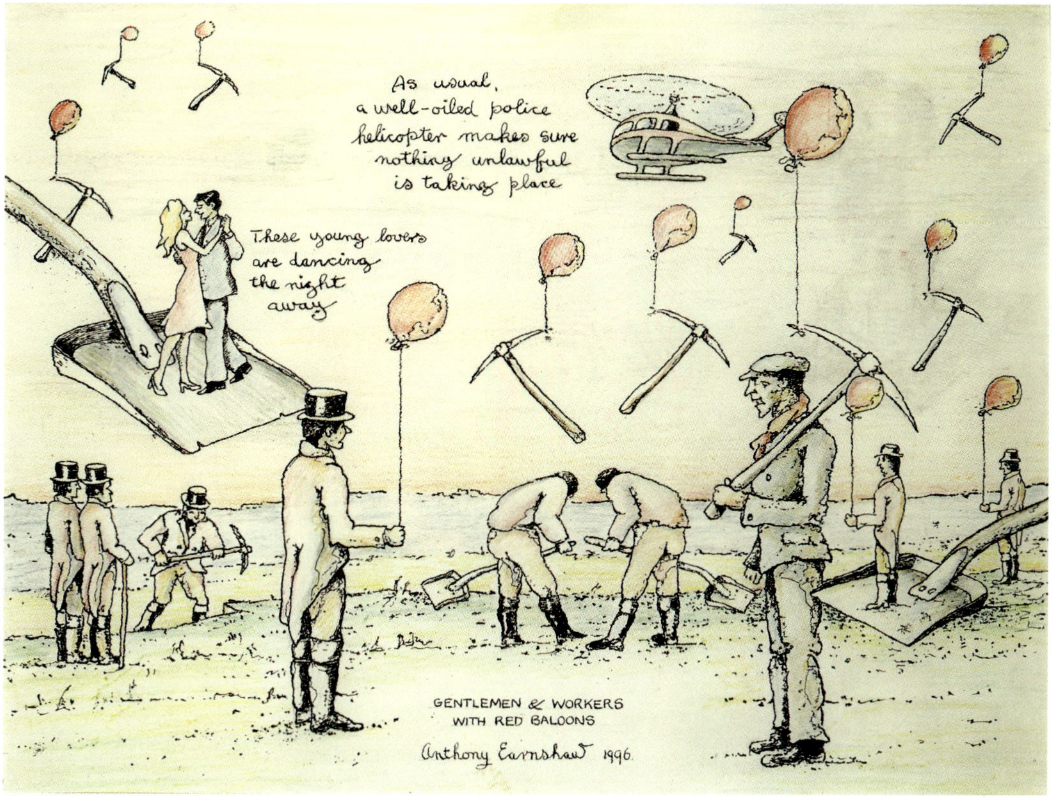

shoulders a pickaxe with a balloon attached. The scene is one of potential confrontation but the balloons suggest all the fun of a carnival, as do a young couple "dancing the night away" on the end of a heavy industrial shovel. "As usual a well-oiled police helicopter makes sure nothing unlawful is taking place."

'Twenty Four Shouting Americans' is a cityscape with skyscrapers. The architecture suggests that this is Manhattan Island but drawn in such a way that it resembles a child's attempt at making New York out of wooden building bricks. The occupants of the buildings—shouting Americans—have been reduced to cartoon speech bubbles giving away their

Gentlemen & Workers
with Red Bal[l]oons, 1996

location by yelling "SHOUT" across the city. Two helicopters fly over the scene and "SHOUT" back. Earnshaw appears to be saying Americans are bombastic loud-mouths.

Never much of a football fan, Earnshaw composes an extraordinary image of a team of eleven, supposedly, scoring

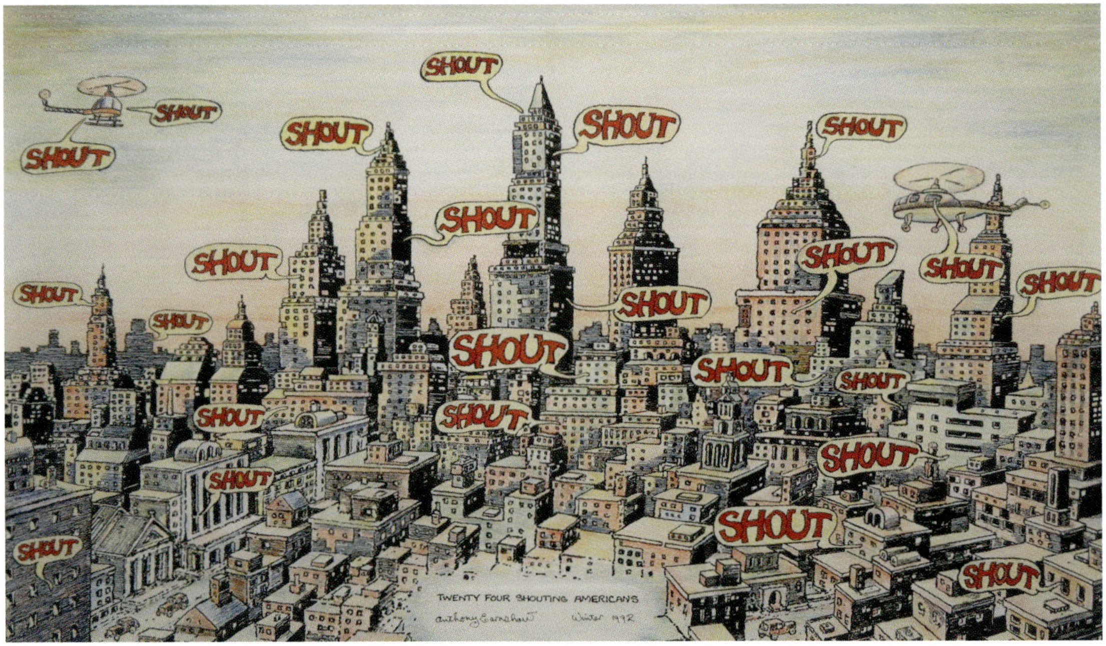

footballers interspersed with another team of eleven cows mooing loudly in a pasture. Each scorer declares "GOAL" while the cows just "MOO". The 'combatants' and speech bubbles recede into the distance between two country churches on the horizon. But the footballers are not playing as a team—no one is defending and there are no goal posts—all the players are isolated. They cannot pass the ball to each other—there is no football as the cows stand around. Has Earnshaw devised an impossible and elaborate 'spot the ball' puzzle?

"Cows are a bit silly", Earnshaw said of this drawing, "because they spend all their time mooing in fields and footballers are the same, aren't they really? They just spend their time scoring goals. At least the cows do something useful, they provide us with milk."[2] Almost hidden in the confusion and ignored in all the noise and futile action is the needy 'pretty doll' in a blue dress sitting on the grass crying for "MAMA".

Twenty-Four Shouting Americans, 1992

Throughout these drawings a remarkable element is Earnshaw's use of line. His line at times seems to have its own agenda, quite removed from the subject of the drawing itself. Sometimes his line will be describing a form, which then wilfully digresses into a decorative motif or a doodle only to return to

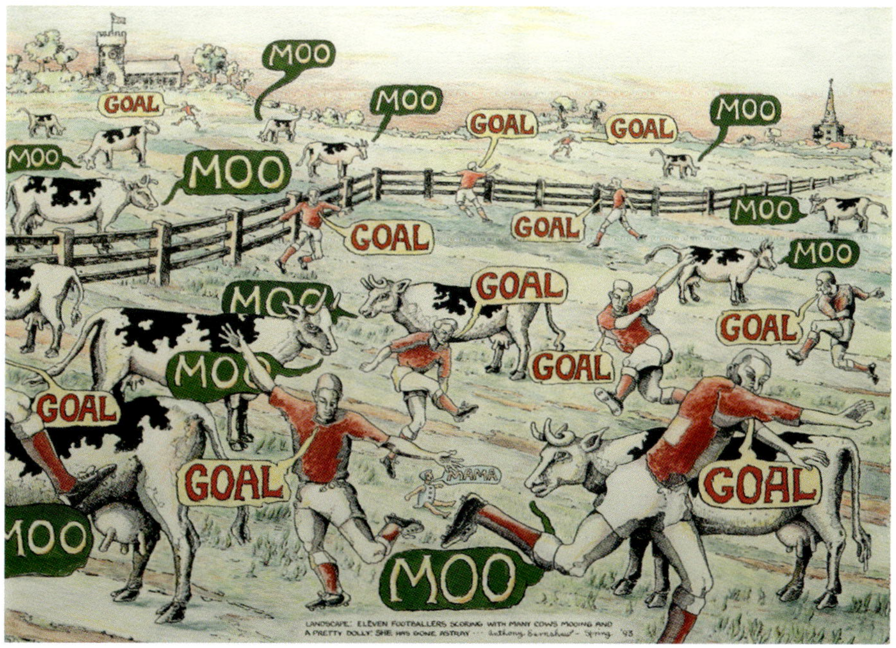

describing form. Like some mischievous child that is mindful of what is expected of it—but then will invent some delaying tactic on the way—Earnshaw's unruly line will stop dead in its tracks and then perform some elaborate dance resembling embroidery or crochet work.

In 'Drama at Sea' Earnshaw substitutes fighter planes for lions and dragons in a commentary on nationalism, sovereignty and chauvinism, bringing to mind our naval history. A large aircraft carrier floats in a decorative heraldic sea where pink lions in various heraldic poses—rampant, salient, passant—fiercely guard the flight deck against an invasion of flying dragons. The pink lions, with the help of the ship's rats, "All rats on deck", and a single, set mousetrap; they appear to be holding the dragons off. Meanwhile, in the sky, there are a series of randomly angular dotted lines tracking the movement of three flies that had unexpectedly landed on the paper as

Landscape: Eleven Footballers Scoring with Many Cows Mooing and a Pretty Dolly: She Has Gone Astray, 1993

Earnshaw was drawing. The chance encounter had prompted a digression apt to the drawing's narrative.

An alternative form of our defence than aircraft carriers is proposed by Earnshaw in 'Aerial Warfare: Good Fairies Turning Evil German Aeroplanes Into Frogs: circa 1940'. Armed with only wands and wings, squadrons of fairies neutralise a 1940s

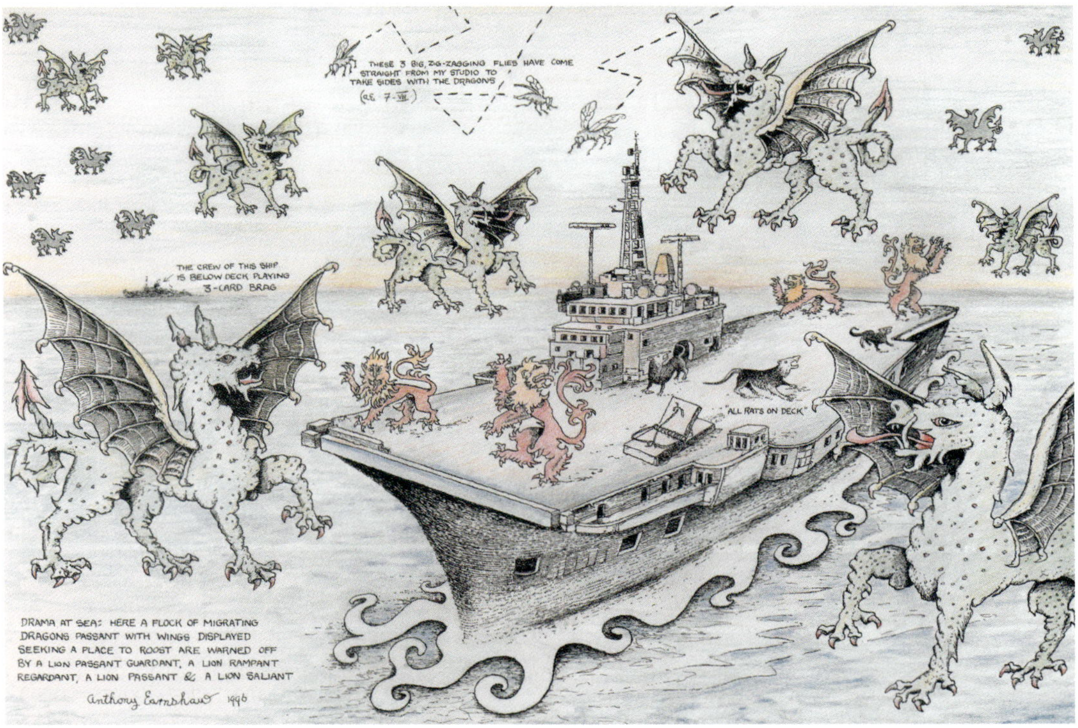

bombing raid by casting spells on the planes thereby turning them into green frogs. In a related piece—'Bees Visit the Fairies Palace: Fairies Visit the Hive'(1988), he proposes a benign weapons' inspection to remove the threat of stockpiling harmful stings and spells—ensuring a peaceful co-existence.

"Incidentally", Earnshaw recalled, "in 1940 the German Air Force dropped stick bombs on Saltburn, one of which landed on the allotment opposite Granny's house. The explosion blew all the tiles off the roof and shattered the windows. I figure Hitler must have thought he stood no chance of winning the war as long as Saltburn-by-the-Sea still stood on the map."[3] These drawings show Earnshaw as a perceptive observer of everyday life and a humorous, but caustic, commentator.

Drama at Sea, 1996

"To move out of this purposeful world one need only take a few paces to the side to find one has entered another facet of the same reality, the world of dark corners and neglect, sounds are subdued and one assumes the role of a sinister watcher."[4]

Media hype, stifling social attitudes, discrimination of all

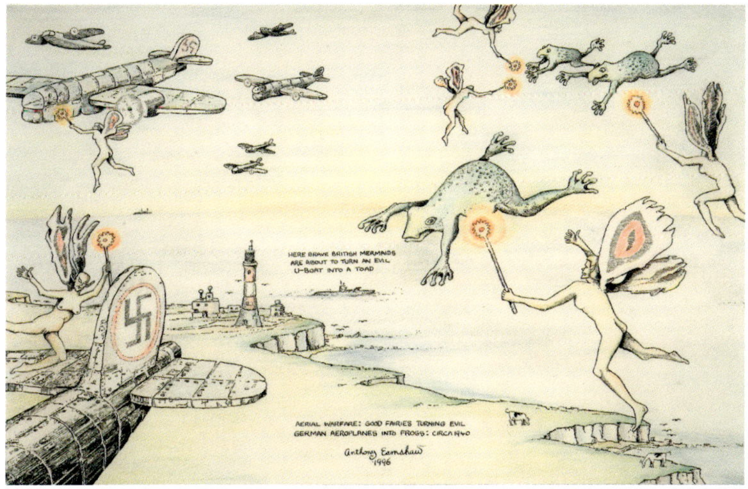

Aerial Warfare, 1996

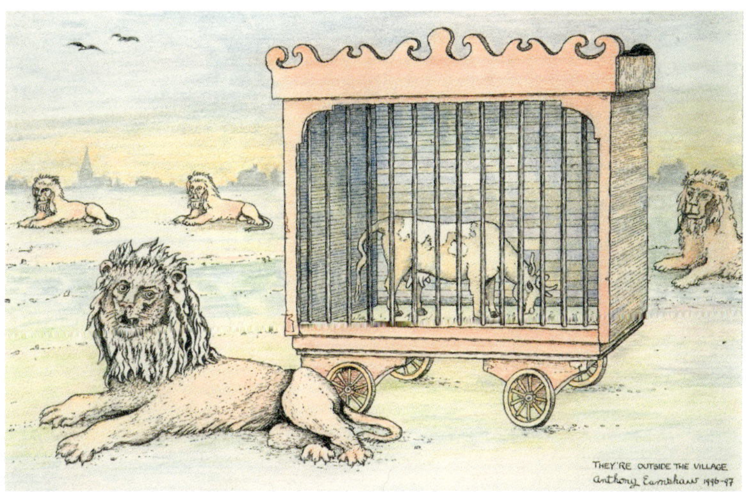

They're Outside the Village, 1996–97

kinds, imposed authority and encroachments on individual freedom by powerful commercial and institutional interests were all targets to be sniped at. Earnshaw's off-centre lens focussed on a critique of events both large and small, which he stored away as ammunition for his personal resistance movement.

In a reversal of roles, a docile cow grazes, locked up in a

circus lion cage, while the big beasts stretch out in the open fields enjoying their freedom. In 'They're Outside of the Village', Earnshaw questions the relative values applied to crime and punishment, where the powerful have the right to roam and are given the Freedom of the City, while the small fry are securely locked up.

'Mickey Mouse in dispute with Karl Marx and F. Engels' is possibly a comment on Walt Disney's refusal to have any employee representation in his animation studio. 'The Bird of Ill-Omen' depicts the media's endless obsession with the single parent and has mothers pushing prams down the street containing baby albatrosses. In 'Two factories and a Teddy Bear' both compete as playthings for their owners and share-holders.

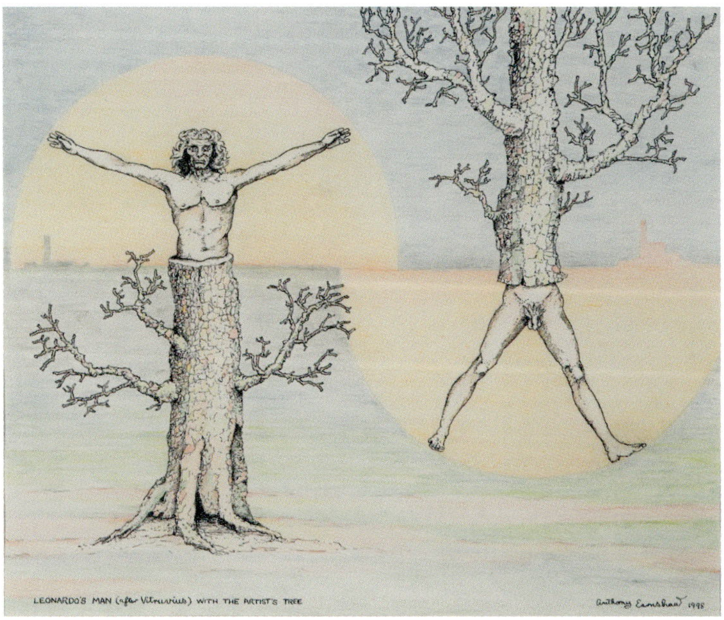

Leonardo's Man (after Vitruvius) With The Artist's Tree, 1998

In a satire on universal proportion and the quest for exactitude, 'Leonardo's Man (after Vitruvius) With The Artist's Tree', Earnshaw takes Leonardo's famous drawing of an encircled human figure with his arms outstretched, and proceeds to cut it in half at the waist. The upper half of the body is grafted onto the lower part of a tree trunk and the bottom half supports the unruly upper branches.

The two resulting tree-figure hybrids are juxtaposed against an industrial horizon. Earnshaw's creative contribution picks up where Leonardo left off. He clearly demonstrate that there is still a lot of work to be done on the analogy of the human body and the workings of the universe and the notion of man as a measure of all things. Earnshaw would probably say he was just trying to help.

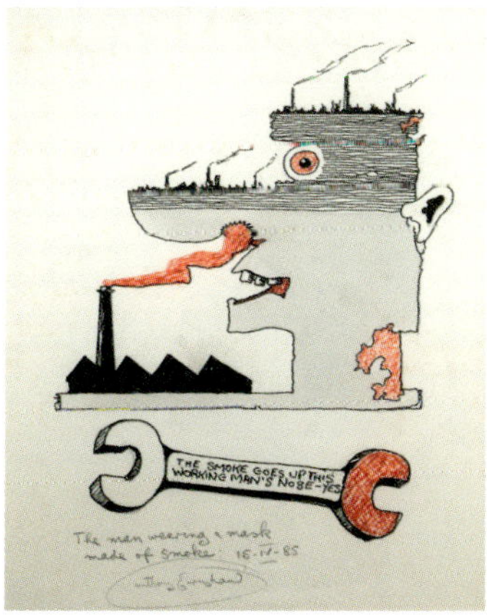

The Man Wearing a Mask Made of Smoke, 1985

There are a small series of pale ink and wash drawings started in the mid 1980s that look quite different to the others—in colour as well as in content. Their origins seem to have come from a variety of sources, including the engineering machinery watercolours Earnshaw produced in the late 1950s and early 1960s and the science fiction novels he read during the same period. They are composed of corroded machine casings, levers, control knobs, ventilation ducts and outlet covers. These parts reform themselves into semi-anthropomorphised figures and structures, existing in bleak landscapes with industrial smoke-filled horizons.

Figures appear throughout the series wearing red and black striped trousers and heavy boots. Devilish operators with spikes for tongues turn knobs and levers, while 'The Man Wearing a Mash of Smoke' inhales the 'intoxicating' pollution from a factory chimney. Cattle are caught up in this nightmare as part of a relentless industrial and agricultural decline. They are dream machines but look intent on total control.

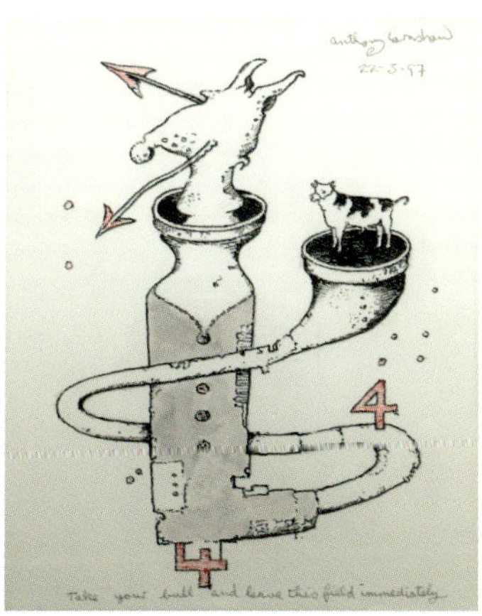

Take Your Bull and Leave This Field Immediately, 1997

The promenade at the bottom of the street in Saltburn where Earnshaw lived had a view of the industrial chemical works of ICI in Middlesborough—a metallic city of pipes, funnels and fumes working day and night.

Earnshaw ended up in hospital in 1994, describing in a letter as having "passed through a very frightening experience".[5] A long-suffering victim of bronchitis, he took new medication to cope with an asthma related chest illness. This brought about an anaphylactic shock which almost killed him—"the enemy was on the way to victory—my death!"[6] During this ordeal he describes the visual effects of the medication—"all I could see was a screen of intense sky blue with shimmering flecks of silver—was it the eye of God with his multitudinous host of angels? After that came the same blue screen—this time with abstract scarlet shapes dancing and moving rapidly in all directions at once—imps and devils inviting me to join them?"[7]

Fortunately Earnshaw did not, preferring instead a stay at the South Cleveland Hospital in Middlesborough.

These experiences feature in a series of drawings that centre around the character of Eve. The backdrops to these visionary drawings are winged angels who form a repeat pattern that suggest depth, hovering in the vibrant blue sky. The angels have their hands together praying—perfect models of piety.

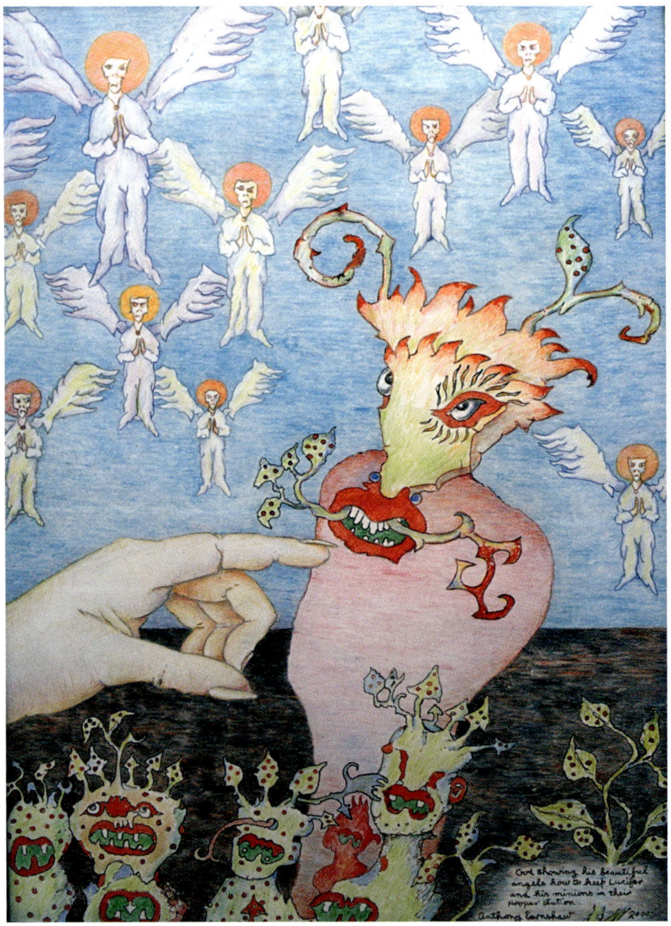

God Showing His Beautiful Angels How to Keep Lucifer and His Minions in Their Proper Station, 2000

Eve, on the other hand, in 'Eve Showing Her Pretty Legs to Some Nngels' flaunts her flesh at the heavenly host wearing only a single flowery garter. She has stiletto heels on her feet that are part of her natural anatomy, bestowed at the moment of creation. 'God Showing His Beautiful Angels How to Keep His Minions in Their Proper Station,' shows Lucifer with a flaming head. He has a bird-like beak which, in turn, is holding a human mouth with teeth gripping an obscure form of plant life. His minions, who are minding Lucifer, resemble the cartoon germs that typically appear in the dirty bathrooms of television disinfectant commercials—one wipe and they would be done for! God's large hand lays down the law by poking Lucifer in the chest. The minions look up fearfully, realising who really is in charge.

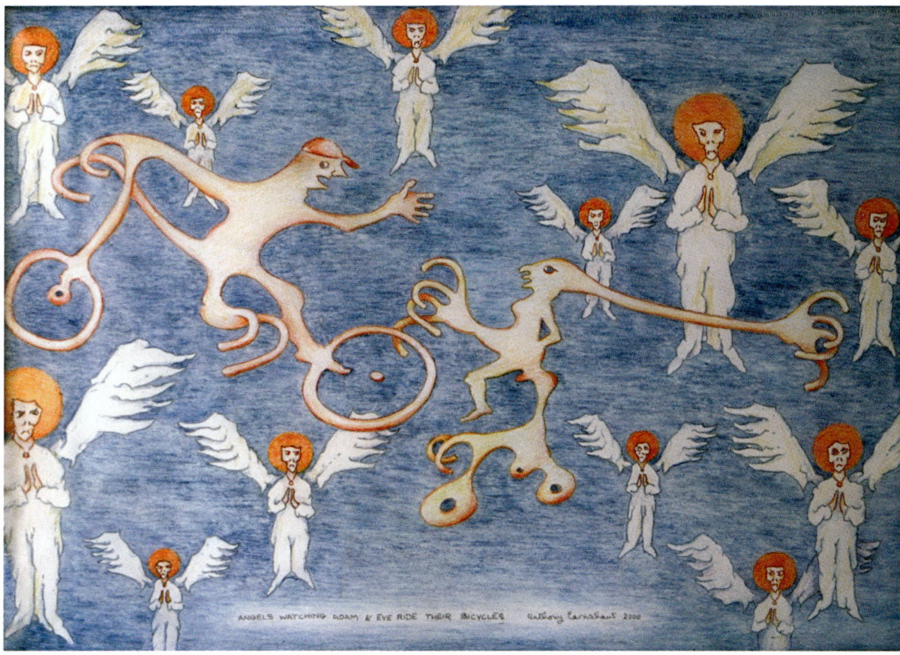

In a drawing from 2000—'Angels Watching Adam & Eve Ride Their Bicycles'. The pair seem to be made of a mellifluous string of ectoplasm in which bikes and cyclists are joined. They speed past the angels, Adam waving, as they journey across the sky.

In 1992 Earnshaw, in collaboration with Ian Breakwell, proposed an exhibition entitled 'Portraits of The Artist's Mother Done From Memory'. The proposal raised the question of "whether an objective visual portrait of one's mother is possible from the reference of personal memory which is based on a subjective, multi-sensory 'picture of the mother'".[8] 'In Memorium: Dorothy Rose Earnshaw nee Myers: (Born 1891–Died 1963)', was Earnshaw's contribution. His mother appears four times in the painting; standing poised to dive on the end of the high diving board at the Redcar Lido, in mid-dive, then

Angels Watching Adam & Eve Ride Their Bicycles, 2000

walking by the pool in bright yellow stiletto heels with a young Tony dressed in a belted, green raincoat and, finally, as a large head and shoulders portrait at the forefront of the picture. Dorothy, in large green hat and pearls, stares intensely out, head tilted. Silhouettes of merchant ships cross the horizon while a flying gull

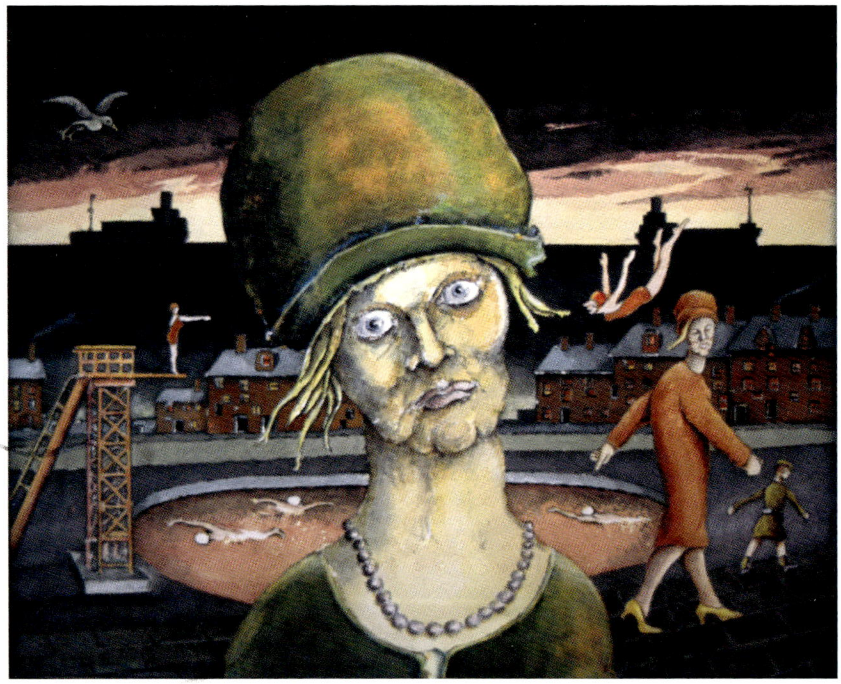

In Memorium: Dorothy Rose Earnshaw nee Myers: (Born 1891–Died 1963)

appears on the left. The painting is a portrait of the artist's mother and a self-portrait of himself as a child. By including his mother four times Earnshaw's portrait implies the compression of time.

A much older Earnshaw riding his bike featured in a double self-portrait watercolour painted in the same year—1992, entitled 'I am riding my H. Rench, waving goodbye to myself: night is falling, Leeds is over the hill and far away, the woman is diving, the gull is speeding to Redcar'.

The diving figure appears again referring to the artist's mother once more. The seagull harks back to Earnshaw's first brush with death—walking on Redcar beach. As he cycles down the road he turns to look over his shoulder. On the jumper of the main older self-portrait, foreground left, there is a question written—"What is it coming quickly down the road behind my back? The rat is staring at it."

Earnshaw's painting resembles a visual synopsis, depicting details from his life. The narrowing road alludes to the passing of time while an unknown future approaches. This prophetic self-portrait with its darkening sky, is an elaborate, yet transparent metaphor, that leaves the viewer suspended in mid-air.

I Am Riding My H. Rench, Waving Goodbye to Myself, 1992

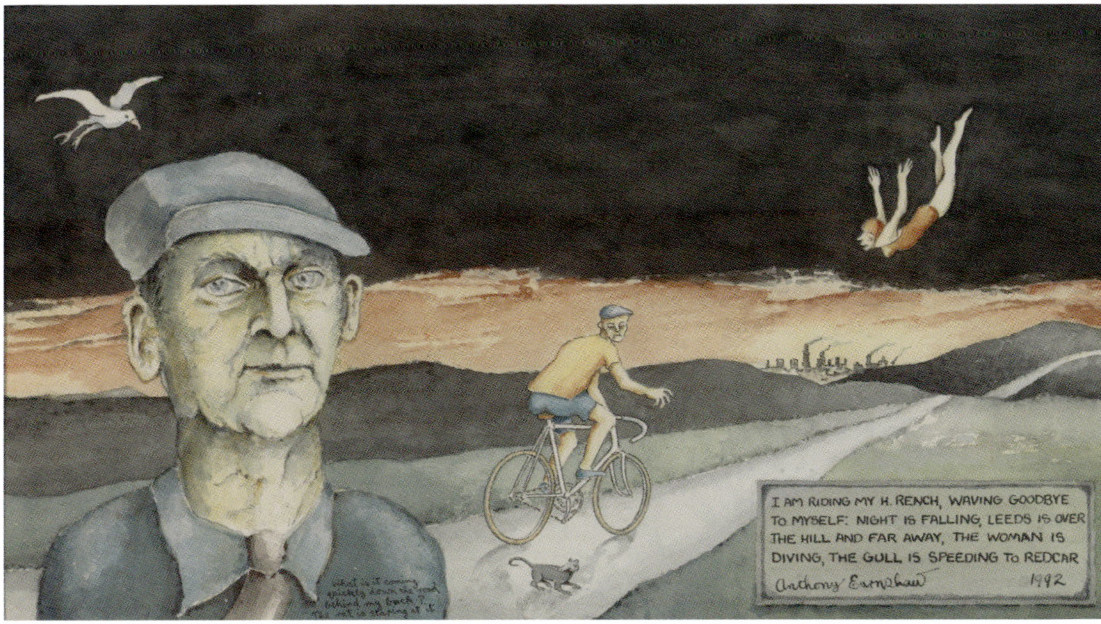

Notes

1. John Slyce, '1978–2000: The Boxed Earnshaw', *Anthony Earnshaw*, Flowers East, 2000
2. Jane Czyzeiska, 'When I Felt Like It', *Artist's Newsletter*, February 1998
3. Anthony Earnshaw, 'Come Out Boxing', unpublished text, 1992
4. Anthony Earnshaw, *Paintings 1945–1965*, Leeds Institute Gallery, Leeds, 1966
5. Letter to Ruth Earnshaw, 1994
6. *Ibid.*
7. *Ibid.*
8. Anthony Earnshaw and Ian Breakwell, unpublished text, 1992

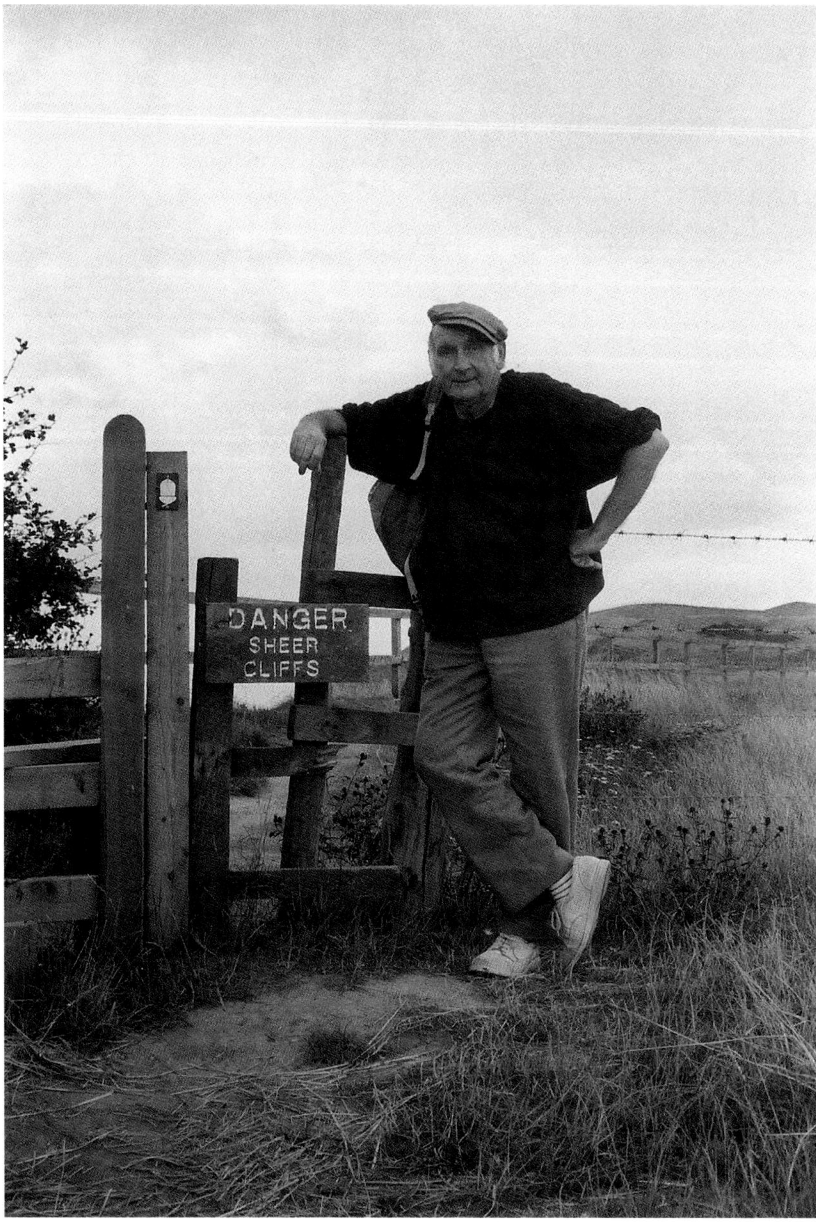

Saltburn-by-the-Sea, 1991

A Miscellany

Earnshaviana

Chris Vine

In the late 1960s Tony was teaching drawing on a textile design project at Bradford Art College. I was one of his students. I had drawn an unfurled flag being blown to the left by a strong breeze. Next to this was a similar flag being blown in the opposite direction by the same breeze.

Tony looked at it suspiciously. He said that it did not look convincing. "For a start, a flag doesn't flap like that. Also the pole is wrong and a flag has a rope attached to allow it to move up and down." I came back from breaktime to find several drawings of flags on my desk, all beautifully drawn by Tony. He pointed out for the drawing to work, the flags would have to look like proper flags as this would help sharpen the visual contradiction.

"For example," he said, "if you wanted to murder someone you wouldn't do it half-heartedly—you'd have to do the job properly. Make sure the knife was sharp and shiny. If your victim was at a dinner party, make sure your suit and bow-tie were freshly pressed and have a flower in your lapel. Have your knife hidden—don't have it clasped between your teeth, it would spoil the surprise. Mingle and chat with the other guests. Then, with a drink in your hand, slowly move around the party. And when you are facing your target, with one swift movement, stab your victim."

Peter Ellis

Les and I had been working hard putting up the exhibition in Liège. There were six artists taking part and we often worked until midnight to hang the show over the five days we had given ourselves.

On Friday afternoon, I was trying to hang one of Tony's boxed assemblages on an uneven wall when Tony and Gail and the other artists arrived for the opening. I was taking extra care hanging Tony's pieces because they were fragile and I had been told that Tony worried about his objects, their transport and safe keeping.

Tony came straight over to me to ask about his work I presumed.

"When's it coming down?"

"What?" I said blankly.

"When's the show coming down?"

I was sweaty, dusty and tired and this staccato interrogation took me somewhat by surprise as there was no comment about the hanging or the look of the show.

"But it's not gone up yet, Tony".

"But when's it gonna come down? I think that we should send Coleman back to pack it up and make sure everything's safe."

"We're still putting it up, Tony."

"I know, but when's it coming down? Let's get Coleman to take it down and pack it safely. He's good."

"But it has not fucking well gone up yet Tony".

"Let's get Les to bring it back, don't you think so, though?"

"Yeah", I said.

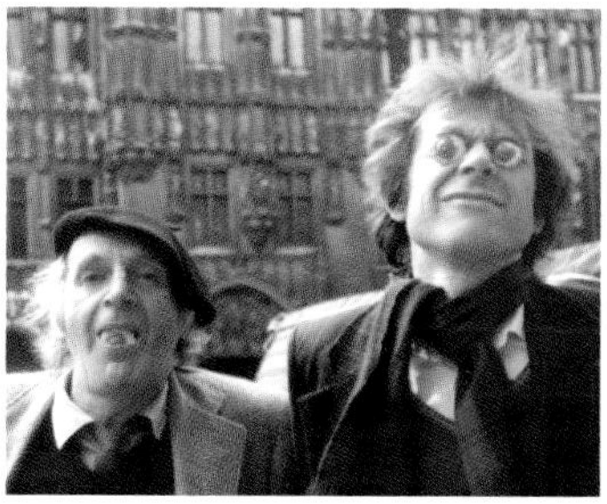

A.E. and Les Coleman, Brussels, 1984

Patrick Hughes

Instead of shoplifting Earnshaw liked to shop-drop. He was proud of being able to substitute picnic mustard or artist's white oil paint for brand-new toothpaste that he had bought, and then to surreptitiously return the toothpaste to the shelves of Boots the chemists to cause consternation to whomsoever bought it. He sometimes sent a letter with a stamp on it but the stamp was the head of Mr Gillette cut from a packet of razor blades. The postman always delivered it. I like the story of Earnshaw only having one glass of wine in the pub. Gail went round after he died, and they showed her how big the glass was, one of those display glasses as big as a vase.

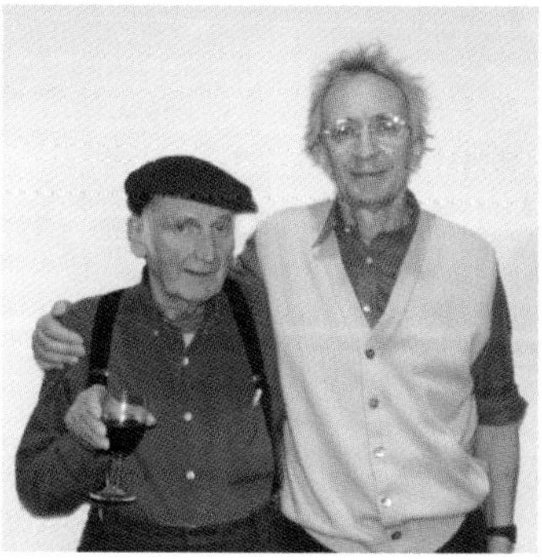

A.E. and Patrick Hughes, London, 2000

John Hyatt

In Leeds in 1980, there used to be some extraordinary meetings involving the Polytechnic fine artists and the University fine artists. The idea was to bring students and staff from both institutions together so a talk could be delivered from which debate, of a polemical nature, would ensue. The Marxist-brigade from the University and the Nietzcheans and poets of the Poly caused a volatile mix, often erupting in some verbal mudslinging.

The main instigator of these evenings from the Poly was Geoff Teasdale supported by Jeff Nuttall and from the University, ex-Art and Language artist, Terry Atkinson. T. J. Clarke, the Marxist social historian of art, was head at the University at a time when both Marxism and feminism were a significant part of the climate within art education. I was a student at the University at the time and seen to be one of a group of 'intellectual guerrillas' by my Poly counterparts.

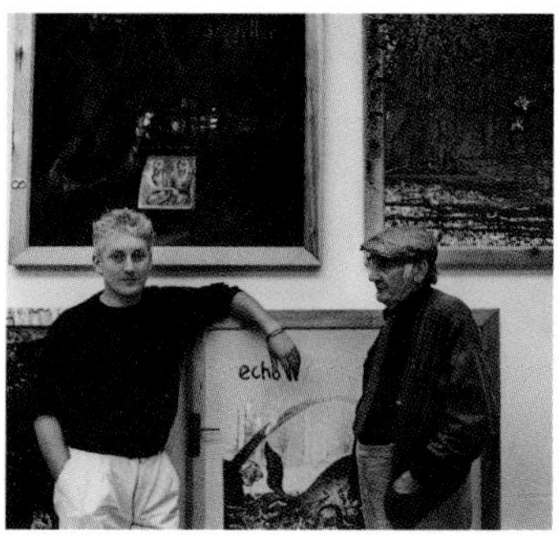

John Hyatt and A.E., Sheffield, 1991

On one of these occasions there were about thirty of us from both camps sitting on plastic seats in an otherwise empty room on the fourth-floor of H-Block at Leeds Polytechnic. Terry Atkinson was talking intently about Marx's theories of surplus value. Suddenly, a man wearing a cap stood up from the second row to intervene on the opposite side of the circle and said, "Well I think Marx was a cunt! Eh? Marx was a cunt!"

In spite of this provocative interjection Atkinson did not break stride, although he acknowledged the comment. "Well you might be right, Tony, in the way that he treated his wife and that." He then carried on as though nothing had happened. That was all Tony said that evening but it stuck in my memory. It was my first encounter with Tony Earnshaw. I took to him instantly. Over the years we became firm friends. Not surprisingly the Marx story became a favourite of mine to recount.

Twelve years later, Tony and I were both teaching Illustration part-time for Dudley Edwards at Cleveland College of Art and Design. We taught on alternate weeks. One week, by an oversight on Tony's behalf, we both ended up teaching together and spent the evening drinking with a group of friends in the Ship Inn on the seafront at Saltburn-by-the-Sea. We were telling stories about absent drunken friends and discussing art and politics when Tony said, out of the blue, "Well I think Marx was a count". I said, "Say that again, Tony." "I said, I think Marx was a count and Bakunin was some sort of lord or something." I said, "Do you realize that for twelve years, you have been famous for saying Marx was a cunt?"

Tony was not amused.

Tony Blundell

A letter I received from Tony sent 19.7.80 recounted how he had recently met a young American student from St Louis, Mississippi, at Leeds University. "Not only has he never heard, but he has never heard of, 'St Louis Blues'… I think I'll shoot him!"

Jean Thacker

We were going to London for a meeting at the publisher Jonathan Cape. Eric and I lived in Shipley, West Yorkshire at the time and I carefully packed an overnight bag. We drove to Leeds to pick up Tony who emerged from his flat with his usual grin, his sole luggage being a bright red toothbrush tucked into his top pocket. Eric's death had a profound effect upon Tony, and yet we would all hope for a friendship such as theirs to enrich our lives. If it were Eric speaking above all else he would have said, "Tony was my friend".

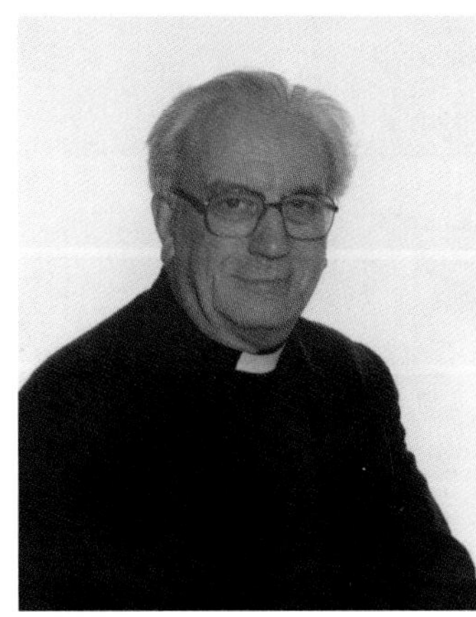

Eric Thacker

Les Coleman

During the course of my friendship with Tony he sent me many letters and postcards. The letters were often illustrated while the postcard images were sometimes altered with witty additions. Many were posted while on visits with Gail to the Yorkshire Dales, "God's country", as he called it. Being friends of Patrick Oliver they had access to his father's cottage Foss Gill at Starbotton in Wharfedale. Patrick's father Bill Oliver was the *Yorkshire Post* art critic of some thirty-year's standing, and it was always understood that on these holidays rent would be settled

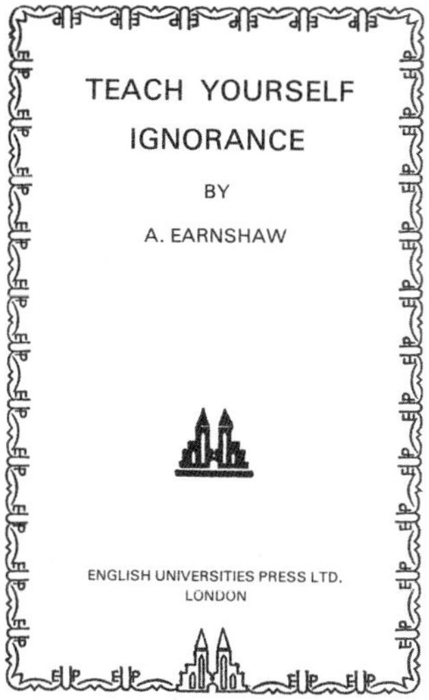

Teach Yourself Ignorance, postcard, 1979

with the gift of a drawing or collage, rather than money.

In 1979 I published Tony's *Teach Yourself Ignorance* as a postcard in my set of 'DisCards'. It was agreed between Tony and myself payment would be a percentage of the print run. Within days of receiving the finished cards Tony sent me this response:

> Dear Les,
> They're lovely. I've sent one to *everybody*. This summer I'm going to sell them on Blackpool prom' and clean-up a million bucks!
> Next week I'll look into outlets. By all means let me know when you're up... we'll get pissed!
> Love T.

Liz Berry

I remember attending Eric Thacker's funeral with Tony. The day did not start well. Gail's car had had its window smashed, so breakfast was cut short and we had to dispatch the car to a nearby garage. We boiled the eggs and ate them en route to Leeds. I noted that Tony was much more dismayed by the fact that I had forgotten the salt, than the state of the car.

Paul Hammond

It must have been the late 1970s when Earnshaw told me of an idea he'd had for a film. It was to be a very short short, since it would consist of a single shot, a single gag. A static camera would film a mousehole in a skirting board at the base of a wallpapered wall, before which the lines of a series of floorboards would radiate. A baited mousetrap—a quintessential Earnshaw prop, as testified to by many a box of his—might well have sat on said floor, although it's a detail I don't remember Tony mentioning, and which I'm adding off my own bat. Nothing would happen in this micro stage set; all would be still beneath the arc lights. That very stillness would nevertheless create a certain tension: when was the mouse to appear? And then from out of the dark semi-circular hole a goldfish would emerge, defy gravity, exit the image at its top edge.

Earnshaw intended to construct his decor inside an

aquarium and to have the edges of the film frame fall well within the confines of the tank, thus ensuring that the latter was invisible to the viewer. The aquarium would be full of water, which when behind glass is forever still, invisible, tantamount to air. A fish would be released at the back of the pseudo wall. It would swim through the mousehole in the direction of the light, and into shot.

At times I have fantasised about making this filmlet myself, in homage to Tony. I've a craving to see it. It's a delight, the idea.*

As an idea, it has something about it that is typical of a beginner to filmmaking, whose own first steps, wittingly or unwittingly, retread those of the pioneers—Méliès, say. Indeed, the movie magician shot several "reconstructed newsreels" of the sinking of the U.S. battleship 'Maine' during the Spanish-American War of 1898: a visit by divers to the wreck on the seabed—a painted backdrop—is lent verisimilitude by the fish that swim before them, for Méliès had interposed a large aquarium between camera lens and stage set.

*Since first writing about the above, I've heard that Chris Vine and other students of Tony's in Bradford actually made the movie, although it has not, alas, survived.

Frances Earnshaw

Sometime in 1990 my father sent me a postcard with the following news: "...I'm working on a new piece: I found a fossil shell on the beach. I'm told it is perhaps 180,000,000 years old and I'm putting it with a plastic prehistoric monster toy, made in Hong Kong last year. They look alike, echo each other."

My father loved the surprising detritus of life and living near a beach he would often make promising finds for his work. Things ended up together, in uneasy juxtapositions in boxes, in numerous notebooks and in his mind.

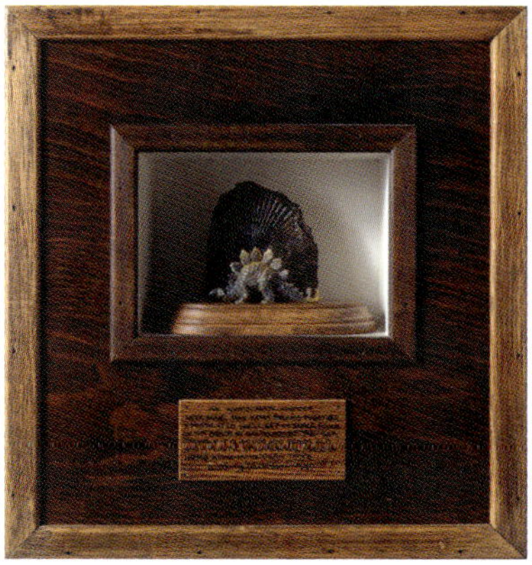

The Windscreen Whipper, 1990

Dudley Edwards

What struck me about Tony above all his other attributes, was his tremendous warmth and affection as a human being. Although he was content with his own company I felt that there was nothing he relished more than time spent in a pub with friends. If a thought came to Tony that in his mind was charged with humour, in his eagerness to share it he would grab your forearm in a vice-like grip and shake it repeating the joke two or three times, chuckling all the while while saying, "Do you know what I mean eh, what do you think, Dudley?" I recall one particular occasion when drinking with Tony when he noticed it was snowing outside, the kind of large snowflakes that float down in slow motion when it is still. Tony nudged me repeatedly saying, "Eh, Dudley, which one do you like best?" He was the only heterosexual Yorkshireman who told me he loved me. Having a similar background I can tell you northerners are very economical with words of affection. I heard a Yorkshire lass of Asian descent priming a couple of cousins before going out to a nightclub—they had just arrived from India. "Remember, if a Yorkshireman says, 'you're alright' with no discernible enthusiasm it means, 'I love you'." Tony would have liked that. He was also a very principled man, who would always stick up for the underdog. An anarchist to the end, I have a lasting memory of Tony, leaning out of the carriage window as the train left the platform at Middlesborough station, with clenched fist raised, shouting, "Up the Rebels."

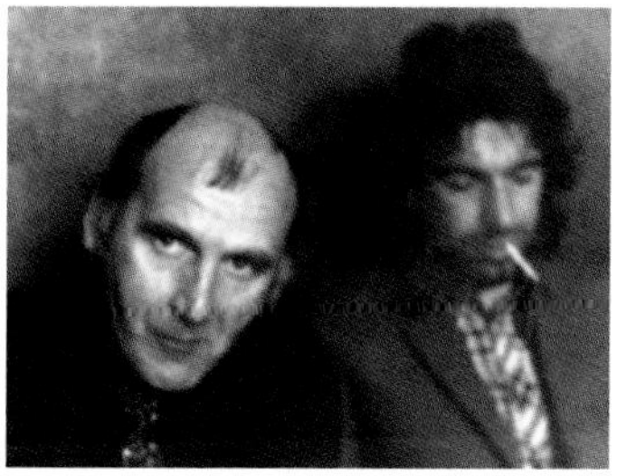

A.E. and Phil Shaw, London, 1981

Phil Shaw

"You must always, *always* look at the world upside down." Tony's advice to me as a student at Leeds College of Art in the early 70s.

Gail Earnshaw

'In Earnshaw's Pantry' consists of a large farmhouse loaf where a mousehole has been dug out of its side. Tony then placed a mousetrap, baited with cheese, next to the mousehole. Exhibited at the South Square Gallery, Thornton in 1985 it attracted the attention of three youths who had come into the gallery to get out of the rain. When they saw the bread work they were less than impressed. "I could have done that myself!" said one of them in a loud voice. Sensing trouble the gallery attendant kept an eye on them but before he could do anything the boys set about the work reducing it to something little more than a pile of crumbs. It became apparent when the youths refused to leave the gallery that a telephone call was necessary. "Hello, is that the police? This is South Square Gallery in Thornton and we are currently showing an exhibition of work and one piece has been vandalised by some youths who refuse to leave", at which point they scarpered.

"What's happened?" asked the police officer.

"One of the youths saw Anthony Earnshaw's bread assemblage and became incensed whereupon he karate chopped it into small pieces. Another youth sprang the mousetrap which was placed next to the mousehole in the loaf and the last lad ate the bait, namely a small lump of cheese."

"Goodness me!"exclaimed the police officer after a pause. "this is more serious than I thought. We're on our way now".

Later Tony rationalised the work's destruction: "It ceased to exist anymore as an actual object but I hope it will exist in their minds as something which provoked them beyond reason".

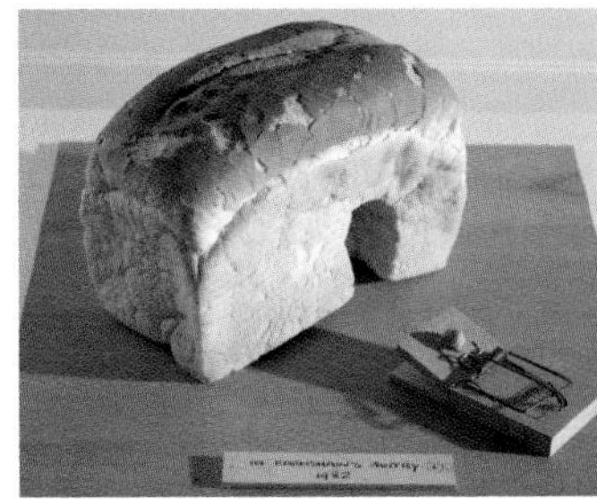

In Earnshaw's Pantry, 1982

Doug Binder

I first heard about Tony while giving a talk at my own exhibition in 1975 at the Cartwright Hall in Bradford. During proceedings I was interrupted by a member of the audience who seemed intent on making sure that I knew the existence of "The best artist around—Tony Earnshaw, a genius!"

Suitably admonished I wondered who this person could be. I would find out some years later when I was introduced to a droll, impish character, sporting a black beret and enjoying a pint of Tetley's bitter.

George Hainsworth

Tony and I worked together as lecturers and colleagues for many years. It was quite late in our teaching careers that I had confirmation that the respect I had long held for Tony's work was reciprocated. We were both prone to retreat on occasion to do a bit of *work* in the woodwork shop at Leeds Poly. Someone,

(I cannot remember who), commented on the fact that I was going to some trouble to frame one of my paintings: to the effect, why bother? On hearing this Tony pronounced, in that distinctive way he had, "Don't take any fucking notice George, you keep doing it."

Glen Baxter

I saw my first Tony Earnshaw when I was a student at Leeds College of Art. I remember being struck by his unique vision and feeling that I wanted to seek out the man who had made such fascinating work. The first things I saw were drawings of guillotines. They were dark and funny, tinged with a surrealist perspective and unlike anything I had ever seen at that time.

Years later I had the opportunity to visit Earnshaw and his wife Gail at their homes in Leeds and Saltburn. I stood in the centre of his studio, surrounded by a host of objects, unfinished collages and boxes—some just awaiting a final addition that would turn the whole thing into a piece of mystery and wonder. It was an Aladdin's cave right there in the heart of the city—a place of poetic reverie and mischief. The perfect setting.

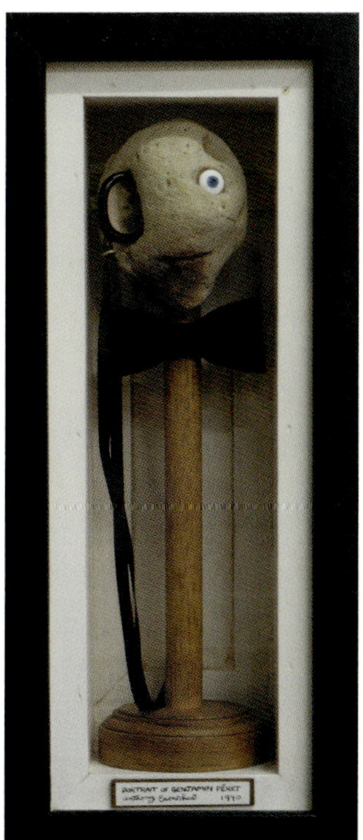

Portrait of Benjamin Péret, 1990

The twentieth century produced two artists who were masters of the box assemblages. Joseph Cornell and Tony Earnshaw, the former internationally renowned and the latter virtually unknown and overlooked even in his own native land.

Whereas Cornell's work is shot through with a melancholic yearning for a lost age of beauty, a world of Medici princes, Russian ballerinas, fragments of an Age of Romance and the faded grandeur of French hotels lost in the mists of time, Earnshaw's work is the polar opposite, provocative, infused with a mordant wit and redolent of a much grittier world. This is the northern industrial landscape, dark, mysterious and, as depicted by this artist, a place of resounding absurdity and menace. Earnshaw was never influenced by Cornell, even stating that as a Christian Scientist, the American artist could never embrace the true surrealist spirit. There is a long Earnshaw box, dated winter 1991, titled: 'As commuters gather on the outskirts of the town the neighbourhood idiot, believing himself to be the ghost of a wild animal, gazes at the head of an old friend, now a trophy hanging on a distant wall, and yearns for the spring to come to the carpark', which depicts what seems at first sight to be a mundane suburban commuting scene but on closer inspection turns out to be closer to the spirit of Samuel Beckett, its title forcing us to engage with a darker undercurrent which belies the clarity of its presentation. How Earnshaw achieves this unnerving presence is in itself remarkable. A series of everyday objects, miniature figures and toy railway lines are seen slightly out of kilter. It is like wandering into one of the scenes in 'Last Year at Marienbad'. Inexplicable and enthralling.

These are the qualities in Earnshaw's work that, whilst questioning the status quo and adopting a stance of defiance, also somehow manage to delight with their poetic resonance and transport us to the enchanted world in which he lived and of which we have now become a part.

John Bell

In 2000 Tony and I decided to reprint his *Flick Knives and Forks*, first published by John Lyle in 1981 and long since sold out. Using the original illustrations but a new design and layout, the second edition was printed and Tony came round to Thirsk Hall to sign and number the 500 copies. Tony's wife Gail was given an orange crayon and the job of being carrot-colourist; it is her handywork you see encouraging the unicorn on the front cover.

I passed the first copy to Tony, who carefully removed the cap from his fountain-pen and with the utmost deliberation signed and numbered it before handing it back to me. He had written:

Anthony Earnshaw 239/500

"Well, you didn't expect me to start at number one, did you?" Tony continued signing copies, picking numbers at random. I soon gave up trying to keep track to avoid duplicates and Tony soon gave up signing altogether.

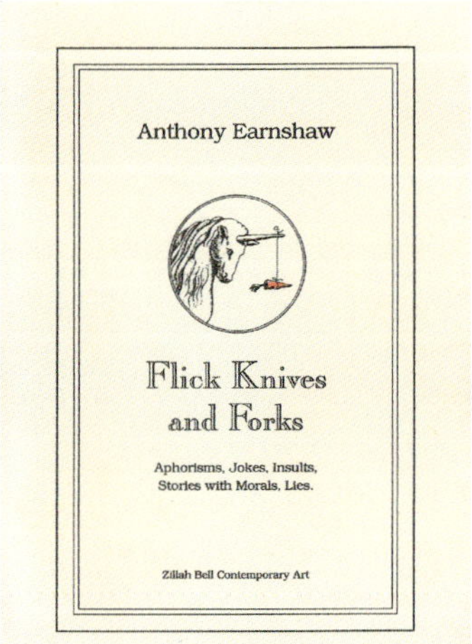

Flick Knives and Forks, 2000

Jack Chesterman

We worked together at Leeds Polytechnic which later morphed into the Metropolitan University, he in Fine Art and myself at the time in printmaking. Our printmaking workshops offered Tony a haven for quiet industry as he rolled out editions of his Secret Alphabets. As an ex-crane driver he liked the cogs, turning handles and the precision rollers of the big Milander offset presses. In particular he liked the whiff of ink, oil and turps which reminded him, he said, of similar smells in the steel works without the need to clock on.

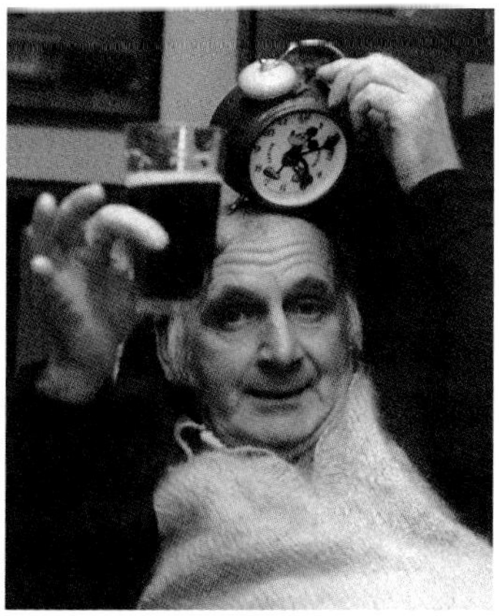

Leeds, c.1987

If working late we would at times repair to The Coburg. The pub's side room presented a kind of universal belvedere from which, if you sat there long enough, we thought you could see the whole world pass before you.

In those days before the sensible drink/drive laws, I would drive Tony back to No.1 Regent Street where the conversation grew more anarchic as we listened to his King Oliver, Armstrong and George Lewis 78s. Art school and traditional jazz seemed wedded at that time and our resident band, the Ed O'Donnell New Orleans Jazz Band, had a loyal following, ourselves included.

The scene now moves to a packed college lecture theatre. We are all there to bask in the wisdom of an eminent apologist of the postwar New York schools of painting. The talk, high on ego and short on wisdom, followed a relentless tedium of name dropping; "Barnett Newman when he visited our house said… While walking across Central Park with Rauschenberg… Talking to Dine in his studio… Morris Louis once told me…" The dreadful litany was only broken when Tony lifted his arm and asked the speaker: "Do you know Mickey Mouse?"

Michael Randle

I became closely involved with Tony through publishing his book *25 Poses,* a series of full frontal male nudes in various settings, with funny insightful captions. The original drawings had gone on display at Bradford College of Art but when the principal, Fred Coleclough, saw them he ordered them to be taken down. It was an open secret that he was having a relationship at the time with an attractive, lively young female working in the college library, and the next issue of an occasional college magazine, which I produced, featured a strip cartoon contributed by one of the students. It depicted in the first two or three frames the top half of the be-suited, pipe-smoking principal carefully examining the pictures on display, with a running caption reading: "It's not that I personally find the drawings objectionable..." and a final frame revealing him naked from the waist down striding towards a door marked Library with the caption concluding "but I have to think of my female members of staff". (His actual words when ordering Tony's drawings to be removed.) I gather from the librarian that both she and Coleclough, far from taking offence, were highly amused by the cartoon.

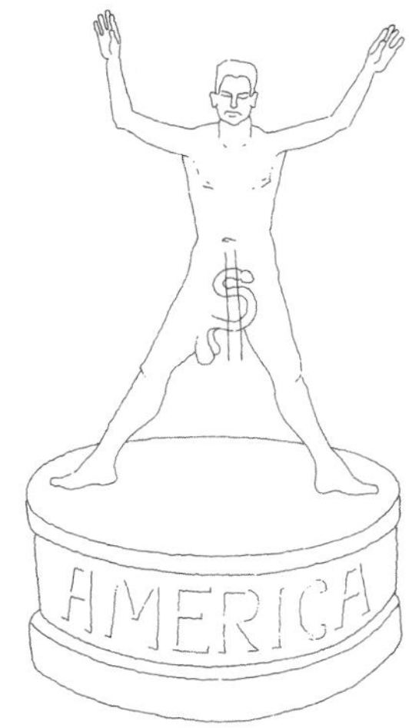

America, previously unpublished, 1972

Sonny Hayes

Tony arrived by train at Bradford where he had taught for many years. Buildings in Bradford had been besieged by massive flocks of starlings for some time and Tony was delighted to see an intrepid hunter, presumably employed by the council, shooting down the civic pests from their perches in the station. Tony suggested to the hunter it would be more effective to employ the services of a golden eagle and relinquish his air rifle. The hunter pointed out, "Yeah, but then the station would be covered in golden eagle shit".

I recall Tony and I reflecting on his work 'Lost Property' made from combs that he had found lying on the streets over a period of one month. We decided that there must be a vast warehouse somewhere where *everything* that was ever lost, was kept. We imagined that magician's assistants, whilst vanished, would sojourn there temporarily. We pictured them smoking, chatting idly and perhaps nonchalantly filing their nails, until they would be needed back on stage.

The truth is I remember little of what was said, only the joy and fascination we felt. To quote Robin Page, Tony's contemporary, 'I don't recall anything that Tony and I talked about. I only know there were moments of genius".

John Welson

I was aware of Tony's work for almost twenty years, exhibiting alongside him in the 70s and 80s, before we actually met. The occasion was the opening of his show 'Pay Attention & Assemble in Orderly Rows, or Else' at Flowers East in 1989. One of the 'gallery groupies', as he referred to some of the visitors, was overheard saying, "oh darling… this stuff is so much fun, so silly." Tony turned, and looking straight at the 'groupie' said, "You should be on the wall, you're silly."

On discovering that I lived and worked in London he saw geography as the cause for our not meeting earlier, saying "Leeds and London are a long way apart in many ways." But distance did not appear to create the same problem when he told me, "I could see the surrealists in Paris from the top of that crane I worked on."

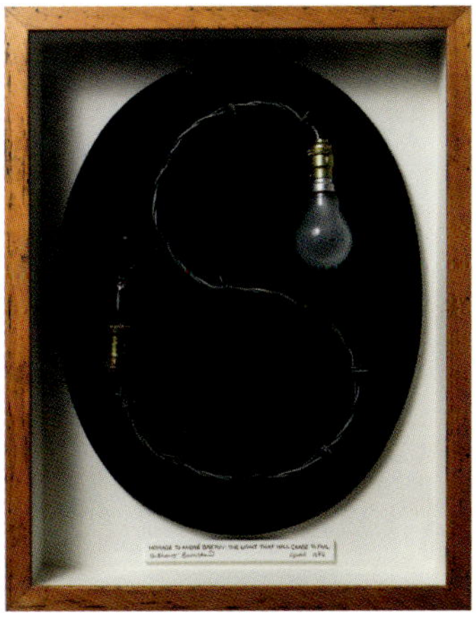

Homage to André Breton: the Light That Will Cease to Fail, 1989

Marie-Odile Gain d'Enquin

When in 1989 I invited Tony to illustrate a collection of my poems 'Clock Lips', translated by Peter Wood and to be published by Hourglass, he happily provided me with seven drawings. This was not without making his own suggestions as to the collection's title and the wording of the poem 'Will Power'. One of the stanzas in the poem reads:

> The pirates came out of the taverns,
> reach the arboretum, with handkerchiefs
> Tied round their torches.

A postcard from Tony reads: "Will Power, 'handkerchiefs' (tied round their torches). Handkerchiefs is a very middle-class term, the common people call them 'snot rags'—snot—nose dirt… pirates would have snot rags tied round their torches, unless, that is, they were bourgeois pirates!" Tony liked to think of his drawings as "secretive and obscure" and complementing my poetry well.

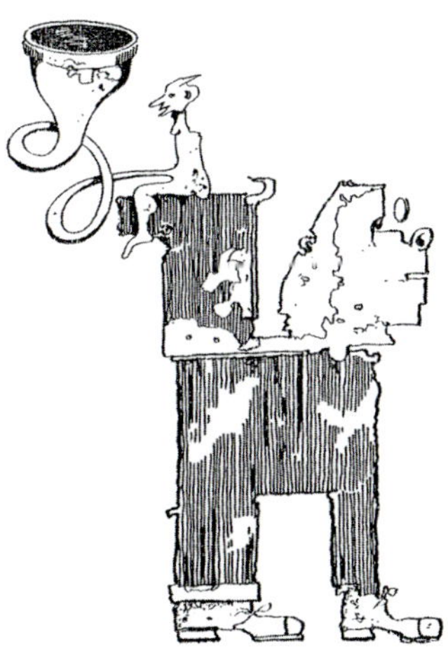

Untitled drawing, *Clock Lips*, 1989

Wedgwood Steventon

Descending into the depths of a Paris Metro station we came across an unfortunate asleep under piles of rags half hidden in a corner. Tony turned to examine the individual and pointing a finger pronounced the diagnosis: "Dead".

On my first walk on the pier at Saltburn we came across a worn and rusted iron railing, once grand, now near its final days. On seeing it Tony's eyes lit up as he proceeded to caress its remains. With his affection and understanding for decay in the inanimate and the way that objects can be discarded, Tony spoke of his desire to take it home and "love and look after it".

Stephen Wierczewski

After Tony's burial in Saltburn cemetery I was asked to drive George Melly to the wake held in the Britannia pub on the seafront. I was driving my low-slung BMW sports car, so it was difficult for George to fit himself in. As we drove away from the cemetery I glanced over to see if George was okay, I was not sure if the look of apprehension on his face was to do with the sad proceedings we had just attended, or because of being squeezed into my car. George turned to me slowly and said in his characteristic deep voice, "Well, the worms will be eating old Earnshaw now." Somewhat taken aback and trying to lighten the atmosphere I replied,"But his work is a death defying act and will live on". After a short pause, George asked me which was my favourite Earnshaw. I replied that it was his box 'The Secret Weapon' (p.96). I particularly admire the bathos of the paper boat defiantly flying the skull and crossbones.

Some months later Gail and I were visiting the seaside town of Whitby and she told me of Tony's wish to fly the skull and crossbones from the roof of every house he had ever lived in. As we walked along, I spotted a shop selling skull and crossbone flags and I went in and bought several. When we returned to Saltburn I decided to fly one on Tony's grave. Over the next few weeks the flag defiantly remained in place. Then one day it disappeared. Was this an act of disapproval or just the wind? Of course, I immediately replaced it with another.

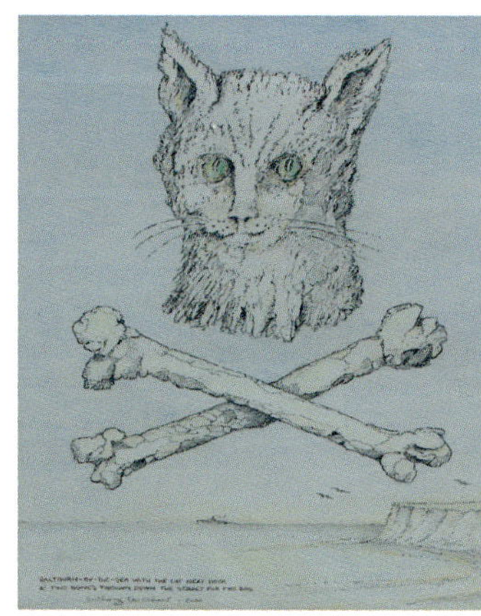

Saltburn-by-the-Sea With the Cat Next Door & Two Bones Thrown Down the Street For the Dog, 2000

Anthony Earnshaw

Collected Writings

The First Cuckoo

Total silence and the act of suicide stand on equal footing. A tenuous thread binds them in the eye of Desolation. The eye blinks once and all thought of future life, of carrying on with the game beyond this point is dismissed—wiped off without trace. The eye blinks twice and behold! There looms the jungle, airless, flashy yet ancient, vast as an empty warehouse, more primitive than the graffiti scratched by tramps on walls in the outer districts, and QUICK WITH MENACE.

The man standing in the clearing has come halfway across the world to arrive at this unlikely spot. Now, it is his intention to do one of three things: to shoot himself, to jump from a high window, or to swallow poison. He will choose which it is to be within the hour. "If this wilderness were for sale who would be the lucky bargain hunter?" he quips, and pushes on...

Beyond the jungle, or, it may be, contained within its bounds, lies the swamp. Frisky neighbours they make too, ever respectful of each other's domain, ever wary lest the one encroaches on the other. Here, silence reigns. The lagoons are silent, the groves are silent, the entanglements and thickets are silent, and all is silent, until broken by the crack of a pistol or the cry of a falling figure or the gagging and writhing of the self-poisoner.

Among a jungle's highlights, a wild beast's lair must rank as a star attraction. It was to one of these that the man, albeit bedraggled and weary, now came. Having gained entry (it was only a cave) he shooed away the deadly little snakes and spiders. "They are not a threat, nothing to worry over," he told himself, and sat crossed-legged on the dirt. "So," he thought, "this is the place. No qualms, no regrets: I'll kill myself here."

In solitude, he draws breath to mouth a strange song, one gauged to soar above the din of industry or a city's racket, and rest a nod from the very Sirens themselves, not to mention King Fool and his buffoon! The song peters out and becomes a formless croon, then a drone. A quondam notion sneaks to mind bringing with it memories of the time when, as a young rebel living in a brash northern town—every street boasted a thousand rooms TO LET—he amused himself with secret games, games devised during those all-too-fleeting moments of imaginative lucidity. For example, the time he pilfered a tube of toothpaste from Woolworth's, took it home, carefully washed out the contents under a running tap, and refilled it with artist's oil paint (Titanium White it was, he remembered—a messy job…), wiped it clean, put it back in its carton and then, having returned to the store, slipped it back among the other cartons … a sort of shoplifter's revenge. Ah yes! Distraught days they had been. Of a sudden, the thought struck him that it had not been until his nineteenth birthday that he had heard tell of Paris.

But enough of that! The time had come to do it! Unsheathing his hunting knife (remember he is squatting in the depths of a jungle) he lingers a moment to see that the blade is sufficiently sharp, and then with a flick, his throat is cut. At the mouth of the cave jackals are gathering… Dinner is served.

Meanwhile, below the horizon, in that same brash northern town, it was the First Day of Spring. Fructify we! Fructify we! Down the gutter raged a torrent of rainwater alive with spawning salmon, young newts nuzzled tab ends in puddles, daffodils sprouted between the flagstones, bluebells between parked cars—even saucy violets peeked from buttonholes. (You can tell the pace of events by this.)

The town was aglow and beautiful. With one accord the traffic stopped to listen to the call of the first cuckoo.

First published: *Surrealist Transformaction,* no.6, 1972

Brooches for Typists

While eating a slice of bread he told me that no one, his parents apart ("I dismiss them: they count for nothing") knew his name. He explained how, after a brief childhood (when tutors drilled him to praise the virtues of Duty and Work, "the contents of a dead god's pockets", as he put it) and a games-free boyhood, he spied his fellow-men engaged in ignoble sciamachy, and concluded they had no need of him.

He slipped from view, "did without them," to use his words. The upshot was a youth spent in stealthy evasion, "like a fly in a dormitory."

"I ventured out at night, crouching behind low hedges, when bossy eyes looked elsewhere. I'm still at it. I keep on the move," he explained, "two nights here, a week there, my life is much the same as a criminal's, the difference being I have never committed a crime." (How, then, is he never without funds? I have yet to see his wallet empty. The pittance he receives as a silversmith barely pays for his drinks.)

On 20th January upon his return to Leeds from Glasgow, I went to meet him at the station. In the bar we settled with a whiskey apiece. "A good trip?" I asked—one has to be polite.

"I enjoyed every revolution of every wheel, every cigarette smoked. It's main line all the way with one stop at Carlisle where heavily-made-up women walk the platform, handbags snap open, slender luggage…"

"Enough of that" I interrupted. One must ward off intimacy.

I met him the following week. After a few drinks he muttered "I'm interested in colours." A person's reason for such an interest is important. The wrong reason can tax loyalty and replace esteem with scorn.

I have always held the symbolism of colour to be a trite device: red for danger, green for envy, and so on. All nonsense! For me, a certain leaden grey tinged with violet is the colour of danger, even as that wan ochre found in wrapping paper embodies the sentiment of envy.

I link either hard flashing colours (cutting blues) or devious, evasive greys with danger; that blue sky mingled with yellow sunlight gives green grass should stop us in our tracks. Bright colours teach us caution.

We each own colours in an intimate way, just as objects do. It is hard to recognize old, battered sofas that are not a particular shade of chocolate brown; faded, inconclusive and remote. Colours clothe the form of reality and make the secret seem austere; does not the Banner of Freedom include every conceivable and inconceivable hue? Is not the rainbow a mere shred from that banner?

Colours in motion shift and assume new chromatic values. Consider how those strings of off-red railway carriages we used to see took on a darker, browner aspect when seen at speed.

Colours have a power in their own right. At different times during the course of my life that have sprung unbidden from an untouched palette in my mind, not understood as hues so much as warning lights, premonitions of an oncoming illness or threat to my well-being. At other times these signals serve to distract my purpose and lull me into a condition of unwariness. As a result I undergo what can only be described as a perplexed flattening or elongation of perception.

Among my childhood memories I list black, mauve, pink and yellow as the colours uppermost in my mind. When a young man, I recollect red, grey, saffron, puce and blue giving a garish splash to my days. Now I am middle-aged I toy with green, turquoise, maroon and that shade, perhaps intensity is a better description, of khaki that has always seemed to me unplaceable, fugitive, a ghost bobbing up when least expected. This colour must be the shade of the eye of the Gorgon.

I wonder which colours will rule my mind as I lie on my deathbed…Whatever, they will be of little account. Colours are as bloodless as the promises of religion.

"Did you know Rin Tin Tin was a bitch?" McQueen's voice thrust a path through my reverie.

The corner keeps the secret, the lake guards the bend…

The following afternoon I called on McQueen at his lodgings. By now he had become the nine of diamonds to my ten of spades. That he was a craftsman, a silversmith, aroused my curiosity. "What is the work like?" I asked myself, "What goes on in the workshop?" I was determined to find out. Armed with a pocket tape-recorder, I sought his confidence. Regrettably, the machine was not in working order. Here is a transcript of his botched words:

…choose one as well above the town centre as possible and well above street-level. A twenty-storey office-block is ideal, I saw one the other day, the lower ten floors unlit as if a gigantic wave had swept by leaving darkness in its wake. Take over the twelfth or thirteenth floor and establish your workshop there. A bench with a vice, electric...... An electric pump, buffing-wheel...... a blowtorch........ tools. OVERALLS GOGGLES GLOVES. Tie back your hair..... start work at 7.30....... LIGHTS...... BROOCHES FOR TYPISTS... MATERIAL... Silver or German silver, G.15........... ½" wide...... check against a straight-edge....... MARKING OUT THE METAL. Divide the piece.... wipe....... accurately with a spitstick.... hole up to stone size. Sand the back...... with a needle-file. PIP WIRE....... and pickle in acid to remove oxide. Mill to G.17........ drawplate.... to form vee pieces............. TEA BREAK...... there's a wind getting up...... that far corner to eat his bun. Why does he do that every day? Some grow old at breakneck speed..... remember a youngster I met..... was an old hand by the time.......... pair of dividers, measure the width of the brooch......... at 45 degree using........ .... check to see the metal has not twisted........ wipe the tools and put them away............ WARNING...... workroom has a fireplace make sure it is...... take my advice you will have it bricked up. The last time I made a brooch for a typist part of the fireplace collapsed, bringing down the fire-back boiler which cracked open spilling a glutinous white fluid..... spread over the floor to a uniform toe-nail depth. It smelt like pig-shit and took six hours to mop up.

NOTA BENE: according to historical reports Nero (54–68 AD) wore shoes shod with silver, while his wife, Poppaea, had hers shod with gold. As it turned out, Nero's footwear proved fatal to Poppaea... he kicked her to death.

First published: *Surrealist Transformaction*, no.9, 1979

Saturday Afternoon Shopping

Being part of a scheme to have the world put away

During a lull in the mad bustle of Saturday afternoon shopping, the sound of a single jam tart being sold rang out eerily. Mouth was the buyer, sensing the presence of a treat it ordered Eyes to look and Hand to grab. On a nearby counter stood rows of rubber balls waiting to be bounced, Mouth scorned them, it had to be the jam tart or nothing and no time for doubt. Rain fell and saliva poured as Feet sped down the street, Hand clutching the bag holding the treat. Shoppers banged and squeaked and lurched. "Pigs!" yelled Mouth, and they shot out of sight double quick and good riddance to them. Feet turned a corner and came to a park with trees and a bench.

Mouth now twists Arm, forcing Body to sit. Hands ransack the bag and Teeth grip the jam tart remorselessly, they will never let go. On the grass a hungry boy is playing with a rubber ball. He has set himself a task: he will bounce the ball two thousand times, non-stop, before he eats the currant bun crumbling in his trouser pocket. He is teaching the ball a lesson.

Perching on an overhanging branch a hungry bird eyes him with the desperation of a cannibal. Imaginary pictures of scattered crumbs, plump and succulent, fill its greedy brain. Its heart bounces with anticipation.

At this same moment, back in the supermarket, a second boy is pestering his mother to buy one of the rubber balls on display. The boy, unable to bide his time, takes it from the cellophane wrapper and bounces it once. Dance! He fumbles the catch and the ball skids on the spot where, half an hour before, a jam tart had ruffled its feathers.

Up goes the bird from the park and races with unruffled feathers across the town's sky to alight on the roof of the supermarket.

Down on the street, not one bustling shopper paid heed to the sound of uneasy wings flapping overhead, and nor did a nest-building owl in the church steeple over the way. The bird, clothed cap-a-pie in black feathers, it must have been a blackbird, had two hours to kill before sundown.

Night had come, the owl is hooting and the shoppers are now dreamers dreaming of cheap goods and how to skimp and save and be a skinflint. Soon, a man, with a black and snowy mind and an icicle-hung reason for living, walks down the street to come to stand in the doorway of a shop, closed and shuttered. He is a supporter of January, this chap, a fan of all things cold and desolate, a winter hooligan, one might say, and he is there to cheer-on a storm from the North that will that night break all the rules and rampage like a lawless blizzard, for was not The Referee out of sight, engaged in another season in another land.

As the Referee sweltered under the shimmer of a southern sun he sank deeper still into the bottomless featherbed called lethargy; and it was a Tuesday, one of the poorest quality, shop-soiled, even more 'Made in Taiwan' than usual, so he thought. He didn't like the look of it one bit, for one thing it had the smell of sweaty working men about it, and that for him would never do. And then came Wednesday. "Let's have a picnic", came the cry from the bedroom. At once a team of servants (for he was a man of wealth and authority) stirred their lazy hands. The grand excursion arrived on the beach and willing hands set to and built all manner of canopies, grottos, sandcastles and a splendid marquee.

When all was ready, The Referee rose from his place and gave the command, "Invite all in sight except working men and their womenfolk, to join us and eat". Lighthouse keepers, drowning sailors, lovers (from the dunes), the Punch and Judy man… all these and more rushed to the marquee where they gobbled as many toothsome delicacies as their greedy bellies could take.

That night when he was back in his secure hotel, tucked-up in his invincible bed, he mused, "I'd rather be an insignificant caterpillar and rule a small cabbage leaf, than a man without money and the authority wealth gives to order the lives of lesser people". Soon he fell into the black pan of sleep, the alembic of fathomless dreams.

This is what he dreamed: it is the height of bitter winter. He sickens of the filthy heat of his quarters and the stink of his own bed. He goes in search of bleak winds. He makes his way up rusty rungs to the roof of the uppermost turret of a rusty castle. He faces the onslaught. He peers through sleet to the blackness beyond. He sees a gleam of light. It comes near. It flickers. It is a lamp held aloft by the man with the icicle-reason for living. The lamp goes out. The Referee is lost in darkness.

How can a game be controlled when the book of rules is out of date?

First published: *Grid* nos. 3/4, 1985

How to Catch a Fish

The wind jumps at breakneck speed from Nor' Nor' East to go madcap down the streets and corridors, flicking tin cans and balefire through a hundred banging doors.

The Great Shoal takes fright. The train and the vans, buses and ferryboats depart bearing both King Mob and Pillars of Society alike. In the time it takes for dust to choke, the town becomes a problem without a solution.

The sky shrinks to a dot and the fog is the ghost of a murderer.

A gun boat lies offshore. A child hoists a dark flag. Paper money and documents float down the gutter. The park is waterlogged, gardens are trip-wired and the outer suburbs bricked up.

THE TOWN IS UNCLEAN, cries the headline. The racing cycle and its buckled wheel, the rows of cinema seats in the gloom, the fixed stare behind the curtain, the woman's thigh and stocking top, all these carry thumbprints and collect unsavoury markings.

> Puffs of dust vanish in the air
> Ragged rats scurry everywhere.

Some few stay-a-beds and laggards miss the bus and are left at the stop. The stay-a-beds gather in groups to recount dreams and examine each other. The laggards read old books and think thoughts such as, "Why didn't the wind come from the Sou' Sou' West?"

At seven-thirty, prompt, a factory whistle blows. The master is calling his dog to heel. Workers rush pell-mell to the clock: to be late means docked wages. In the market place one or two stallholders take down the shutters. Bankrupt stock is for sale.

The town is hard pressed and it shows: one lamp to light two streets, one sewer to serve two suburbs, little signs like that.

The hungry ones take note and hurry from blank wall to empty square, tricky footwork is needed, greasy patches are treacherous.

The situation could get out of hand, when it's one loaf to feed both rich and poor the indicator swings to a mark beyond danger.

An ever-present mystery rests in the way whole areas of the

familiar world evade notice, wear masks, so to speak. Consider any public gathering place, the passenger concourse at a railway station will serve as an example, we move down well tried yet invisible tracks to the booking office, bookstall, snack bar and trains. To leave this purposeful world we need take but a few paces to one side to find another facet, one of rusty corners and neglect where sound is subdued; we merge with the background and assume the role of a sinister watcher.

Unemployment, too, sheds new light on the world we accept without thought. Small things normally ignored gang-up and throw day-to-day life out of kilter. Unemployment means deep water and many a sprat wriggles in the inky depth until caught in a trawl.

One such sprat lived in a sombre district beyond the allotments.

On the morning after the night of The Great Fright he counted his pennies and went to the market to buy a pair of second-hand shoes. When back home he found the fit not only good but PERFECT, as if he had broken in and worn them over a number of months. Every intimate curve and bulge in his feet found agreement with the warmth of the leather: a snug fit was what he had and it disconcerted him. Who had worn them, he asked. None other than his "double," he concluded and vowed to track down and have him laid.

In zigzag up Main Street and straight down the Back Alley; from hovel to hotel, from doss house to dark arch, from park bench to rubbish tip he went yet not a glimpse of his quarry did he see. He was chasing a wraith.

Days and weeks pass and the reward for effort is a down-at-heel look and scuffed toecaps. Five more hours come and go and yawning holes gape in beaten soles; and then foul weather sets in and his room becomes a reeling deck with cargo secure under tarpaulin breaking loose to menace with a bulk that can crush.

The lighthouse began to flash.

By now it is a bleak evening in November. The sole activity in the town is the feverish construction of a concrete clinic on a site where garages and lock-up shops once stood.

In a kitchen down a sulking alley sits Irene, gazing with rapture-blunted eyes at her new coat. "Delicious," she murmurs, as her fingers smooth the last of the creases and slither over the first of the buttons. "MODES de LUXE, Paris & London," reads the label. What excitement!

Wriggling with pleasure, she strips off down to stockings, suspender belt and shoes. Into the coat she slips and out of the house she slides. "This will stop the traffic," she breathes, as she steps from the pavement onto the road and across the path of an oncoming speedster.

In the streets the foul weather rages on and the lighthouse flashes its warning.

The sprat is sitting by the grate reading his paper. HALF DRESSED WOMAN INJURED BY CAR, reads the headline.

A young woman wearing nothing but an overcoat and shoes was knocked down and seriously injured by a speeding motorist in Regent Street last night. A police spokesman said, "She was carrying no means of identification."

Now comes a rap at the street door and a voice shouts, "Come here with my shoes!"

Leaving his emerald chair, the sprat goes to the door and swings it open. A fisherman dressed for all kinds of weather stands before him.

"They're my shoes, I bought them from a stall in the market, I paid good money for them," he bubbles.

"Your shoes and your bait," cries the fisherman and so saying casts his net and hauls in his catch.

That night the fisherman and his family ate red meat and small potatoes.

The lighthouse keeper smashed the lamp and the coast went dark.

In the early hours the wind dropped and The Great Shoal swam home, wriggling its fin.

First published: *Entrance*, no.2, 1988

The Child's Brain

King Kong plunges to his death from a great height and the real death of a bird in the sky, events dramatic enough for the whirring imagination of a seven year old to cope with.

In the early 1930s part of my childhood was spent at Redcar on Teesside, then as now a down-at-heel seaside resort surrounded by steel works and wind-swept dunes. Yet I hold the town close to my heart, for it is the birthplace of many a dream and memory: it is winter, it was always winter and cold, I am alone on the beach building a secret world, a sand landscape of hills, mountains, ravines with bridges, towns and harbours. Of a sudden a gull which has died on the wing crashes to the sand at my feet, its feathers brushing my forehead as it falls. There it lies, twitching, huge as gulls are huge, and dead, a weird visitor to my private world.

Of the three flea-pits the town boasted my favourite was the Pavilion, at the Coatham end of the prom. It was, in truth, all that remained of what had been the North Pier, blown away by a great storm in the 1920s. Films like dreams come and go and are soon forgotten, yet 'King Kong', which I must have seen in 1933, or early 1934, with its scenes of adventure in a fabled land, was the one to overwhelm my mind and stay with me to the present day. And of those scenes my hero, for that is what Kong had quickly become, tumbling head-over-heels from the roof of the skyscraper to his death on the street was the one to dominate my mind. Death from the sky, again. In my child's brain he crashed at my feet as I walked through a strange city.

First published: *Seeing in the Dark*, Serpents Tail, 1990

The Frog of Ill Omen

Tadpoles they are legion, in every direction there they are beyond count, many more than umpteen, flapping their tails in the murk and the mud.

When I was a lad back in the '30s, living in Leeds, I and my pals used to spoon every speck and last seed of raspberry jam from the jars, gulping the lot down with bread, margarine and pleasure. Then we set forth adventuring to a stagnant pool we knew of in Harehills (alas, no longer there: semi-detached houses now stand where the swamp once stank).

Quite soon what had been jars full of jam became jars full of tadpoles: the "duff" (Duff or Dare) was to eat them. You close your eyes and swallow, they taste like tadpoles, a kind of Tadpole taste, not quite Frog.

Some few months passed, I applied my time to a pen and ink drawing, depicting strange events taking place in the air over the White Cliffs of Dover, circa 1940; the foremost of these being that of good fairies turning evil German aeroplanes into frogs, which at that time was just how things should be.

To tell the truth, this drawing was a second version with minor variations of one I drew back in 1993, now in the collection of Marie-Odile Gain d'Enquin. I wanted a second version simply to please myself; I like the ambience—dare I use that word here—of it.

And so, after three weeks of painstaking work, my drawing came to a stage where it was nearly done with. All that was left was to dot the i's and cross the t's, so to speak.

It was Saturday morning, time to go shopping. On my way home, stepping out down my front street, I was of a sudden brought to an abrupt halt. There, before my feet, squatting on the pavement was a frog, yes a frog, not a tadpole, a frog waiting for me outside my own front door. I stooped to prod, as one does with frogs, but it didn't budge, not one millimeter. I tried again, and it opened one eye and blinked (or was it a wink?).

With that I picked it up and took it indoors that I might investigate the frog more.

It sat on my table, immobile, eyes shut. "Croak," I yelled. Not a word came forth. "Jump then," I coaxed. Not a twitch, only the dull thud of its willful heartbeat. "Right lad," I said to myself, "city life is not for you."

Up to the top of Emerald Street I went with the silent one clasped in my hand. A right turn along Milton Street soon bought us to Hazel Grove, a pleasant wooded valley with a stream flowing through it, used by the local townsfolk as a park.

On the bank of the stream I found a decaying hollow log.

"That's your home," I thought, and placed Froggy safely inside… safe as a frog in a log, listening to the crepitation of the trees.

An hour later, back in my studio, putting the final cross-hatching to one of the frogs (I had three of them included in my composition), I reached over to dip my pen in ink. Guess what, yes, disaster galore, over went the full bottle engulfing all my brave and gorgeous fairies along with the frogs, once aeroplanes, in a dank, black impenetrable swamp of Indian ink.

The following day I returned to the log by the stream. The frog had leapt.

First published: *Manticore*, no.1, 1997

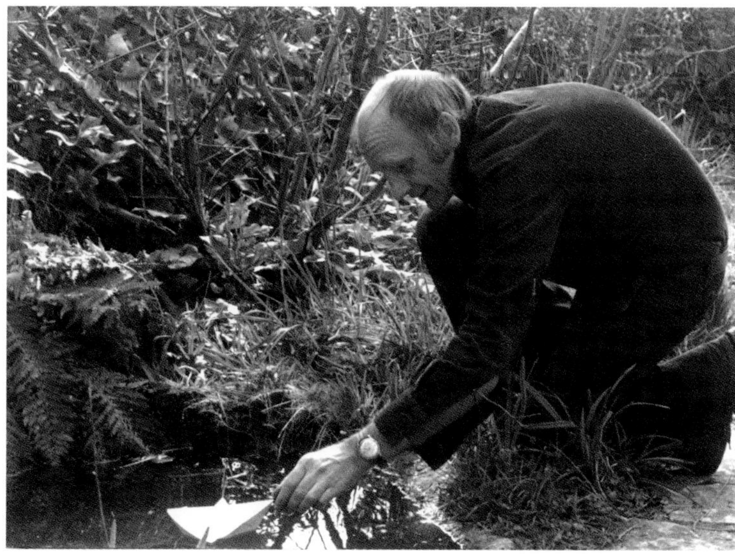

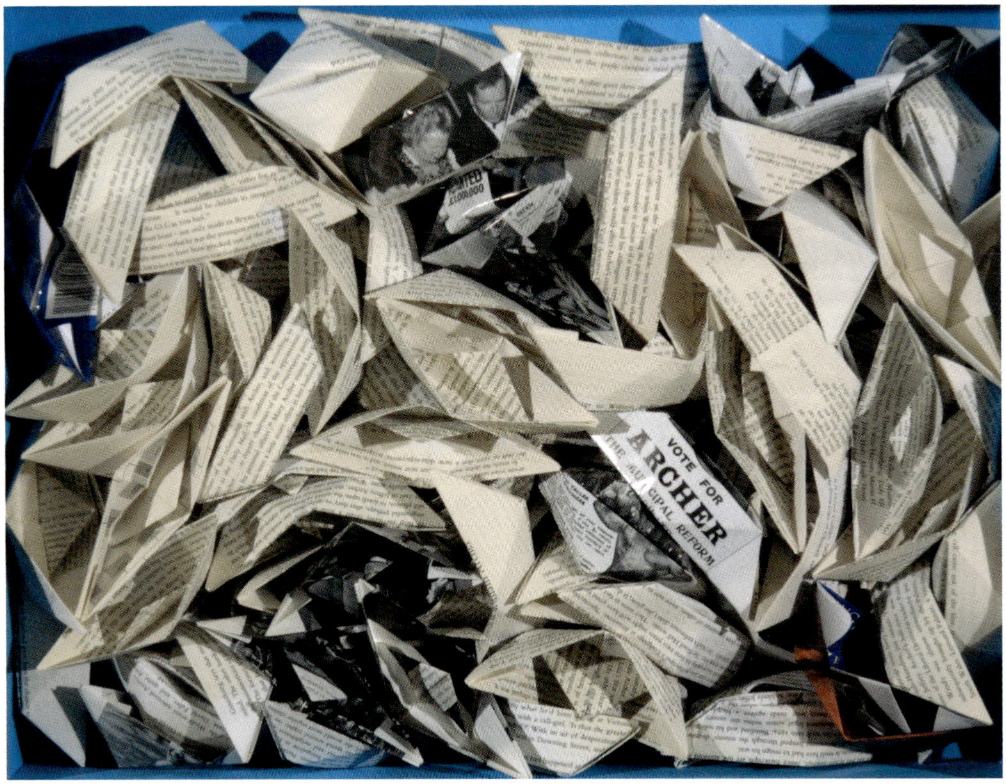

All at Sea, 1995

In response to the Site Gallery's 'Rebound' project, I took the book, Michael Crick's biography of Jeffrey Archer, *Stranger than Fiction*, and at random tore out 101 pages: these I used to make 101 paper boats which I then 'launched' higgledy-piggledy into a glass-fronted box of my own construction. To this I gave the title 'All at Sea'. Finally, to add THE END to my project, on the 23 September I went with what was left of the book and a photographer friend to the end of the pier at Saltburn-by-the-Sea, Cleveland and threw it into the sea. Once stranger than fiction, now all at sea.

—*A.E.*

Aphorisms

The Sea

The sea with all its marvellous oceans and freedom is one vast, rambling mansion haunted by fish. It is these alone who know the way through the countless, unlit rooms and which black corridors to glide down, to come in time to Stygian vaults where ghosts of an early age walk on the bed.

Fish are the bearers of the sea's secrets and when captured by the enemy refuse to speak even under torture by hook, gaff and threat of the skillet.

Clouds, the sea's allies, move with stealth to spy on the land.

The sea views harbours and ports as territories annexed by the enemy and fumes.

None of us will get anywhere without wet seaboots.

A world without a sea is like a rainy day without a waterfall.

If truth be told, men build lighthouses to warn off the sea.

The sea will never be calm until the last hill has been splashed.

The Pacific Ocean firmly believes in the abolition of storms and shipwrecks.

The hardened land-lubber feels seasick when the tide is in.

The sea will curb its unruly waves only when the land lies flat and behaves itself.

The sea rations its waves to so many per beach and not one more than is necessary.

One wave in ten leaves home and comes to the land after a stormy night out.

Some few waves come to the shore seeking useful employment in peaceful reservoirs.

Even experienced waves get in difficulties when up against dangerous cliffs.

When distracted by a flighty raindrop brushing its crest, the mountainous wave quickly became a harmless ripple only fit to paddle in.

Round-the-clock shift work is the lot of tides. If the moon paid good wages tides would be rich, they could retire to some other planet nearer to the sun and stagnate.

The littoral zone is a battleground. The sea sweeps in with waves glittering in the sun and then retreats before an advancing army of determined children brandishing heavy buckets and sharp spades. (Maybe after all, children are on the side of human beings?)

Yet his first ripple sent by the sea heralds the downfall of the most steadfast sandcastle, no matter how firm the builders make the foundations.

Not many King Prawns employ children to build their castles.

The sea's disdain for paddling day-trippers is fathomless.

Rain is the sea's answer to holiday-makers.

Sand is the sea's dust. Holiday-makers travel from far to lie on it. They then catch the train home to dust the ornaments on the mantelpiece.

The most interesting waves spread themselves luxuriously on the beach when holiday-makers are back at work.

The bucketful of worn-out sand from Blackpool beach went on holiday to the Gobi desert. It was lost in admiration.

The captive goldfish in its heart know its bowl is as near as it will ever get to the sea and shrugs its fins with resignation.

Suburban Frigidaires crouch fearfully in the kitchen when a wild iceberg is in the neighbourhood.

Cod and haddock eat 'Man Overboard' raw, without chips, salt or vinegar.

When shanghaied, shrimps and prawns form the crew of the good ship 'Chop-Suey'.

For mackerel the Whitby cobble floating lazily overhead is as innocent as a cloud on a July day.

The pretty, young flying fish had a brief flirtation with a big, strong albatross.

Do sharks, whales and octopuses dream of exotic holidays in faraway ponds, lakes and tarns?

Short story: ROVER went on deck to beg for a bone. Of a sudden the ship gave a lurch, up he went in a somersault and backwards he fell into the foam; it was more fun to watch than being at the circus. A dogfish named SPOT, latrating under a nearby reef heard the splash, came out wagging his tail and ate the poor little fellow, name tag and all. The End.

What men call 'Civilization' is a sort of ocean on land. It has sharks and pirates and murky depths where denizens caught in treacherous currents drown.

If the entrepreneur knew how to drain the sea he'd switch the pumps on today, and tomorrow start building office blocks.

Finding they had things in common from the old days and to relieve the boredom of it all, Amber and Pearl struck up a friendship while decorating the person of the business man's wife.

At the dinner party the string of pearls huddle for company round the elegant neck of the Dowager and recall the whisper of the sea to drown the inane clack of the guests.

King Neptune and Others

King Neptune sinks in his throne and storms over the sloppy behaviour of his young typhoons and wayward tidal waves.

For Neptune the frenzied activity of a Moscow, a Chicago or a London is little more than a storm-in-a-teacup.

Neptune, set in his ways, thought 'The Titanic' new-fangled and sent one of his icebergs to put it to the test.

Jehovah keeps a Dove in a cage, Neptune has his Stormy Petrel fly free.

Jehovah caused The Flood, but first of all he had to gain King Neptune's permission.

King Neptune didn't hear about The Ark until it was too late.

Just as Jehovah knows the name of every sparrow that falls to earth, Neptune mourns for every shrimp tangled in a net.

Pearly tears come to Neptune's eyes when he contemplates the fate of his oysters.

Neptune prefers beautiful mermaids swimming free to ugly sailors locked in submarines.

In Neptune's Kingdom Mount Everest is a traveller's tale brought home by driving rain.

Neptune is proud of his garden and resents the way ignorant humans dismiss his cherished plants as 'seaweed'.

In retaliation King Neptune has decreed that corn and wheat, and buttercups and daisies are 'landweeds' and must be swept away.

The brave King of Atlantis lashed himself to his throne as his Kingdom went down with all inhabitants.

If only the Incas had built a canal across Panama and Columbus had kept his eyes closed the 'Western Hemisphere' would not have been discovered; the Sioux would still be hunting bison.

First published (shortened version): *Copy Book*, no.6, 2005

Corners Without Let

Corners rarely bother themselves with daylight, preferring as they do the company of shadows, ghosts and the stealth of night.

Corners, dust, neglect and smells in league against straight lines, hygiene, order and civilization.

Dutiful Day marches in a straight line from Dawn to Noon to Dusk and then, worn out, goes to bed. Night slithers from Dream to Nook to Corner with Dawn a thousand years in the future, brushing its teeth and pulling on its jackboots.

Down in the machine shop the lathes spun in a hurry turning ugly corners of one sort or other. At the same time the turners stared at the clock, it announced a corner of another kind, at a quarter to the end of the shift it stood and a night full of beautiful corners to turn beckoned. (It was pay-day).

The lights went out, dust began to settle, spiders came, webs went up, flies got eaten and then the wallpaper began to peel. Left to their own devices corners get on with life at a steady pace.

Corners seldom know the pleasure of visitors. When a snarling rat backs into one it is welcomed like a dear friend and all the spiders smile and spin their finest webs for the occasion.

The corner had a fair view of the room: a table leg, flaunting itself, plenty of skirting board to admire and beyond that the Butler kissing the Maid; and heaven only knows what else was going on out of sight round the other corners.

Setting the beasts of the city an example, the rats from out of town turned a corner and gnawed the banquet clean.

In a castle's 49,999 corners is where he lives. He is not a happy man, he wants 50,000 of them. (I own to it, I am he.)

Like God, Foreman can see round corners.

Once upon a time, long ago, the owner of the house pasted wallpaper pattened with roses in his corner, and then went to his lounge to read his newspaper. The Dorothy Perkins flourished vigorously, thanks to rising damp.

Throughout history rampaging hordes of house-proud women have scourged innocent specks of dust, cowering helplessly in the folds of their motherly corner.

In the length of time as specks of dust grow old they come to yearn for a peaceful eternity in an ideal corner in a heavenly attic far from the busy housewife and the brutal disturbance of her duster.

Captains of Industry and Mrs. House-Proud alike have yet to breed the HOOVER with the courage to venture into the darkest corner of the house.

When dust settles Mrs. House-Proud can't settle.

Dust knows a good corner when it sees one.

Dust and only dust has set foot in the Four Darkest Corners of the world.

Outlandish corners of the world such as America and even as far afield as Australia are marked on our charts, while the nethermost corners of the cellars in our own homes remain unexplored.

For plenty of townsfolk the centre of the universe is the shop on the corner.

A world without corners is like an idiot without anyone to annoy.

A subversive rumour is abroad that the world has one corner too many (or one too few).

Childhood means spending a thousand and one nights looking in a thousand and one corner shop windows.

The 'Big Bang' came about when God spring-cleaned Heaven and shook his duster.

An apocryphal account has Adam and Eve fashion aprons out of fig leaves for another reason: dusty Eden needed spring-cleaning.

Corners mean doubt, Heaven can have none: Hades has more than it knows what to do with.

We humans must hand over the government of our lives to the care of corners, for they alone know which way to turn.

Gadabout zigzags tend to fall in love with virginal straight lines.

It takes a few curves to make a circle.

The zigzag is the black sheep of the Corner family.

When it comes to zigzags scientists study flies.

The cube is the intellectual member of the Corner family.

The Corkscrew is the skeleton-in-the-cupboard of the Corner family.

Floodlit sunshine outdoors, indoors black and snowy corners: it's a funny old town.

Given leeway town planners and policemen would have bent corners go straight.

Humanity could neither knock on doors nor punch faces without those useful corners called 'knuckles'.

What people think of as 'God' is something or nothing lurking round the corner they call 'Death'.

Clouds scud by above while the town goes up in flames below, and yet rats in the sewers scurry merrily for they know a hot meal is waiting to be wolfed round every twist and bend and corner, and they can hardly contain themselves before getting their sharp teeth in.

Little Miss Corner SAT and yelped like a whipped bitch. "YAWOOO!" she went, "My skirting board is being gnawed by a big, handsome mouse."

By chance the wooden parts of the trap came from the same tree that had provided the planks for the skirting board. What a time they had raking over ancient scandals of the forest and nattering about the old days. Meanwhile, unnoticed, mice from every corner in the house came to nibble the bait and smack their little lips with glee, and soon after, mice from next door came to see what was going on and then they too got their teeth in.

God's elbow is the Cornerstone of Creation.

God's scribble was the original Labyrinth.

Would you trust signposts in a Labyrinth?

The hither and thither fly is at home in the Labyrinth.

The fly is the Spirit of the Labyrinth incarnate.

Flies take dangerous corners in their stride.

The endless corridor without a turning is the inescapable Labyrinth.

Of course the Minotaur has a sense of humour, didn't it erect a DANGEROUS CORNER AHEAD sign in its home?

With the Minotaur in its Labyrinth and the rabbit in her cunningaire, all's well and the world is not yet lost.

When the interminable corridor eventually came to a corner, fear and trembling filled its soul and the Apocalypse itself fell upon it.

Gentle curves have no truck with headstrong zigzags.

Sedate curves pray that one day young Zigzag will straighten himself out and toe the line.

All over the world straight lines are queuing to go round corners.

It is straight lines that drag their feet, corners show a clean pair of heels.

In an ideal world corkscrews shall be made on the upper floor of the factory, with a spiral staircase for the hands to trudge to and fro.

Bottle and Cork were having a quiet night when corkscrew gatecrashed and very soon after the booze went.

The darkest shadows in town gathered to witness the marriage of Miss Straight Line to Master Sharp Corner.

First published (shortened version): *Extrance*, no.4, 1990

Radio Interview

Interview at Leeds City Art Gallery for the exhibition 'A View From Back o' Town', broadcast Radio Leeds, April 1987.

Where's the title from?
It's from an old Louis Armstrong Blues number called 'Back of Town Blues'.

Jazz music is very important to you isn't it?
Very, sure, I took an interest in it perhaps instinctively in 1939.

Actually we can hear one of your pictures over here. It's very good for art on radio, let's just have a listen to this picture.
[...tick tock tick tock]

Now what's that one called?
That one is called 'The Faithful Servant'. It is what seems to be a thermometer mounted on a small box and it ticks. Whoever heard of such a thing? But to let the listener into a secret, contained within the box is an old alarm clock. The whole work of art needs to be wound up once every twenty-four hours.

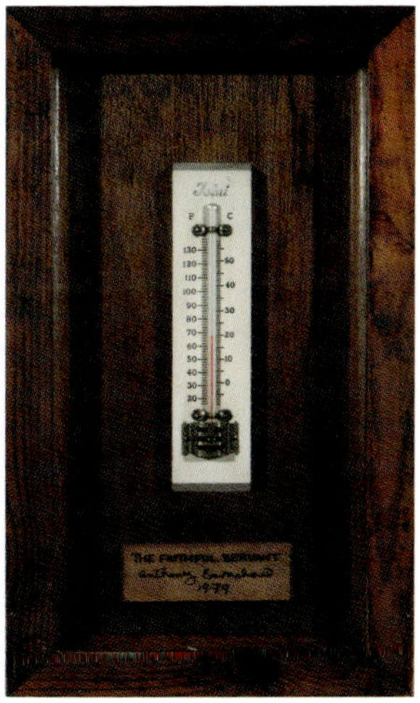

The Faithful Servant, 1979

Now then, there is a piece of work over here which I believe is certainly topical for last week. What's that one called?
'The April Fool', it's a plastic bottle which used to contain bubble-foam, in the shape of a Snowman. I saw this in a chemist shop down Chapeltown Road and went inside and bought it and then built a bonfire around it and gave him a match with which he can light the bonfire if the snowman wanted to. If the bonfire was lit the snowman would begin to melt and put out the bonfire so it is a kind of circular contradictory joke.

Even my two and a half year old would enjoy that one.
Oh yes, children like my work, more so than grown-ups I may add. That's because I myself, am a child in my heart.

Quite a lot of the work... that one is in three dimensions and there's quite a lot of work here which is three-dimensional tell me about this one next to it: again an unusual combination of images, we've got a mousetrap with a flower on it. Tell me about that.
That one's called 'Agony in the Garden' and it's a Little Nipper mousetrap baited by a rose and it has caught a bee... so I don't know what else there is to say... It's a kind of sadistic image I think, a cruel one. The idea of rebellion and an alternative way of looking at life has always been with me and still is and I think that art and poetry which interests me greatly too has always been an ingrained aspect of my personality.

So the titles of these pictures are very important for you?
Yes they are, yes.

Next to that we have got a high heel shoe and a footprint in the sand.
That one's called 'Crusoe's Dream'—I've always thought that when Robinson, poor chap, shipwrecked and alone as he was on his desert island, when he saw the footprint in the sand, he must have thought to himself 'goodness gracious, heavens above, a woman has arrived on the scene an Eve for me, Adam, that I am here in this Eden and that's what that one is about, but alas it wasn't to be [laughter] as we all know, or at least those who have read *Robinson Crusoe* must know.

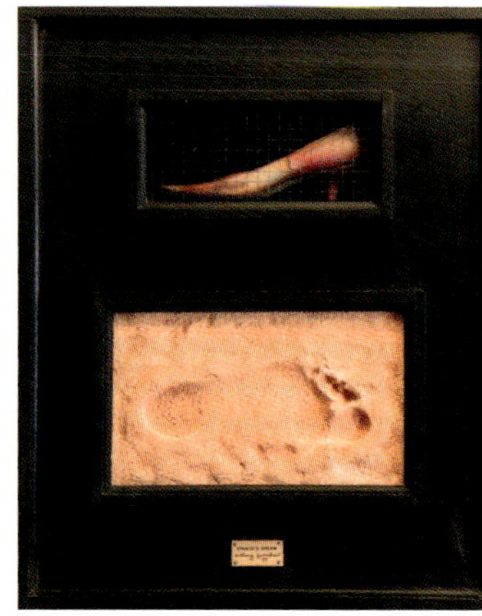

Crusoe's Dream, 1979

Yes and actually looking at the footprint in the sand, to me it looks more like a Man Friday than a Woman Friday's foot. I don't think I would have been too intrigued by that.
Enamoured shall we say? [Tony laughing] Actually, the footprint is made by an old pal of mine but that's another story. [laughs]

You've lived in this part of the world, Yorkshire all your life. Is it important to actually have an exhibition of your work in the Leeds Art Gallery?
It certainly is, it's of enormous importance to me because even though it is a sleazy old twopence-halfpenny town and I love it still. It's my home.

How do you feel as a working artist when you see a painting going for twenty-five million?
Oh, good luck, it's better than the money the government spends on things like Trident Missiles and stuff like that and Centurion tanks which are made up the road at Barnbow, or at least they were, they cost about fifty million don't they, eh? I'd rather see money going on Vincent's sunflowers who's a bit of a lad as I am. I bet Vincent's rolling in his grave laughing, he never sold anything, you know I think he sold one once for about twopence.

Back to the title of the exhibition with these eight pen and ink drawings that we've got over here. What can you tell us about those?
Well they are eight from a series of pen-and-ink drawings I have been making over the past four years which currently amount to some fifty in all. I call them my social-realism drawings, er, I called the whole series 'A View from Back o' Town' so that's really where the title of the exhibition comes from. They are comments on society at large as it is now, as I see it.

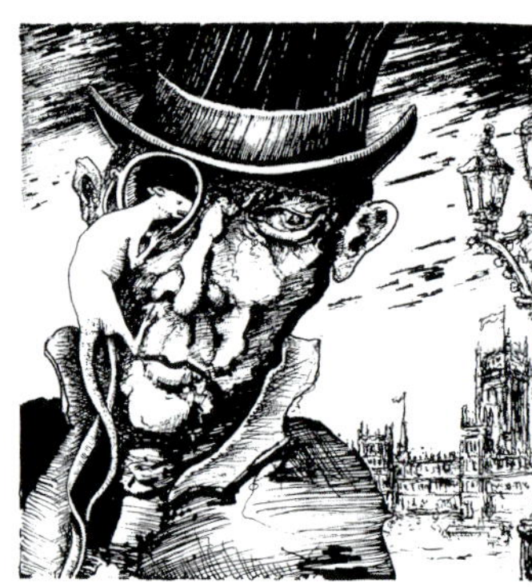

An old acquaintaince caught his eye, on the way from The House, c.1983–86

And you have a fairly jaundiced view of society from the look of these.
An anarchistic one, I think. Yes certainly I am against the bosses, against the Establishment.

For instance we have got somebody here who obviously is a toff and presumably from the House of Lords, we've got the House of Lords in the background, what can you tell us about him?
Well the title of that little pen-and-ink drawing is called 'An old acquaintance caught his eye away from the house' and it depicts a rat crawling up his face and peering through his monocle at his brains which presumably don't exist in my view.

And over here I believe this is the second one of a sequence actually.
It is out of sequence; even so it's called, 'He has been playing with his toys' and it shows a factory and a teddy bear and a toy engine and I am sure that's the way the bosses indeed do see the things that they own which include factories and the people who work in them too.

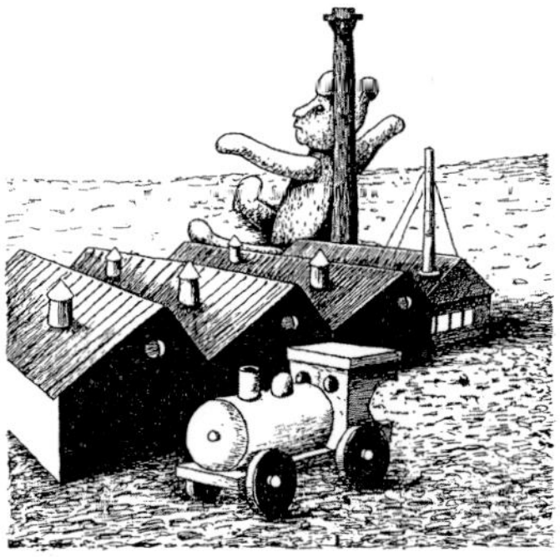

He has been playing with his toys, c.1983–86

As just their playthings?
More or less, yes. That's why they pay them so much an hour, so much a minute, I know, I've worked in such places. If you clock in minutes late you get five minutes docked off your wage at the end of the week.

Now this one could be a portrait of us in here really… it's people looking in an art gallery, what can you tell us about that one?
This one depicts two ladies wearing headscarves and carrying shopping baskets and popping out of the shopping baskets can be seen pig's heads and they are looking at paintings on the walls of the art gallery, which are oil on, canvas paintings of pig's heads and the title is, 'They don't know much about art but they know what they like', and I think that that is at large the general public's attitude to art and poetry.

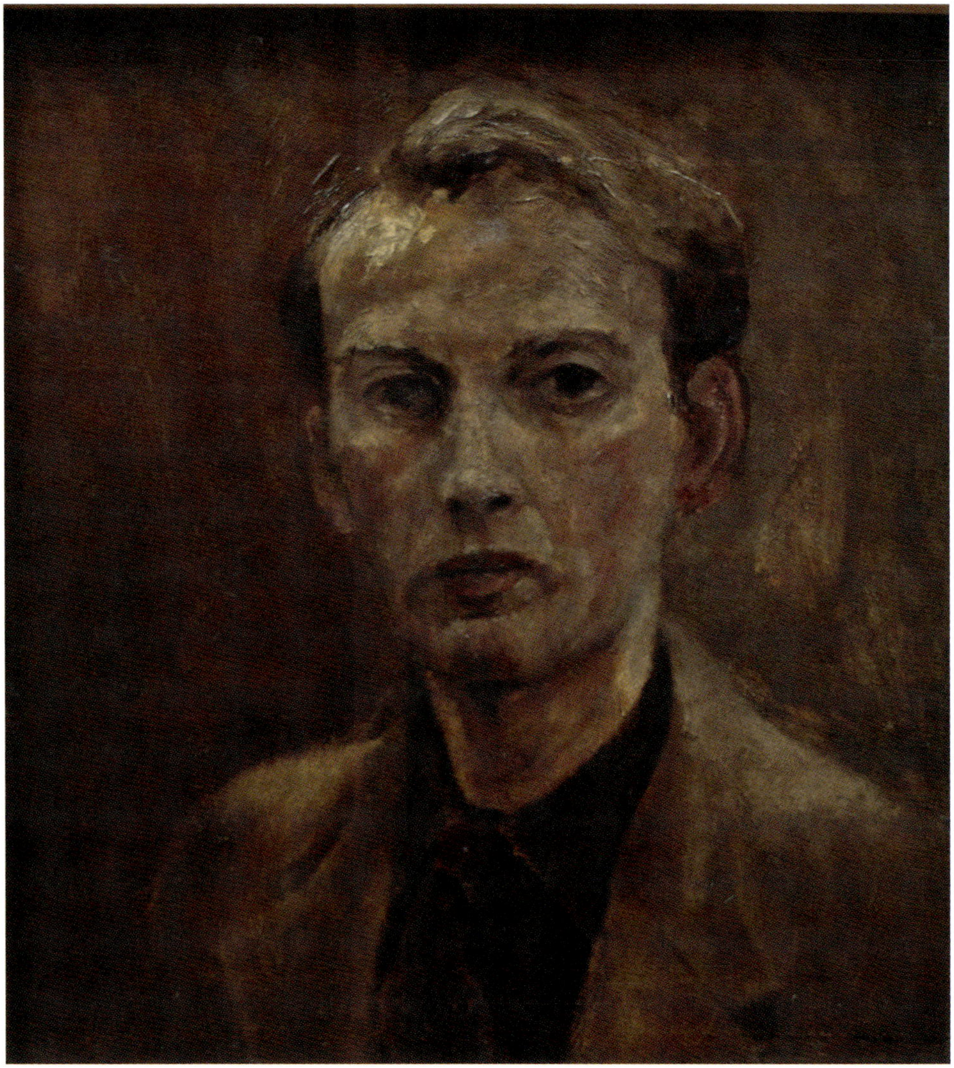

Self-Portrait, 1951

Earnshaw brought many examples of his work to show to students in his drawing class at Bradford College of Art. Along with a series of his early watercolours he showed us a small oil painting. Earnshaw would have been twenty-seven years old at the time he made the painting. The portrait shows a slim-faced, serious young man—using a difficult medium to capture a good likeness. After many days of painting he achieved the task he had set himself. Earnshaw then made this point: "After I had completed the picture, I realised that I was not in the least bit interested in external reality". The painting had been a watershed, a pivotal experience that helped confirm his belief in the imaginary.

—*Chris Vine*

Anthony Earnshaw

Chronology

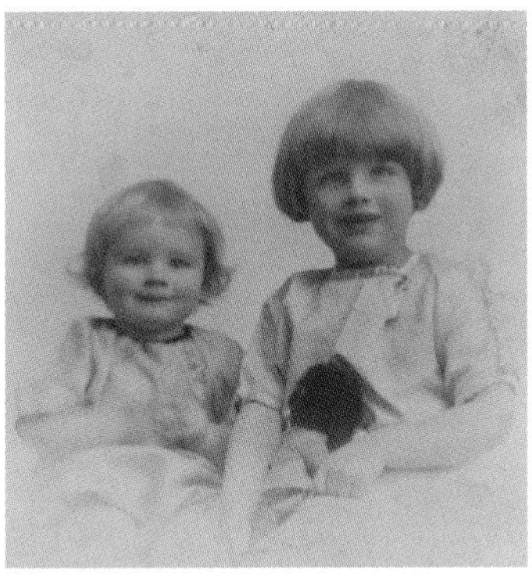

Anthony and Peter Earnshaw, 1926

1910
—Paternal grandfather murdered in Bradford, West Yorkshire.

1921
—Peter Earnshaw, older brother of A.E., born.

1923
—The Industrial Workers of the World, founded in 1905, is at its peak. The IWW contends that all workers should be united within a single union and that the wage system should be abolished.

1924
—Born Ilkley, West Yorkshire, 9th October at 42 Brooke Street, the second son of Ernest Earnshaw and Dorothy Earnshaw. Ernest Earnshaw dies after developing meningitis and pneumonia in August, two months before A.E.'s birth.
—Franz Kafka dies in Prague, Lenin dies in Russia and André Breton publishes the first surrealist manifesto in Paris.

1930
—The family jewellery business in Ilkley is declared bankrupt. Dorothy Earnshaw, Peter, Tony and Aunt Winnie, Dorothy's sister, move to 6 Cedar Grove, Redcar, a small seaside town on the North Yorkshire coast. A.E. and his brother attend John Batty Primary School, Redcar.

1931
—Fred Myers, A.E.'s maternal grandfather, retires and moves from Ben Rhyding with his wife Alice to live in Saltburn-by-the-Sea to be near their daughter Dorothy and their two grandsons.

1933
—The film 'King Kong' is released. Seen by A.E., it makes a profound impression and Kong will feature in his art many years later.

1934
—The Earnshaw family move to 33 Spencer Place, Leeds.

1936
—A.E. and his schoolfriends watch in fear as a German airship passes over Harehills School.
—A diptheria epidemic breaks out in Leeds. A.E., who suffers from severe bronchitis, is briefly moved from Leeds to live with his grandparents in Saltburn-by-the-Sea. He attends Saltburn School.

1938
—Leaves Harehills School at Easter to work as an apprentice fitter and lathe turner at Ingleby Motors, Leeds, where Peter has worked since 1935.
—Develops an interest in the history and origins of New Orleans jazz and blues.

1940
—Meets Eric Thacker at Leeds Rhythm Club. As well as jazz they both have an interest in Surrealism. This friendship lasts until Thacker's death in 1997.

1942
—On 9 October, his birthday, receives call-up papers. Graded C3 unfit for active service, due to ill-health.

1945
—A.E. publishes letter in *Freedom* inviting anyone interested in anarchism in Leeds/Bradford area to make contact with the idea of forming an anarchist discussion group. There is no support for the proposal.

1946
—A.E. writes poem about Ingleby Motor Company which he pins on the factory notice board, for which he receives the sack.

1947
—The Institute of Contemporary Arts, London, established by Roland Penrose.
—Meets George Melly at the London Gallery, Brooke Street, London, where Melly works. This is the beginning of a loyal friendship in which Melly will later become a collector of A.E.'s work. Starts to make small drawings and collages.

1950
—First exhibition with friends in a shoe shop on Briggate, Leeds. A.E.:"We put our work up on the walls between the shoe racks."
—Visits the ICA, London, where he briefly meets Roland Penrose to show him an early drawing. Penrose looks at it perfunctorily before leaving for a meeting.

1956
—Works at Leeds College of Art as a part-time portrait model. Meets Monica Simpson, who attends evening painting classes.

1957
—Marries Monica Simpson in March at St Augustin's Church, Leeds. They move to 64 Northbrook Street, Leeds.
—Birth of daughter Ruth Mary Earnshaw on 15 December, in Leeds.

1959
—Birth of daughter Frances Jane Earnshaw on 9 January, in Leeds.

1960
—Starts to make larger paintings.

1961
—Meets the artist Patrick Hughes in The Wrens pub, Leeds. They become close friends, a friendship that continues until A.E.'s death.

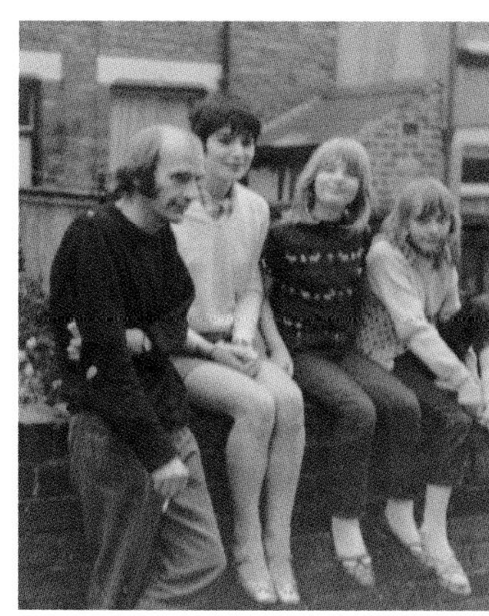

Anthony, Monica, Ruth and Frances Earnshaw, Northbrook Street, 1965

1964
—Melly gives a lecture on Magritte at Leeds College of Art, and later with Patrick visits 64 Northbrook Street, where he purchases a painting by A.E.

1965
—Makes first assemblage using a found object, after discovering a bayonet socket with only one slot in it for the bulb. A.E.: "I wired it up using a piece of flex attached it to a lamp-holder and put it on a backing to represent the ceiling. It ceased to be a mass produced utilitarian object because it was flawed. I gave it a new identity."

1966
—Re-establishes contact with Eric Thacker and they start corresponding regularly. The germination of 'Musrum' and 'Wokker' date from this time.
—Dorothy Earnshaw dies in Ben Rhydding, Ilkley. Buried in Ilkley cemetery next to her husband Ernest Earnshaw.
—Collaboration with Patrick Hughes, Robin Page and Ron Swift to collect and name leaves taken from a sycamore tree in Gledhow Valley Woods, Leeds. Four hand-printed copies of *The Sycamore Tree* are made. Trevor Winkfield: "Under Earnshaw's supervision, we coated each leaf with ink and pressed them against sheets of paper. At the end of an exhausting day, we bound the sheets into a book: Earnshaw's portrait of a tree. It was a wonderful conceit, using both the subject and its fundament, wood, to make the leaves of a book."
—'Painting 1945–1965', Institute Gallery, Leeds: exhibition of eighty oil and watercolour paintings organized by Patrick Hughes. The success of the exhibition enables A.E. to stop working as a lathe turner and start working as a lecturer one day a week at Harrogate College of Art.

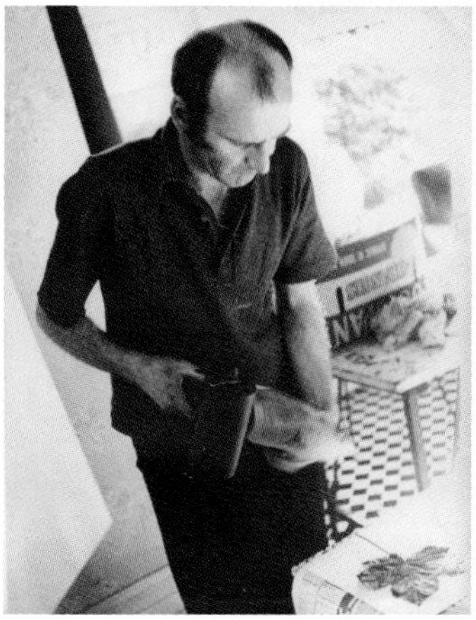

A.E. inking leaves for *The Sycamore Tree*, Leeds, 1966

1967
—Starts teaching two days a week at Bradford College of Art in the Textiles Department.
—Exhibits a work in 'The Enchanted Domain' exhibition in Exeter organized by John Lyle; their friendship continues until A.E.'s death.

1968
—Contributes to *Surrealist Transformaction* edited by John Lyle.
Musrum, in collaboration with Eric Thacker, published by Jonathan Cape, London.
—Teaches on Foundation Course at Bradford College of Art with Jeff Nutall, Alistair Park and Roddy Carmichael, with Albert Hunt running complementary studies. Participates in 'Festival of Chance' where he shows the film 'King Kong' backwards. Other participants in the festival include Robin Page, John Latham and Bruce Lacey.
—Meets Gail Blackstone, a student on the Foundation Course.

1970
—Exhibits original 'Wokker' strips in 'Comics' at the ICA, London.

1971
—'Wokker' appears weekly in the *Times Education Supplement* from 8 October, for one year.

—Patrick Hughes introduces A.E. to Angela Flowers and her gallery.
—*Wintersol*, in collaboration with Eric Thacker, published by Jonathan Cape, London.
—Awarded a fellowhip at Department of Fine Art, Leeds Polytechnic to produce lithographic prints of his pictorial alphabets. A.E. is contracted to teach there two days a week which continues until 1985.
—Takes part in a street performance in Leeds with Fine Art students. They are arrested for disturbing the peace and, along with the other members of the group, A.E. is given a two year suspended sentence.

1972
—*Seven Secret Alphabets* published by Jonathan Cape, London. Exhibition at Angela Flowers Gallery, London of alphabet prints and original pen and ink drawings combined with book launch.

1973
—*25 Poses* published privately with the aid of a Yorkshire Arts Association grant.
—'Hughes & Earnshaw', Ferens Art Gallery, Hull.

1974
—Paints Wokker's portrait. Exhibited at Cartwright Hall, Bradford.

1978
—'Dada and Surrealism Reviewed', Hayward Gallery, London. Angela Flowers Gallery, London mounts 'Transformaction Review,' to coincide with Hayward Gallery exhibition.
—Declines to take part in 'Surrealism Unlimited 1968–1978', Camden Arts Centre, London, on 'ideological' grounds.

1979
—Exhibits in touring exhibition '…a cold wind brushing the temple' showing works purchased by George Melly for the Arts Council of Great Britain.

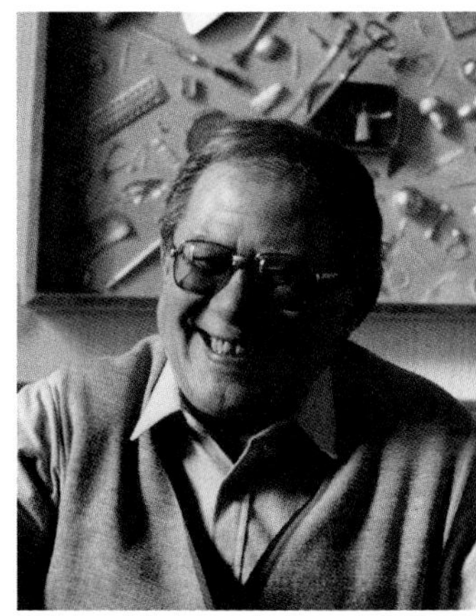

Marcel Mariën, Brussels, 1984

1981
—*5 x 5*, an anthology edited by Asa Benveniste, published by Trigram Press, Hebden Bridge. Contributors are Anthony Earnshaw, Glen Baxter, Ivor Cutler, Ian Breakwell and Jeff Nuttall.
—*Flick Knives & Forks* published by Transformaction, Harpford.

1983
—Meets artist and poet Peter Wood in The Nags Head pub, Leeds. Originally from Yorkshire, Wood was now residing in Paris.

1984
—Visits Marcel Mariën at the time of Mariën's exhibition 'Mise en oeuvres', Galerie Isy Brachot, Brussels.

1985
—Marries Gail Blackstone, 5 January at Leeds Registry Office.
—*Carping & Kicking*, published by Hourglass Press, Paris.

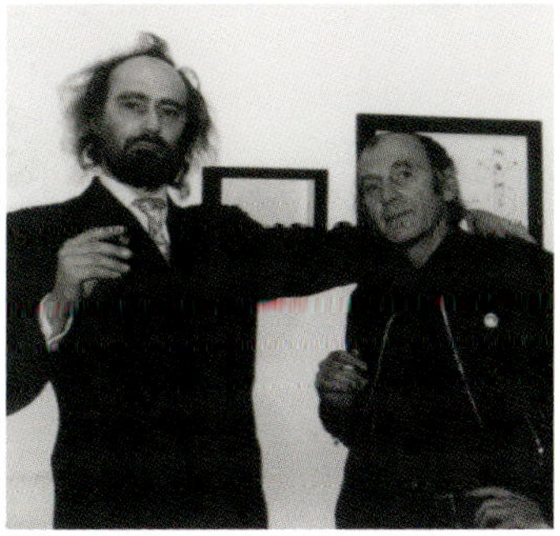

John Lyle and A.E., London, 1978

1986
—Contributes to 'Contrariwise: Surrealism and Britain 1930–1986', Glynn Vivian Art Gallery, Swansea.

1987
—F.O.E. (Friends of Earnshaw) buy and donate 'Raider's Bread' to Leeds City Art Gallery.
—Attends lecture given by Sir Roland Penrose. During question time A.E. asks Penrose to explain how he could accept a knighthood from the establishment while claiming to be a surrealist. After a long silence Penrose says he will discuss the matter in private, an offer he reneged on.
—Retrospective exhibition 'View from Back o' Town', Leeds City Art Gallery, Leeds and Cleveland Gallery, Middlesbrough.
—An eighteen-minute film on A.E. and his work, by Alex Marengo, is screened as a Saturday Review special, 'Two English Surrealists', on BBC2, 10 October.

1988
—*An Eighth Secret Alphabet*, published by Hanborough Parrot Pieces, Oxford.
—*Aspects des Bas-Quartiers*, published by Camouflage, Paris.
—'Works Ancient and Modern', Graves Art Gallery, Sheffield. Eduardo Paolozzi is exhibiting in the adjoining gallery and they exchange works.

1989
—*Clock Lips*, by Marie-Odile Gain d'Enquin with illustrations by A.E. published by Hourglass, Paris.
—A ten-minute film 'On the Edge,' about A.E. and his work, screened on Tyne Tees Television, 7 December.
—Moves from Leeds to 4 Emerald Street, Saltburn-by-the-Sea with Gail who is employed by Cleveland Gallery, Middlesbrough. A.E. has his own studio for the first time.

1991
—'Funny Looking', Cirque Divers, Liège; an exhibition of six English surrealists organized by Les Coleman. A.E. is among the exhibition contributors who visit Marcel Mariën in Brussels.

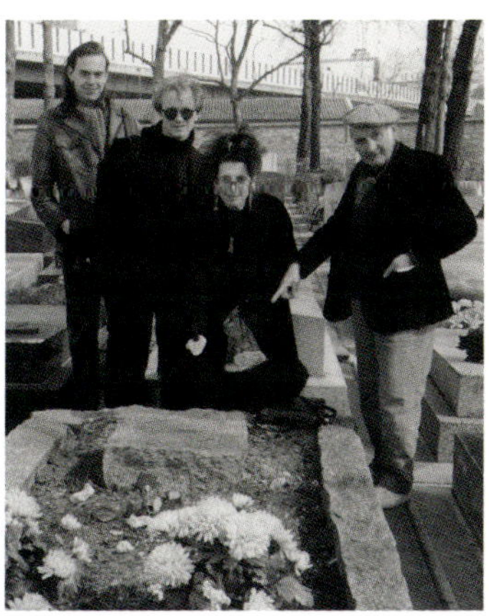

Stephen Clark, Ken Cox, Gail Earnshaw and A.E., Péret's grave, Paris, 1995

1992
—'Portrait of the Artist's Mother Done from Memory', Angela Flowers Gallery, London, is the result of a suggestion by A.E. and Ian Breakwell.

1994
—Exhibits in 'Worlds in a Box' (South Bank Centre touring exhibition) travelling to Edinburgh, Sheffield, Norwich and at Whitechapel Art Gallery, London.
—Visits André Breton's grave in Paris.
—Health starts to deteriorate and A.E has several spells in hospital.

1995
—Exhibits in 'The Discerning Eye', Mall Galleries, London, at the invitation of Patrick Hughes.
—Makes second visit to Batignolles cemetery, Paris, where Breton and Péret are buried. The inscription on Péret's grave reads: "Je ne mange pas de ce pain-là."

this translates as "I do not eat that bread!" and was the title of a collection of his poems published by Editions Surréalistes in 1936. A piece of bread is placed on his grave.

1997
—Visits Chicago with Gail for A.E.'s exhibition 'I Only Want to Help' at Belloc-Lowndes Fine Art Gallery, Chicago. While there they visit the surrealist collection at the Art Institute of Chicago.
—*Flick Knives and Forks* (second edition), published by Zillah Bell Contemporary Art Gallery, Thirsk.

1998
—Peter Earnshaw dies of Parkinsons Disease.

2000
—'Anthony Earnshaw', Flowers East, London. An exhibition of selected work from the last twenty years. This is the last exhibition A.E. attends.

2001
—John Clayton visits Saltburn-by-the-Sea to make his film 'Flick Knives & Forks'.
—Despite being ill, A.E. sees Wokker animated by Dave Brunskill shortly before his death. Dies from cancer on 17 August in James Cook Hospital, Middlesbrough. Buried in Saltburn Cemetery.
—Memorial exhibition mounted at Leeds City Art Gallery, Leeds.

2002
—'Earnshaw & Friends', Dean Clough Art Gallery, Halifax. An exhibition of his, and friends work, in his collection.
—John Lyle dies in France in August.

2003
—'Anthony Earnshaw, His Own Collection', Dean Clough Art Gallery, Halifax.
—John Clayton's short film 'Flick Knives & Forks' completed.

2005
—'Boxes', Flowers Central, London where John Clayton's film is shown for the first time.

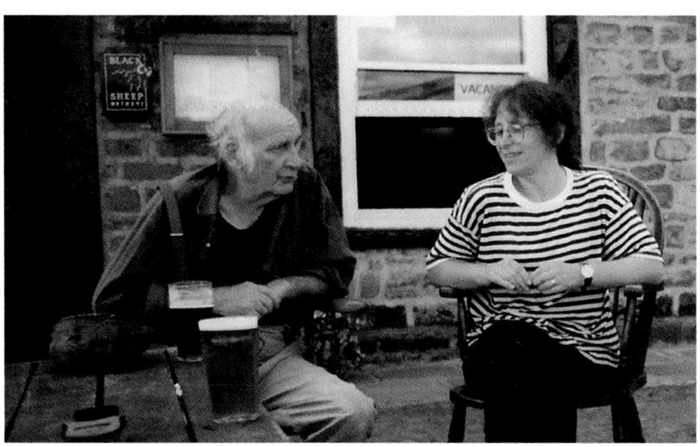

Anthony and Gail Earnshaw, Reeth, Yorkshire, 1998

Biography

Biographical details tend to be boring or pretentious (or both), unless, that is, they read, "Exhibited at the Armory Show, fought alongside Durutti in Spain, married to Mae West…"

—A.E., letter to Tony Blundell, July 1980

Solo Exhibitions

1966—Paintings 1945–1965, Leeds Institute Gallery, Leeds
1972—Anthony Earnshaw, Angela Flowers Gallery, London
1973—Anthony Earnshaw, Exe Gallery, Exeter
1977—Anthony Earnshaw Prints & Drawings, Oxford Gallery, Oxford
1986—Alphabet Prints, Dean Clough, Halifax
1987—A View from Back o' Town, Leeds City Art Galleries, Leeds and Cleveland Gallery, Middlesbrough
1988—Wokker, Dean Clough, Halifax
1989—Works Ancient and Modern, Graves Art Gallery, Sheffield; Pay Attention and Assemble in Orderly Rows or Else, Flowers East, London; Boxes, Roupell Street Gallery, London
1991—On the Corridor, Chelsea Arts Club, London
1992—Anthony Earnshaw, Fouts & Fowler Gallery, London; Come Out Boxing, Dean Clough, Halifax
1993—Dial M for Earnshaw, Gallery M, London
1997—Lucifer Contemplating the 21st Century & Other Boxes, Gallery M, London; I Only Want to Help, Belloc-Lowndes Fine Art, Chicago
1998—Because I Felt Like It, Dean Clough, Halifax
2000—Anthony Earnshaw Selected Works from the last 20 years, Flowers East at London Fields, London
2001—Memorial Exhibition, Leeds City Art Galleries, Leeds
2002—Earnshaw and Friends, Dean Clough, Halifax
2005—Boxes, Flowers Central, London
2006—Pinboard Gallery, bookartbookshop, London

Group Exhibitions

1961—London Opportunity, Salford City Art Gallery, Salford
1962—West Riding Artists, Wakefield City Art Gallery, Wakefield; The Royal Society of British Artists, Federation of British Artists London; CEMA Open Exhibition, Belfast (prizewinner)
1963—Red, White and Blue, London Galleries, London and Leeds University, Leeds
1964—About Round, London Galleries, London
1965—Midland 21, Midland Group Gallery, Nottingham
1966—Form & Image, Leeds Institute Gallery, Leeds
1967—Yorkshire Artists Exhibition, Leeds City Art Galleries, Leeds; The Enchanted Domain, Exeter City Gallery, Exeter
1969—Homage to Appollinaire, ICA Galleries, London
1970—Work by Patrick Hughes, Eric Thacker, Tony Earnshaw, Jeff Nuttall and Robin Page, Lane Gallery, Bradford; Comics, ICA Galleries, London
1971—Trouble at t'Cartwright Hall, Cartwright Hall, Bradford
1972—Artichokes, Greenwich Theatre Gallery, London; British Drawings 1952–1972, Angela Flowers Gallery, London; Illustrated Books 1967–1971, Victoria & Albert Museum, London; Gradiva, Galerie l'Escalier, Brussels; Phases, Nice; 3rd International Print Biennale, Cartwright Hall, Bradford; Wokker in Bradford, (with Eric Thacker) New Lane Gallery, Bradford
1973—Anthony Earnshaw and Patrick Hughes, Park Square Gallery, Leeds; Pen and Pencil, International Culture Centre, Antwerp and Bibliotheque Royal, Brussels
1974—Hughes & Earnshaw, Ferens Art Gallery, Hull and St Paul's Gallery, Leeds; A Priori, Cartwright Hall, Bradford
1975—Envelopes, JPL Fine Art, London and Ferens Art Gallery, Hull
1978—Transformaction Review, Angela Flowers Gallery, London
1979—Leeds Fine Art Club, Leeds City Art Galleries, Leeds; A Cold Wind Brushing the Temple, Arts Council of Great Britain (touring exhibition); Triptych, Victoria Gallery, Harrogate
1980—Made in King Kong, (with Tony Blundell and Les Coleman) Greenwich Theatre Gallery, London; Leeds Fine Art Club, Harrogate Art Gallery, Harrogate
1981—5 x 5, Holdsworth Gallery, Hebden Bridge; Badge Art, Angela Flowers Gallery, London
1982—Anthony Earnshaw, Terry Hammill and Frank Jennings, St Paul's Gallery, Leeds
1984—Exposicao Internacional Surrealismo e Pintura Fantastica, Lisbon; The Spirit of Surrealism, Oliver Bradbury and James Birch Fine Art, London; Lurking in Weeds, Huddersfield Art Gallery, Huddersfield
1985—Third Yorkshire Artists' Biennial, Scarborough Art Gallery, Scarborough; Still Life, New Life (touring exhibition); Friends of Dunganon, Meyers Gallery, Esbjerg, (touring exhibition); The Irresistible Object, Leeds City Art Galleries, Leeds; Exhibition, James Birch Fine Art, London
1986—Surrealist Revelation, James Birch Fine Art, London; Modern Art, It's a Joke, Cleveland Gallery, Middlesbrough; Contrariwise: Surrealism and Britain 1930–1986, Glynn Vivian Gallery, Swansea, (touring exhibition); The Artist Publisher, Crafts Council Gallery, London
1987—The Day Book, Smith's Gallery, London (touring exhibition)
1988—Surrealism is Dead: Long Live Surrealism, Crawshaw Gallery, London; New Acquisitions, Dean Clough, Halifax; Contemporary Portraits, Flowers East, London

1989—Badge Art 2, Flowers East, London; Tricks and Transformations, Museum and Art Gallery, Hanley; A Public Hanging, Polytechnic Gallery, Leeds
1990—Les Micquets, Centre Culturel Courbevoie, Paris; Another G'n'T (with Gail Earnshaw), Dovecot Arts Centre, Stockton
1991—Drawn to Humour, Cleveland Gallery, Middlesbrough; Funny Looking, Galerie Cirque Divers, Liège; Hourglass Group, Galerie Nurf, Paris; Art in Boxes, England & Co., London
1992—Another G'n'T in York (with Gail Earnshaw), University of York, York; Art in Boxes, England & Co, London; Super-Real, East West Gallery, London; Portrait of the Artist's Mother Done From Memory, Flowers East, London; Small is Beautiful part X, Flowers East, London
1993—Self Portraits, Angela Flowers Gallery, London; Art in Boxes, England & Co., London and Castle Museum, Nottingham; Art for Sale, Whiteleys, London; Small is Beautiful part XI, Flowers East, London; Christmas Show, Fouts & Fowler Gallery, London; The Dean Clough Collection, Dean Clough Gallery, Halifax
1994—Bill Gainham Memorial Exhibition, South Square Gallery, Thornton; Box Show, Peter McMillan Gallery, Cambridge; Brought to Book, Angela Flowers Gallery, London; Small is Beautiful part XII, Flowers East, London; Worlds in a Box, City Arts Centre, Edinburgh (The South Bank Centre touring exhibition); Miscellanea, Newcastle College, Newcastle
1995—Curiouser & Curiouser, Espace U.V.A, Paris; British Surrealism 1935–1995, England & Co., London; 18 ans de la Galerie du Cirques Divers: Musée d'Art Moderne et Art Contemporain, Liège; Rebound: Book Art, Site Gallery, Sheffield; The Discerning Eye, Mall Galleries, London; Small is Beautiful part XIII, Flowers East, London; Christmas Show, Saltburn Artist Gallery, Saltburn
1996—Diverse Memories: The Company of Things, Manchester Museum, Manchester; Another G'n'T (with Gail Earnshaw), Zillah Bell Gallery, Thirsk; Julie Sparne Memorial Exhibition, Bradford College of Art; Small is Beautiful part XIV, Flowers East, London
1997—Boxing Clever, The American College in London, London; All the World's a Globe, Gallery 27, London; An Alphabet of Art, Leeds City Art Galleries; The Middlesbrough Open Exhibition, Cleveland Gallery, Middlesbrough; Small is Beautiful part XV, Flowers East, London
1998—Small is Beautiful,part XVI, Flowers East, London
1999—Angel of Mercy: Aspects of British Surrealism, Leeds City Art Galleries, Leeds; Small is Beautiful part XVII, Flowers East, London; Un peu de casse-croûte, La Papeterie, Brussels
2000—The Box Show, Zillah Bell Gallery, Thirsk; Things, Norwich School of Art Gallery, Norwich (touring exhibition); Ville De Conches, Maison des Arts, Paris; Ubu in UK, Mayor Gallery, London
2001—Showtime, Manor House, Ilkley
2005—Pinboard Gallery Review, bookartbookshop, London
2007—'says the junk in the yard', Flowers East, London
2008—Wings of Time, Shandy Hall, Coxwold; British Surrealism & Other Realities, The Sherwin Collection, Middlesbrough Institute of Modern Art, Middlesbrough
2009—British Surrealism in Context: A Collector's Eye, Leeds City Art Galleries, Leeds
2010—What a Relief, Flowers, London

Public Collections

Arts Council of Great Britain
Leeds Art Gallery, Leeds
Graves Art Gallery, Sheffield
Dean Clough, Halifax
Provident Insurance, Leeds

Books

1966—*The Sycamore Tree* (with Patrick Hughes, Robin Page and Ron Swift), hors commerce. (edition of 4)
1968—*Musrum* (with Eric Thacker), Jonathan Cape, London
1970—*Musrum,* Grove Press, New York
1971—*Wintersol* (with Eric Thacker) Jonathan Cape, London; *Musrum*, Jonathan Cape, London (paperback edition)
1972—*Seven Secret Alphabets,* Jonathan Cape, London
1973—*25 Poses*, hors commerce, (edition of 90 signed and numbered), Bradford
1980—*Seven Secret Alphabets,* Jonathan Cape, London (paperback edition)
1982—*Flick Knives & Forks,* Transformaction, Harpford
1987—*Carping & Kicking,* Hourglass, Paris; *Aspects des Bas-Quartiers*, Camouflage no.19, Paris
1988—*An Eighth Secret Alphabet*, Hanborough Parrot Pieces, Church Hanborough
1996—*Musrum and Wintersol,* German translation, hors commerce, (edition of 8)
2000—*Flick Knives and Forks,* Zillah Bell Contemporary Art, Thirsk (second edition of 500 copies signed and numbered)
2002—*Looking for a Carnival: Four Versions*, Copy Book no.5, London
2005—*The Sea*, Copy Book no.6, London

Contributions to Books and Pamphlets

1966—*Dongdeath and Jazzabeth*, Eric Thacker, Location, Leeds;
1981—*5 x 5*, Trigram Press, Hebden Bridge
1983—*More on Oxymoron*, Patrick Hughes, Jonathan Cape, London
1985—*La viande brave sur le dos merchant,* Pavel Reznícek, Camouflage, Paris
1989—*Clock Lips,* Marie-Odile Gain d'Enquin, Hourglass, Paris
1990—*Seeing in the Dark*, Serpent's Tail, London
1991—*Funny Looking,* Collection Papier Journal, Editions du Cirque Divers, Liège;

1994—*Brought to Book*, Penguin Books, Harmondsworth; *Bill Gainham*, South Square Gallery, Thornton
1996—*Craven Sur Craven*, Marie-Odile Gain d'Enquin, Editions du Rewidiage, Lonpre
1997—*Variations on a Theme*, Les Coleman, Copy Book no.4, London
1998—*Redstone Diary of the Absurd*, Redstone Press, London
1999—*Dying for Eternity*, Andrew Lanyon, hors commerce (edition of 200); *Pour Peter Wood*, Hourglass, Paris
2000—*We Shall Strike for More Dreams*, Peter Wood, Hourglass, Paris
2001—*Surrealism in Britain*, Michel Rémy, Lund Humphries, London; *Écoutons Voir*, Supplement to S.U.R.R…, no.4, Paris
2006—*Dr Clock's Handbook*, Redstone Press, London
2008—*Left to Write*, Patrick Hughes, Flowers, London; *British Surrealism & Other Realities*, The Sherwin Collection, Mima, Middlesborough
2010—*Pandorama*, Ian Duhig, Picador, London
2011—*Paradoxymoron*, Patrick Hughes, Reverspective, London; *Le fonds Paul Destribats*, Paris; *On the Thirteenth Stroke of Midnight: An Anthology of British Surrealist Poetry* (edited by Michel Rémy), Carcanet, Manchester

Contributions to Journals and Periodicals

1968—*Surrealist Transformaction*, no.2, Transformaction, Sidmouth; *The Magazine*, no.8, I.C.A. London; Surrealism in the City, *Architectural Review*, December
1970—*Surrealist Transformaction*, no.3, Transformaction, Sidmouth; *Blue Food*, nos.1, 2, Transformaction, Sidmouth.
1971—*Surrealist Transformaction*, no.4, Transformaction, Sidmouth
1971/2—Wokker (with Eric Thacker) *Times Educational Supplement*, London
1973—*Surrealist Transformaction*, nos.5, 6, Transformaction, Sidmouth; *Gradiva*, no.4, Brussels
1974—*Blue Food*, no.3, Transformaction, Sidmouth; *Les Lèvres Nues*, no.10, Brussels; *Brumes Blondies*, no.5 Amsterdam
1975—*Les Lèvres Nues, La fausse sortie*, Brussels
1976—*Surrealist Transformaction*, no.7, Transformaction, Sidmouth
1977—*Surrealist Transformaction*, no.8, Transformaction, Sidmouth
1979—*Surrealist Transformaction*, no.9, Transformaction, Sidmouth; *Les Lèvres Nues, Le cache–sexe des anges*, Brussels. *Le La*, no.6, Geneva
1981—*Not Poetry*, Galloping Dog Press, Newcastle; *Event*, no.10, London; *Illustrators*, no.37, Association of Illustrators, London
1982—*Ellebore*, no.8, Paris; *Camouflage*, no.2 Tomahawk Supplement, Paris
1983—*Camouflage*, nos.4, 5, Tomahawk Supplement, Paris
1984—*Camouflage*, no.6, Tomahawk Supplement, Paris; *Camouflage*, nos.7, 8, Tomahawk Supplement, Paris; *The Hourglass Review*, no.1, Hourglass, Paris
1985—*Homnesies*, Paris; *Camouflage*, nos.9, 10, Tomahawk Supplement, Paris; *Grid*, no.2, Paris; *Grid*, no.3/4, Paris; *De sac et de cord,*, no.1, 2, Paris; *Knuckleduster Funnies*, nos.1, 2, 3, 4, Todmorden
1986—*Grid*, no.5, *English contributions to surrealism*, Paris; *The Looker*, no.8, M5 Press, Winscombe
1987/9—*The Truth*, London, (Wokker included in all 20 issues)
1988—*Annual Jissom*, G.T.O.G. Huddersfield; *Freedom*, 1988/1989, Freedom Press, London
1989—*Extrance,*, no.3, Bolton; *Les Lèvres Nues, Le moment venu*, Brussels
1990—*Extrance,*, no.4, Bolton; *The Looker*, no.14, M5 Press, Winscombe
1991—*Les Lèvres Nues, Le Zénotage*, Brussels; *Mensuel*, nos.126, 128, Cirques Divers, Liege; *Hotel Ouistiti,*, no.11, Paris
1992—*Les Lèvres Nues, Le Qui–vive*, Brussels; *Les Lèvres Nues Terre-à-terre*, Brussels
1993—*Les Lèvres Nues, La Claire–voie*, Brussels
1995/9—*The Whistler Journal*, Wokker, Chelsea Arts Club, London
1996—*Au Nord de quoi?*, no.1, Editions Bonneville, Lille
1997—*Manticor*, no.1, 2, Leeds Surrealist Group, Leeds; *S.U.R.R…*, no.2, Editions surrealists, Paris
2000—*Manticor*, no.5, Leeds Surrealist Group, Leeds
2001—*Carnets Trimestrials du Collège de 'Pataphysique*, no.3, Clamercy
2002—*Manticor*, no.6, Leeds Surrealist Group, Leeds
2003—*S.U.R.R…*, no.4, Editions surrealists, Paris
2007—*Au Nord de quoi?*, no.2, Editions Bonneville, Lille

Bibliography

1961—W.T.O. Oliver, Factory hand's enigmatic watercolours, *Yorkshire Post*, 31 November
1968—George Melly, Musrum, *Observer Colour Supplement*, 6 October; Philip Norman, Profile: Ahead of the Wolves, *Sunday Times*, 31 March; Jonathan Miller, Madly Lucid, *Observer*, 10 November; Robert Nye, Fable or Joke, *Birmingham Post*, 23 November; Anon., Odd looks for minister who writes 'as I feel', *Morning Telegraph*, 27 December; Pat Williams, Weird Word, *Sunday Telegraph*, 27 October; Ivor Cutler, Dressing-table book, *Sunday Times*, 27 October; Anon., Bumper Fungus Book, *Times Literary Supplement*, 24 October; Ray Gosling, I gave my copy to the trombonist, *The Times*, 26 October; Martin Dodsworth, Duldrum, *The Listener*, 24 October; David Piper, The poet dies again, *Guardian*, 8 November; Anthony Powell, Surrealists at large, *Daily Telegraph*, 19 December; Edward Lucie-Smith, Christmas Books 1, *New Statesman*, 29 November; Anon., Private Joke Book, *Guardian*, 28 October; Anon., 'Indescribable' is the word, *Halifax Courier*, 25 October; Alan R, Radnor, Visit a fantasy world, *Evening Express*, 2 November; Anon., Musrum Developers; Neil Spencer, Musrum

1969—Douglas Wollen, Bookshelf, *Methodist Magazine*, March
1970—George Melly, *Revolt into Style*, Allen Lane, The Penguin Press, Harmondsworth
1971—Michael McNay, A misanthropic Christmas, *Guardian*, 25 November
1972—W. L. Webb, Books of the Day, *Guardian*, 30 November; Peter Fuller, Anthony Earnshaw, *Arts Review*, 18 November; George Melly, Signs and portents, *Guardian*, 30 November; Anon., Too trendy for words, *Daily Mirror*, 6 November; Anon., Tony's seven ways of saying ABC, *Yorkshire Evening Post*, 29 December
1973—Anon., *The Star*, 1 March; Peter Mackarell, Surreal Humour, *Times Educational Supplement*, 23 February; I.B., Secret's of an Artist's Visual Humour, *Express and Echo*, Exeter, 9 January
1979—George Melly, *A Cold Wind Brushing the Temple* (catalogue), Arts Council of Great Britain
1980—John Lyle, *The Assassination of Pierrot*, Greenwich Theatre Gallery (catalogue), London; Jeff Nuttall, Three Artists, *Guardian*; Tony Pusey, *Melmoth*, no.2, London
1982—'Rover', *Leeds Other Paper*, 26 March; W.T.O. Oliver, *Yorkshire Post*; Rosanna Negrotti, Anthony Earnshaw, *What's On*; Ian Breakwell, Illustrated Lies and Jokes, *Art Monthly*, December
1985—Miranda Strickland-Constable, *The Irresistable Object* (catalogue), Leeds City Art Galleries, Leeds
1986—Ian Walker, The Spirit of Surrealism, *Contrariwise* (catalogue) Glynn Vivian Gallery, Swansea; David Briers, Contrariwise, *Art Monthly*
1987—Terry Waldron, Teeside vision mingled with a mean old world, *Middlesbrough Evening Gazette*, 3 July; Peter Inch, Anthony Earnshaw, *Arts Review*, 24 April; Robson's Choice, Submarines crewed by ex-miners, *Workers Press*, 17 October; George Melly, *Anthony Earnshaw*, Leeds City Art Galleries (catalogue) Leeds; Patrick Hughes, Earnshaw, *Art Line*, April/May
1988—Chris Bunyan, Anthony Earnshaw assemblages and Prints, *Darts*, 29 June; Robert Clark, Anthony Earnshaw, *Guardian*, 10 June; Les Coleman, A View from Back o' Town, *Escape*, no.16, London; Ian Breakwell, *City Limits*, 29 December–5 January; Marie-Odile Gain d'Enquin, Les Jardins Du Roi Tony, *Camouflage*, no.19, Paris
1989—Ian Breakwell, Tomes from the Tomb, *City Limits*, 5–12 January; Maria Klein, Tim Lewis & Tony Earnshaw, *Art Line*, no.7
1991—Marcel Mariën, *Indeed*, Collection Papier Journal, Cirque Divers, Brussels; George Melly, *Paris and the Surrealists*, Thames and Hudson, London; Jean-Marie Wynants, Non-sens Dessurs Dessous, *L'instant*, 4 April; Jean-Marie Wynants, Surrealiste, n'est-il pas, ce non-sens britanique, *La Sori*, Brussels, 4 April; Bernice Saltzer, The Magnificent Seven, *Mail*, 19 March; Pru Farrier, Laughter and tears over the rainbow, *Northern Echo*, W.E. Johnson, Drawn to Humour, *Arts Review*
1993—Sue Hubbard, Anthony Earnshaw, *Time Out*
1994—Anon., *Worlds in a Box* (calalogue) The South Bank Centre, London
1995—Tony del Renzio, *Art Monthly*; Marie-Dominique Massoni, *Eclairs d'eau*, Editions Surrealistes
1996—Robert Clark, Wall Game, *Guardian*, 2 January
1997—Jane Czyzelska, When I felt like it, *Artist's Newsletter* February 2000—Anon., *Anthony Earnshaw*, Flowers; Patrick Hughes, *Lurking in Weeds*, Flowers East (catalogue); John Slyce, *1978–2000: The Boxed Earnshaw*, Flowers East (catalogue); Glen Baxter, *Observer*; Paul Hammond, From the Palearctic to the Tropics, in Phillip West, *The Surrealist Found in Saragossa* (catalogue) Palacio de Sastago, Zaragoza
2001—Anon., Anthony Earnshaw, *Yorkshire Post*, 21 August; George Melly, Anthony Earnshaw, *Guardian*, 22 August; Patrick Hughes, Anthony Earnshaw, *Independent*, 23 August; Anon., Mr. Anthony Earnshaw: artist with eye for the absurd, *Darlington and Stockton Times*, 24 August; Anon., Anthony Earnshaw, *The Times*, 25 August; Dave Robson, In death as in life, *The Evening Gazette*, 31 August; Anon., Tony Earnshaw 1924–2001, *The Whistler Journal*, no.23, Chelsea Arts Club; T.F. Griffin, For Tony Earnshaw, *Artscene*, September
2002—Les Coleman, The Rich Sardine Lives in His Own Tin, *Manticor*, no.6; Gail Earnshaw, Anthony Earnshaw 1924–2001 (catalogue), Leeds Art Fair, Leeds
2003—Robert Short, Anthony Earnshaw, Sculpture in 20th Century Britain, Henry Moore Institute, Leeds
2007—George Melly, A homage to A.E., *Au Nord de quoi?*, no.2, Editions Bonneville, Lille
2009—Julia Weiner, GP who had his stethoscope turned into Surrealist art, *The Jewish Chronicle*, 11 September

Television and Radio Programmes

1987—A View from Back o' Town, BBC Look North; Two English Surrealists, Saturday Review, BBC2, 10 October; A View from Back o' Town, interview, Radio Leeds.
1989—On the Edge, Tyne Tees Television, 7 December
1993—Kaleidoscope, BBC Radio 4, 11 January

Contributors

Dawn Ades (b.1943) is Professor of Art History and Theory at the University of Essex. Exhibitions curated or co-curated include: Dada and Surrealism Reviewed, (Hayward Gallery, London, 1978); Fetishism: Visualising Power and Desire, (Brighton, 1995); Dali's Optical Illusions (Hartford, Connecticut and Edinburgh, 2000); Undercover Surrealism: Georges Bataille and Documents (Hayward Gallery, London, 2006). Publications include *Photomontage* (1976); *Salvador Dali* (1982); *Andre Masson* (1994); co-author, *Marcel Duchamp* (1999).

Les Coleman (b.1945) studied at Hull, Leeds and Goldsmiths Colleges of Art. He has held twenty-four solo exhibitions and curated a further seven including Funny Looking (Liège, 1991); Foo Zap Yow and Now (ICA, London, 2003) and Written, Drawn and Stapled (Conway Hall, London, 2009). Selected publications: *The Jewish Banana* (1981); *With My Right Hand* (1989); *180 Grammes* (1990); *Unthoughts* (1992); *Unthinking* (1993); *Impensées* (1994); *Meet the Art Students* (1997); *Meet the Art Students: Now in Glorious Crayon* (2002); *Unthunk* (2002); *Thunks* (2008); *Dirt & Other Works* (2009).

Gail Earnshaw (b.1950) was a student on the foundation course at Bradford College of Art, where, in 1968, she met Anthony Earnshaw. They married in 1985. They exhibited together in a series of shows titled Another G'n'T, the first being held at the Dovecot Arts Centre, Stockton, in 1990. Since Anthony's death she has continued to teach art in schools, and to promote his work, as she did throughout their long relationship. In 2007 she married Stephen Wierczewski.

Paul Hammond (b.1947) was another student 'Lurking in Weeds' (1966–1969) where he studied painting. He continued his studies in painting and film at the Slade School of Fine Art, London. His interest in Surrealism and film led to him organising a programme of surrealist films at the National Film Theatre in 1978. This coincided with the editing and publication of *The Shadow and its Shadow: Surrealist Writings on Cinema.* Published titles include: *Marvellous Méliès* (1974); *French Undressing* (1976); *L'Âge d'or* (1998); *Constellations of Miró, Breton* (2000). Since 1992 he has lived in Barcelona.

George Hardie (b.1944) studied graphic design at St Martin's and the Royal College of Art. In the 1970s he partnered in Nicholas Thirkell Associates, designing many record covers with Hipgnosis. He is a member of the Alliance Graphique Internationale, a professor at University of Brighton, and in 2005 was elected a Royal Designer for Industry. Publications include: *Book design (with a pictorial alphabet)* (1978); *Also Available in Other Colours* (1993); *Scraps di Londres* (1994); *Shop: Batch Production, Limited Edition, Multiples, Self-Publishing and the Small Run* (1994); *Dènouement: Ten Detective Stories Destroyed* (1996); *Manual* (2004).

James Heartfield (b.1961) writes and lectures. Books written by him are: *The 'Death of the Subject' Explained* (2001); *Creativity Gap* (2005); *Let's Build!* (2006); *Green Capitalism* (2009); *The Aborigines Protection Society* (2011). As a freelance journalist he wrote for *Living Marxism* and *Fiji Times* and more recently *Blueprint* and *The Telegraph.* He is a Doctor of Philosophy, completing his studies at the Centre for the Study of Democracy, University of Westminster in 2010.

Patrick Hughes (b.1939) is an artist. His first exhibition was at the Portal Gallery, London in 1961. Since then he has shown internationally and his work is included in many public collections: Arts Council of Great Britain, Museum of Modern Art, Glasgow; Tate Gallery, London, British Council, British Library; Contemporary Art Society; and the Victoria & Albert Museum. He is co-author with George Brecht of *Vicious Circles and Infinity* (1975); co-author with Paul Hammond of *Upon the Pun* (1978); *More on Oxymoron* (1983); *Left to Write* (2009) and *Paradoxymoron* (2011). Books on Hughes: *Behind the Rainbow* (1983) and *Perverspective* (1998).

Michel Rémy (b.1946) is Professor at the University of Nice and a leading authority on Surrealism in Britain. He was a member of the Phases movement, and founder of the short lived review *Flagrant Dèlit* (1978–1984). He is author of *The Surrealist World of Desmond Morris* (1991); *Surrealism in Britain* (1999), the first study of surrealist writings, painting, sculpture and politics in Britain; and *On the Stroke of Midnight*, an anthology of surrealist poetry in Britain (2011). He has co-curated several surrealist exhibitions in France and England.

Michael Richardson (b.1951) is an anthropologist who has made a special study of Surrealism. He is currently Visiting Fellow at the Centre for Cultural Studies at Goldsmiths, University of London, and has previously been Visiting Professor at Waseda University, Tokyo. He is the author of *Georges Bataille* (1993); *The Experience of Culture* (2001); *Surrealism and Cinema* (2006) and *Otherness in Hollywood Cinema* (2010). He has edited and translated several anthologies of surrealist writing including two collections of short stories, *The Dedalus Book of Surrealism: The Identity of Things* (1993) and *The Myth of the World* (1994).

Roger Sabin (b.1961) teaches at Central Saint Martins College of Art and Design, University of the Arts, London. He is best known for his books *Adult Comics* (1992) and *Comics, Comix and Graphic Novels* (1996). He is the editor of *Punk Rock: So What?* (1999) and co-editor of *Below Critical Radar: Fanzines and Alternative Comics* (2004). He wrote regularly on comics for *The Observer* and currently writes for *Eye,* a magazine about graphic design.

Chris Vine (b.1949) studied at Bradford College of Art (1965–1970) where he was taught for two years by Anthony Earnshaw. In 1969 he was co-founder of the touring company, Bradford Theatre Group, which ran until 1978. He studied anthropology and Middle Eastern Studies at Bradford University (1975–1979). He continues to exhibit his paintings and drawings and in 1983 started working as a freelance illustrator. In 2006 he illustrated *The Girl Who Swallowed the Wind* by Carol Rutter and is currently undertaking a commission to illustrate the complete plays of William Shakespeare.

Works illustrated

Dimensions are in centimetres: height by width by depth. Works not attributed to collections are in the estate of Anthony Earnshaw.

p.2 Found Object, 1965. *Private Collection.*
p.6 The City, 1950. Watercolour, 53 x 53. *Collection: Les Coleman.*
p.8 Distribution of Wishes, 1965. Oil on canvas, 104 x 63. *Collection: Patrick Hughes.*
p.10 Field Fall, 1965. Oil on canvas.
p.12 A Pillar of Society, c.1984–86. Ink on paper, 29.5 x 26.
p.13 Who is This Who is Knocking on My Banging Door? (2), 1997. Boxed assemblage, 43 x 51 x 7. *Private collection.*
p.14 The Red Sea, last Saturday night, 1997. Crayon on paper, 43 x 51 x 7.
p.15 Untitled drawing, from *Musrum*, 1968.
p.16 Y for Yeggman, from *An Eighth Secret Alphabet*, 1988.
Wokker, n.d.
p.17 142 Ballerinas Jitterbugging to Basie's 'One O'Clock Jump', 1998. Boxed assemblage, 35.5 x 35.5 x 7.5. *Private collection.*
p.28 Me Mam, c.1944. Welded metal, 26.5 x 6.5.
p.29 Phantoms & Shadows Playing With Ropes & a Rusty Helmet, 1949. Pen, ink and gouache, 36 x 24.
p.31 Untitled, 1946.Watercolour, 30 x 38.
p.32 Many Levers to Push and Knobs to Pull, 1961. Watercolour, 40 x 54. *Collection: Dean Clough, Halifax.*
p.34 The End of a Perfect Day, 1946. Watercolour, 24 x 20.
p.36 In Aylesbury's Ancient Days (II), 1948. Pen, ink and crayon, 57 x 41.
p.37 The Future of Pets: Whatever Became of Rin Tin Tin, 1966. Oil on canvas, 97.5 x 62.
p.38 In Aylesbury's Ancient Days, Parts 4–7, 1948. Pen, ink and crayon, 34 x 22.5.
p.39 Black and Snowy Night, 1950. Watercolour, *Collection: Tom Maschler.*
p.40 One Bent Ventilator, One Severed Hand, Two Phantoms Playing With a Length of Rope, 1949. Pencil, ink and gouache, 31 x 20.5.
p.41 The Castle Where the Birds Live, 1953. Watercolour and soap, 26 x 21. *Collection: Dean Clough, Halifax.*
The Citizen, 1952. Watercolour, 24.5 x 20.
Luminous Skull, 1953. Watercolour, 24 x 19.
p.42 The Wheel That Will Trundle Round the World, 1955. Watercolour, 68 x 53.
p.43 Two Ghosts, 1958. Watercolour, 46 x 32.
p.44 Letter to a Bird, 1954. Watercolour, 44 x 34. *Collection: Dean Clough, Halifax.*
p.45 The Wand, 1960. Watercolour, 48 x 32.
The Chinese Dragon, 1962. Watercolour, 53 x 74. *Collection: Dean Clough, Halifax.*
Semi-detached Washbasins, 1963. Oil and sand on canvas, 85 x 112.
p.46 Dressing Table, Number 4, 1963. Oil and sand on canvas, 79 x 119.5.
Dressing Table, Number 6, 1963. Oil and sand on canvas, 76 x 110.5.
p.48–59 Drawings reproduced from *Musrum*, dimensions and whereabouts of originals unknown.
p.61–67 Alphabetical letters, c.1970–72. Ink on paper, 21 x 15.
p.71 Shame, c.1972–73. Ink on paper, 33 x 19.5.
Liberty, c.1972–73. Ink on paper, 33 x 19.5.
p.72 Irreverence, c.1972–73. Ink on paper, 33 x 19.5.
Sainthood, c.1972–73. Ink on paper, 33 x 19.5.
Surrealism, c.1972–73. Ink on paper, 35.5 x 25.5.
p.74 Perversity, c.1972–73. Ink on paper, 33 x 19.5.
Fantasy, c.1972–73. Ink on paper, 35.5 x 25.5.
p.76 Freud, c.1972–73. Ink on paper, 33 x 19.5.
p.78 Nightwork: Wokker's Eyesight Fails While He is Guarding a Factory on a Tray, 1974. Watercolour, 79 x 57. *Collection: Marie-Odile Gain d'Enquin.*
p.80–91 Wokker strips, n.d. Ink on paper, 22 x 33.
p.92 The Four Elements, 1993. Boxed assemblage, 35 x 54 x 6.5. *Collection: John Bell.*
p.96 The Secret Weapon, 1980. Boxed assemblage, 38 x 46 x 12. *Collection: Stephen Wierczewski.*
p.97 Raider's Bread, 1979. Mixed media, 34 x 24 x 12. *Collection: Leeds City Gallery.*
p.98 Pele's Old Age, 1979. Mixed media, 104 x 162. *Collection: Diane Atkinson.*
God Creating Eve, 1997. Boxed assemblage, 43 x 51 x 12. *Collection: James Heartfield.*
p.99 The Bride with Her Bachelors, Again: after Marcel Duchamp, 1991. Boxed assemblage, 44 x 40 x 10.
Weary and Bewildered: The Spirit of the Century meets the Angel of Death, 1996. Boxed assemblage, 28 x 30 x 7. *Collection: Damien Hirst.*
p.100 Mariën en Cachette, 1985–95. Boxed assemblage, 33 x 41 x 17. *Collection: Patrick Hughes.*
p.101 The Adventures of Bryant & May, 1990. Boxed assemblage, 35 x 63 x 10.
Delilah's Tools, 1979. Boxed assemblage, 46 x 38 x 7. *Collection: Glen Baxter.*
p.102 Up On the Mantelpiece Again, 1996. Boxed assemblage, 32.5 x 32.5 x 8.5. *Collection: Patrick Hughes.*
In the Canteen at the Headquarters of Doubt (Second version), 1983. Boxed assemblage, 54 x 50 x 7. *Collection: Angela Flowers.*
p.103 The Bottomless Pit, 1980. Boxed assemblage, 54 x 34 x 5. *Collection: Diane Atkinson.*
The April Fool, 1978. Boxed assemblage, 51 x 34 x 15. *Collection: Arts Council of Great Britain.*
p.104 Lucifer Contemplating the 21st Century, 1996. Boxed assemblage, 43 x 33 x 8.
The Rules Discarded, 1986. Boxed assemblage, 37 x 31 x 11. *Collection: Patrick Hughes.*
p.105 Boyhood of Don Juan, 1980. Boxed assemblage, 33.5 x 47 x 7.5. *Collection: Louisa Buck.*
Mickey has Chopped off Dumbo's Left Ear, 1999. Boxed assemblage, 27.5 x 42.5 x 9.5. *Collection: Geoffrey Sherwin.*
p.106 Lost Property, 1979. Mixed media, 128 x 160 x 5. *Collection: John Bell.*

p.107 Philosophy in the Boudoir, 2000. Boxed assemblage, 52 x 42 x 12. *Collection: Diane Atkinson.*
The Hungry Infant Circles the Locked Pantry and Stamps Her Tiny Feet, 1997. Boxed assemblage, 24 x 26 x 7. *Collection: Patrick Hughes.*
p.108 The Death of Henry Moore O.M., 1970. Ink on paper, *dimensions and whereabouts unknown.*
p.110 Observatory Time For A Second Time (after Man Ray), 1988. Crayon on paper, 35.5 x 55.5. *Collection: Les Coleman.*
p.111 Trying to catch his patron's eye, c.1983–86. Ink on paper, 29.5 x 26.
p.114 Looking for a Carnival, c.1983–86. Ink on paper, 29.5 x 26.
p.115 Adapted postcards, 1985–87. Ink, crayon and felt pen, 15.5 x 10.5. *Collection: Les Coleman.*
p.116 Many parliamentary candidates believe a kite is a yo-yo, c.1983–86. Ink on paper, 29.5 x 25.5.
p.118 With his teddy in a grip of steel, the bosses son eyes a 25mm twist drill and plumbs the puddle of his brain to fathom what purpose it serves, c.1983–86. Ink on paper, 29.5 x 26.
One of these rats is a politician, c.1983–86. Ink on paper, 29.5 x 26.
p.119 Snubbing a vulgar pork pie, at the Conservative Club,, c.1983–86. Ink on paper, 29.5 x 26.
p.120 They don't know much about art but they know what they like, c.1983–86. Ink on paper, 29.5 x 26.
Ever willing to help, our artist, A.E., has redesigned the NF trademark, 1980. Felt pen on paper, 20 x 23.5.
p.122 Village Life, 1994. Crayon on paper, 54 x 69.
p.124 Prince Kong Distracted From His Toys by an Apparition of Fay Wray in the Guise of a Fairy, 1996. Crayon on paper, 52.5 x 68.5. *Collection: Florent Chopin.*
p.125 Street Life—Alas, 1996. Crayon on paper, 55 x 64.
p.126 No Buttons, 1995. Crayon on paper, 59.5 x 47.
p.127 Gentlemen & Workers with Red Baloons [sic.], 1996. Crayon on paper, 48 x 56.
p.128 Twenty-Four Shouting Americans, 1992. Pen, ink and crayon on paper, 39.5 x 65.5. *Collection: James Heartfield.*
p.129 Landscape: Eleven footballers scoring with many cows mooing and a pretty dolly: she has gone astray, 1993. Crayon on paper, 52 x 77. *Private collection.*
p.130 Drama at Sea, 1996. Crayon on paper, 40 x 51. *Collection: Dudley Winterbottom.*
p.131 Aerial Warfare, 1996. Crayon on paper, 58.5 x 80.
They're Outside the Village, 1996–97. Crayon on paper, 51 x 67.
p.132 Leonardo's Man (after Vitruvius) With the Artist's Tree, 1998. Crayon on paper, 62.5 x 67.
p.133 The Man Wearing a Mask Made of Smoke, 1985. Pen, ink and crayon on paper, 24 x 19.5.
Take Your Bull and Leave This Field Immediately, 1997. Pen, ink and crayon on paper, 24 x 19.5.
p.134 God Showing His Beautiful Angels How to Keep Lucifer and His Minions in Their Proper Station, 2000. Crayon on paper, 60 x 42.
p.135 Angels Watching Adam & Eve Ride Their Bicycles, 2000. Crayon and ink on paper, 38 x 52.
p.136 Leaving the Swimming Pool at Redcar, circa 1931, 1992. Watercolour, 41 x 49.
p.137 I am Riding My H. Rench, Waving Goodbye to Myself, 1992. Watercolour, 27 x 50. *Collection: Bill Bingham.*
p.144 The Windscreen Whipper, 1990. Boxed assemblage, 35.5 x 33 x 12.
p.146 In Earnshaw's Pantry, 1982. Mixed media, 36 x 33.
p.147 Portrait of Benjamin Péret, 1990. Boxed assemblage, 41 x 18 x 12. *Collection: Mary Rose Beaumont.*
p.150 America, 1972–73. Ink on paper, 35.5 x 25.
p.151 Homage to André Breton: the Light That Will Cease to Fail, 1989. Boxed assemblage, 56 x 42 x 10. *Private Collection.*
Drawing, from *Clock Lips*, 1989. Ink on paper, *dimensions and whereabouts unknown.*
p.152 Saltburn-by-the-Sea With the Cat Next Door & Two Bones Thrown Down the Street for the Dog, 2000. Crayon on paper, 47.5 x 36. *Collection: John Bell.*
p.166 All at Sea: Portrait of a Politician, 1995. Boxed assemblage, 49 x 53 x 10.
p.175 The Faithful Servant, 1979. Boxed assemblage, 33 x 19.5 x 10. *Collection: Nancy Fouts.*
p.176 Crusoe's Dream, 1979. Boxed assemblage, 73 x 38 x 7. *Collection: Leeds Art Gallery.*
An old acquaintaince caught his eye, on the way from The House, c.1983–86. Ink on paper, 29.5 x 25.5
p.177 He has been playing with his toys, c.1983–86. Ink on paper, 29.5 x 25.5
p.178 Self-Portrait, 1951. Oil on board, 49 x 45. *Collection: Leeds Art Gallery.*

Photographic credits

Arts Council Collection: p.103; Isabelle Blondiau: p.141; Andrew Darke: p.184; Dean Clough, Halifax: p.41; Frances Earnshaw: p.149; Gail Earnshaw: p.123, p.165; Marie-Odile Gain d'Enquin: p.138; Leeds Art Gallery: p.97, p.176; Sarah Metcalfe: p.183 (Paris); John Timbers: p.182; Michael Woods: cover, p.30.